LAROUSSE
Complete Guide to
INDOOR PLANTS

Key to coloured tabs

The plants in this book are divided into the groups listed below. Use the coloured tab in the corner of the pages to help you find the different groups as you flick through the book. Within each group the plants are arranged alphabetically.

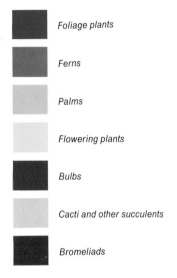

Foliage plants

Ferns

Palms

Flowering plants

Bulbs

Cacti and other succulents

Bromeliads

LAROUSSE
Complete Guide to
INDOOR
PLANTS

KEN MARCH & JILL THOMAS

LAROUSSE

LAROUSSE
Larousse plc
Elsley House, 24–30 Great Titchfield Street,
London W1P 7AD

This edition published by Larousse plc 1995

10 9 8 7 6 5 4 3 2 1

Material in this book was previously published by
Kingfisher Books in *The Kingfisher Complete Guide
to Indoor and Conservatory Plants* in 1992

This edition © Larousse plc 1995
Text copyright © Ken March and Grisewood & Dempsey Ltd, 1991, 1992
Illustrations copyright © Grisewood & Dempsey Ltd 1991, 1992

British Library Cataloguing in Publication Data
A catalogue record of this book is available from the
British Library.

ISBN 0 7523 00245

Printed in Portugal

Editor: Stuart Cooper
Consultant: Brian Davis
Design: Heather Gough, Terry Woodley
Picture Research: Elaine Willis
Artwork: Jonathan Adams, Wendy Bramall,
John Davis, Will Giles, Sandra Pond

CONTENTS

Introduction

All too often, plants are allowed to become leggy, dehydrated specimens, which struggle for survival in our homes and conservatories. Properly cared for, though, they provide tremendous benefits in terms of visual appeal, botanical interest, and even mental well-being. People are happier when surrounded by plants, and they do much to mitigate the so-called 'sick-building' syndrome that afflicts many modern offices.

The wide variety of plants available means there is something to suit almost every taste, growing environment and level of horticultural skill. Elegant palms can be used to enhance older-style interiors, while bold plants, such as the Strelitzia, produce striking effects in modern rooms. Damp, shady places, such as bathrooms, can be filled with ferns; warm, dry living rooms are ideal for growing succulents. The novice indoor gardener can achieve success with hardy ivies and figs, then move on to the more demanding exotics such as orchids and bromeliads.

The enjoyment of indoor and conservatory plants is enhanced by the many different techniques that have been developed for displaying them. Container manufacturers produce a vast array of pots, wall pots, hanging pots and baskets, planters, troughs, terrariums and bottle gardens in which to grow plants. In the conservatory, open soil beds offer the opportunity to grow many exotic varieties to full size.

The key to growing indoor and conservatory plants successfully lies in understanding and responding to their needs. They must be provided with just the right amount of warmth, light, humidity, water and food; potted in the correct pot containing a suitable compost; and placed in the best position. This book gives detailed instructions on all these points for over 500 of the most attractive, interesting and unusual plant varieties.

Plant names

Most indoor plants have a common name, e.g. Mother of Thousands, and they all have a botanical name, e.g. *Tolmiea menziesii*. While the common name may be easier to remember, the botanical name should be used to identify and order plants. Apart from the fact that all plants have a botanical name, this name is also unique to each plant. A common name, however, may refer to two different plants. For instance, Mother of Thousands is used for *Saxifraga stolonifera* as well as *Tolmiea menziesii*. Botanical names are also internationally recognized and more stable, although they do change or are disputed from time to time as our understanding of plant relationships advances. This book gives any former or alternative botanical names.

Botanical names usually have two components, denoting the genus (*Tolmiea*) and the species (*menziesii*). Some names also have a third component. If this begins with a lower-case letter the plant is a subspecies; if it starts with a capital letter and is in quotation marks the plant is a hybrid that has been raised in cultivation. Because of limitations of space, it has not always been possible to list all the hybrids or subspecies of each plant in this book.

Closely grouped Anthuriums, Chrysanthemums, Azaleas, Cyclamens, and Chamaedoreas produce a magnificent display on a windowsill.

How to Use this Book

The plants in this book are presented as single page entries that focus on a single species, on a species and its varieties, or on a group of closely related plants. Each entry contains a description of the plant or plants, including any common or alternative botanical names that are used; a photograph for identification; a facts panel that lists the plant's characteristics, season of interest, care requirements, availability, uses and the related varieties; and a line drawing that illustrates a useful care, display or propagation method. All these features are identified and described in the panel opposite. The terms used to describe plant characteristics are explained below.

There are a number of ways in which this book can be used to select plants. Refer to the index to find a particular plant, the colour key to flick through a group of plants, the photographs to work out schemes for associated planting and the facts panel for selecting the varieties that might suit a particular location.

Plant type
The plants in this book are arranged according to type, as explained on page 8 of this Introduction. The plant type descriptions in the facts panels also include details of the plant's habit. This is the overall shape and direction of the growth and may be erect, upright, bushy, shrubby, prostrate, trailing or climbing, or a combination of two or more of these qualities.

Season of interest
This is the period during which a plant is considered to be at its most attractive. For the foliage plants, ferns, palms, bromeliads and many of the cacti, this tends to be all year round. For the flowering plants, bulbs and some cacti it is generally the flowering period.

Size
Plants grown in containers rarely attain their full natural size. They are constrained both by the limited space for root development and by the need to keep them to a manageable or attractive size by regular pruning. If a plant can achieve its full potential in a container, this size is given. If it cannot, the size is described in terms of a range within which the plant is

considered to look at its best and is practical to keep. Some specimens will be able to exceed this range if space allows or conditions are ideal. Plants grown in conservatory beds can achieve their full natural size.

Flower
In the flowering plants, bulbs, cacti and bromeliads the flowers or flower heads are a major feature of the plant and are covered in some detail. In the groups where flowers are small and insignificant they are described only briefly to aid identification.

Leaf
The leaves are described to aid selection and to facilitate the identification of unknown plants. The descriptions are for plants that are in good health; the foliage of unhealthy plants may appear quite different.

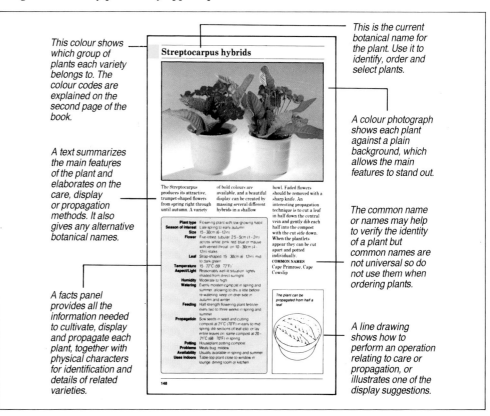

This colour shows which group of plants each variety belongs to. The colour codes are explained on the second page of the book.

This is the current botanical name for the plant. Use it to identify, order and select plants.

A text summarizes the main features of the plant and elaborates on the care, display or propagation methods. It also gives any alternative botanical names.

A colour photograph shows each plant against a plain background, which allows the main features to stand out.

A facts panel provides all the information needed to cultivate, display and propagate each plant, together with physical characters for identification and details of related varieties.

The common name or names may help to verify the identity of a plant but common names are not universal so do not use them when ordering plants.

A line drawing shows how to perform an operation relating to care or propagation, or illustrates one of the display suggestions.

Plant Types

The following sections outline the groups into which the plants in this book are divided. These groupings are a mixture of traditional and scientific categories and are the ones used in retail outlets and catalogues.

Foliage plants

Flowering plants

Foliage plants
All foliage plants produce flowers but they are usually small and insignificant. These plants are grown mainly for their leaves, which may be green or variegated, or more unusual colours such as yellow and red. Some plants have leaves that change colour in the autumn. Leaves may be hand-shaped, oval, lance-shaped or divided into leaflets; many are toothed.

Ferns
Ferns bear no flowers but reproduce by dispersing spores. These are borne on the underside of the leaves, known as fronds, which are either bold and tongue-shaped or divided into leaflets.

Palms
Palms produce flowers but their main attraction lies in the arching, finely divided leaves, which are known as fronds, as in the ferns. Palms are slow-growing plants and are relatively easy to maintain.

Cacti

Bulbs

Flowering plants
Flowering plants are grown mainly for their flowers although some also produce berries and fruits. Plants come into flower in all seasons of the year and some produce blooms all year round. The duration of flowering varies with each plant, ranging from just a few days to several months. A number of flowering plants are treated as annuals when grown indoors, to be discarded after the first flowering.

Bulbs
Although they could be included with the flowering plants, bulbs are usually treated separately because of their particular growing requirements. The bulb is the underground storage organ of the plant. True bulbs consist of fleshy scales surrounding the central bud, but the terms is also used to cover other storage organs such as corms and tubers.

Bromeliads

Cacti and other succulents
Cacti do not bear leaves but have instead thick, succulent stems, which store water. Succulents have thick, fleshy stems and leaves, which also act as water reservoirs. Both types of plant have evolved the ability to store water in order to survive the arid or semi-arid conditions of their natural environment.

Bromeliads
Bromeliads produce a rosette of glossy green foliage and a vividly coloured flower head or spike. The spike is formed by a series of modified leaves called bracts; the flowers themselves are small and insignificant.

With their elegant, arching fronds, palms are ideal for growing in large pots, either on or close to the floor.

Plant Care and Cultivation

This book provides specific instructions on care and cultivation for every plant included. The following sections explain why plants require the types of care prescribed and give some general advice on the techniques for providing it.

Temperature

The temperature range given for each plant is the optimum at which it will sustain its rate of growth and overall health. It is essential to provide a stable temperature, preferably towards the middle of the range. Plants that are kept too warm during the day and then too cold at night often shed their foliage. For the same reason it is important to keep plants away from draughts.

Problems caused by temperature occur most often in late autumn, winter and early spring, when many plants are in their vulnerable resting phase and fluctuations of heat and cold are most likely.

Aspect/Light

All plants need light to manufacture the foods that enable them to grow and produce healthy foliage and flowers. The amount of light needed varies between the different species so the positioning of plants is of vital importance. Ferns prefer rather more shade than other plants as their deep green foliage has evolved to collect relatively low levels of light. Conversely, highly coloured foliage plants will lose their bright colours if they are deprived of the sunlight that creates them.

Humidity

The amount of atmospheric moisture a plant needs depends upon the rate the water drawn up from its roots is lost through its leaves – the process known as transpiration. Cacti and other succulents have fleshy tissue, which can store water, so they do not need high humidity. Ferns and some other plants have thin leaves, which lose water rapidly and will soon become shrivelled if the air is too dry. Without high humidity they soon shrivel and turn brown at the leaf edges.

Most problems occur with plants that require high humidity, as many homes have a dry atmosphere due to central heating. Misting helps to increase humidity but with species that also require bright sunlight, this can cause marking of the foliage. Another solution is to place the pot on moistened pebbles so that moisture evaporates below the plant. Alternatively, group plants in a bowl, planter, bottle garden or simply in their pots, so they create a humid microclimate.

Watering

More plants fail because of problems with watering than for any other reason. The amount of water needed varies greatly between the different groups of plants, and it is also dependent on temperature, light, time of year, size of pot, and even air movement.

Tap water is acceptable for most plants, although it should be allowed to adjust to room temperature before use. If rain water is recommended, the rain should be collected and stored hygienically.

A bed of pebbles, half covered with water, will help to maintain the humidity level.

Humidity can also be provided by regularly misting the foliage with tepid water.

LIGHT NEEDS OF SOME PLANTS

Full sun		Well-lit situation		Moderate light		Light shade	Shade
Agave	Hippeastrum	Abutilon	Cycas	Adiantum	Ficus benjamina	Anthurium	Ficus pumila
Ananas	Hyacinthus	Aphelandra	Dizygotheca	Aglaonema	Gardenia	Aspidistra	Fittonia
Aucuba	Gymnocalycium	Aporocactus	Dracaena	Asplenium	Guzmania	Calathea	verschaffeltii
Bougainvillea	Lithops	Asparagus	Ficus	Begonia masoniana	Howea	Cryptanthus	
Ceropegia	Narcisssus	Begonia boweri	Hedera	Cissus	Hoya	Fittonia verschaffeltii	
Codieaeum	Nerium	Begonia rex	Laurus	Columnea	Nidularium	argyroneura nana	
Echeveria	Notocactus	Billbergia	Monstera	Dieffenbachia	Philodendron	Maranta	
Euonymus	Opuntia	Chlorophytum	Peperomia	Dracaena marginata	Rhipsalidopsis	Pellaea	
Euphorbia	Pelargonium	Chrysanthemum	Phoenix	Epipremnum	Saintpaulia	Pteris	
Faucaria	Sansevieria	Coffea	Schefflera	Episcia	Schlumbergera	Spathiphyllum	
Fuchsia	Yucca	Coleus	Tradescantia	Fatshedera	Vriesia	Stromanthe	

Plant Care and Cultivation

Most plants can safely be provided with water through the surface of the compost, as long as it is allowed to drain into a saucer below and the surplus is discarded. Unless the plant is an aquatic species it should not be left standing in water, otherwise the roots will rot and the plant will die. Avoid splashing water on the foliage, as this will cause it to rot or become scorched or marked.

Frequency of watering is also important. Ferns, Azaleas and some other plants should be kept constantly moist. Cacti and succulents should be watered infrequently, with more in the spring and summer when they are actively growing, but the barest minimum in autumn and winter to prevent them from drying out completely. With most other plants it is usually a good policy to allow the compost to get on the dry side before re-watering. Do not let it dry out too much as the plant will wilt and the compost will shrink back from the pot and allow water to drain away rather than absorbing it. A final point to note is that not all plants that wilt are too dry; they often wilt when they are too wet. It is therefore important to judge the condition of the compost very carefully before each watering, not just by looking at it, but by probing beneath the surface with a finger.

Feeding

Feeding should take place only during a plant's active growing season, never when it has slowed its rate of growth or is dormant. Moisten the compost before applying the fertilizer and ensure that it is used at the strength recommended for the plant.

The type of fertilizer to use depends on the plant and its stage of growth. A general houseplant fertilizer, high in nitrogen, can be used for most foliage and flowering plants to promote lush foliage. With flowering plants, once the foliage is established it is best to switch to a flowering plant fertilizer, rich in potassium. This will help produce better quality flowers. Tomato fertilizers achieve the same result.

Slow- or controlled-release fertilizers save the trouble of mixing and can be applied as pellets or sticks that are sprinkled over, or inserted into, the compost.

Training

Plants with a climbing habit need some means of support. Small plants simply require a small stick or stake, while loose, leggy plants should be provided with a light framework of sticks placed around the pot and linked with string. Climbing plants with a bushy habit need a trellis or hoop. In all these cases, attach the plant to the support with small wire rings or string.

More vigorous plants need a moss pole for support. Attach the plant to the pole with string, hairpins or bent wire, and moisten the pole often with a mister. Plants that both climb and trail can be grown in a hanging basket where the stems will both hang over the sides and climb up the supporting ropes or chains. When training plants up conservatory walls, the stems should be tied to galvanized or plastic-coated wires, which are placed about 50cm (18in) apart and attached to the wall with the eyed screws known as vine eyes.

Pruning

Pruning is necessary to maintain a compact habit and to encourage bushy growth. In most cases it is simply a matter of pinching out the foliage using the thumb and forefinger. Woody-stemmed subjects, however, require the use of secateurs or a pruning knife, and plants with very thick stems must be pruned with a saw.

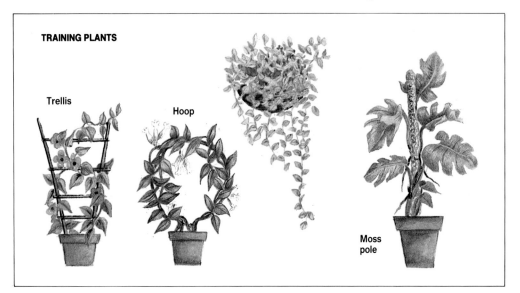

TRAINING PLANTS

Trellis

Hoop

Moss pole

It is important when pruning to leave a clean wound with no bruised or ragged tissue that could become infected with disease. Trim back to a position just above a leaf or bud, as long lengths of bare stem can 'die back', leading to disfigurement or loss of the plant. A few species ooze a milky sap when pruned. This can be dealt with by sprinkling charcoal over the cut.

Some plants produce leggy and untidy growth that requires rather more than a light trim. They should be cut back by a half to two thirds in order to produce a reasonably compact plant the following season.

Grooming and cleaning
Dead flowers and brown leaves should be pinched out or trimmed off immediately to maintain the appearance of the plant and to prevent the spread of disease. After removing diseased tissue, clean and disinfect any cutting tools before using them on other plants.

It is not usually necessary to clean leaves more than a couple of times a year. Avoid leaf shines or oily sprays as these may damage the plant. Plants with tough, waxy leaves should be wiped gently with a damp cloth to remove dust and grime. Clean the top surface only. Other plants can be cleaned by spraying the foliage with tepid water. Soak up excess water with a kitchen towel and allow the plant to dry away from sunlight.

Cleaning is best carried out when plants are actively growing; during their dormant period they are more susceptible to damage.

Pots and potting
Whether to use clay or plastic posts is a matter of personal preference as there are arguments for and against both types. Plastic pots are cheaper, lighter, and less breakable. Clay pots, on the other hand, can absorb and release moisture, allowing the roots to 'breathe', and they are more stable than plastic pots.

Repotting into a larger pot is necessary not only to provide a plant with more space for its roots but also to increase the reserve of nutrients and the moisture-retaining capacity, and to give the plant more stability. Repotting is best carried out in the plant's growing season. Frequency depends on the plant, but once every two to three years is enough for most varieties. Select a pot that is no more than 7.5–10cm (3–4in) larger in diameter than the previous one. Do not re-pot plants that are diseased or stressed.

When plants reach a certain size it may be impractical to re-pot them into a larger pot so replace the compost in the existing pot every three years or so.

All the plants in this book can be grown in ordinary houseplant potting compost. However, when potting cacti and succulents, orchids or bromeliads, try to obtain the composts that are produced for these plants.

Bottle gardens and terrariums
Bottle gardens and terrariums make an attractive feature and also protect plants from fumes and draughts and enable them to create their own humid microclimate. As space is restricted it is best to use smaller plants, such as Fittonia, Maranta, Peperomia and Pilea. Planting the garden requires some skill as well as improvized tools. First pour in some gravel or charcoal for drainage and cover this with compost. Next insert the plants and firm around them. Finally, give the plants a light spray and trickle a tiny amount of

When roots fill the pot, knock out the plant. Keep the root ball intact.

Place the old pot into a slightly larger one and fill around with compost.

Remove the old pot, place the root ball in the hole, firm around the sides, and water.

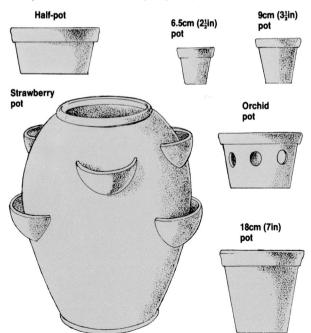

Half-pot

6.5cm (2½in) pot

9cm (3½in) pot

Strawberry pot

Orchid pot

18cm (7in) pot

Plant Care and Cultivation

Pour drainage material, such as charcoal, through a funnel, then add a layer of compost.

Use improvized tools to scoop out holes, insert the plants, and firm around them.

Spray the plants lightly and stand the bottle in good light, away from direct sun.

water down the sides of the bottle to remove any dirt. Place the bottle in good light but out of direct sun. Do not seal it. Keep a check on the compost to ensure it remains moist; the plants should not need spraying very often, if at all. Remove dead leaves.

Pests and diseases

This section explains how to combat the pests and diseases that affect plants. Remember, though, that prevention is better than cure. A plant that has been well cared for should be strong and healthy enough to resist most infections so follow the care instructions strictly. Carry out regular check-ups for pests and diseases and put sickly plants into quarantine to prevent the problem spreading to healthy plants.

Most pests and diseases can be dealt with using the range of products detailed in the chart below. Follow the manufacturer's guidelines for the safe use, storage and disposal of these products. Chemicals are available in liquid concentrate or powder form to be mixed with water and applied through a mister, or as dust or aerosol sprays. Check that sprays do not contain CFCs (chlorinated fluorocarbons), which damage the ozone layer. If possible, use sprays outdoors, but away from direct sunlight to avoid scorching. Some chemicals can be applied with a paintbrush or a cotton swab. If in doubt as to whether a chemical can be used on a plant, test it on just one or two leaves first. In conservatories the use of known pest predators provides an effective and environmentally friendly form of pest control.

PESTS AND DISEASES TREATMENT CHART

Aphid Attacks soft, fleshy plants, such as flowering plants. Spray repeatedly with soft soap or pyrethrum.

Red spider mite Pest of many plants growing in hot, dry conditions. Spray repeatedly with derris.

Scale insect Affects many plants. Spray young with pyrethrum or derris; remove adults with fingernail.

Thrips Attacks flowering plants, e.g. Chrysanthemum. Spray repeatedly with pyrethrum or derris.

Whitefly Minor pest of many plants. Larvae hard to eradicate; spray adult flies repeatedly with pyrethrum.

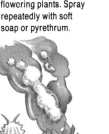

Mealy bug Attacks many plants, especially cacti. Spray with derris or dab bugs with methylated spirits.

Mildew Disease of relatively few plants. Hard to treat so dust plants with sulphur as preventative.

Rust Affects very few plants, including Fuchsia. Difficult to control but removal of infected leaves will help.

Botrytis Affects soft-fleshed plants. Remove dead matter before rot sets in; dust plants with sulphur as preventative.

Sooty mould Disease of plants affected by insect pests. Remove with mild, warm solution of detergent.

12

Propagation

An enjoyable way of obtaining new plants is to propagate them yourself. The basic techniques of propagation are sowing and germination of seeds or spores; rooting of cuttings; layering; and separation and rooting of offsets. The text entries describe the method to use for each plant and the following sections provide some general guidelines on each technique. Make sure that pots, trays, knives, scissors and other tools are spotlessly clean, preferably sterile. Use only proprietary potting composts, never garden soil as it may contain disease organisms. The best time to propagate plants is early in their growing season, which for most varieties is spring or summer, when conditions will be right for germination or rooting.

Seeds or fern spores
Fill a seed tray or half pot with seed sowing compost and sprinkle the seeds or spores thinly on the surface. If the seeds are small to large, cover them lightly with compost. Very fine seeds or spores should be left uncovered. Moisten the compost with a fine-rosed watering can or a mister. Cover the container with

The Kalanchia, or Devil's Backbone, has tiny plantlets on its leaves, which can be dislodged and potted.

glass and maintain the temperature at 19–24°C (66–75°F). Once the seeds or spores have germinated, remove the cover. Prick out the seedlings when they are large enough to handle and pot them singly.

Cuttings
There are several methods for propagating plants from cuttings, using either the growing tips and stems, the stems only, or the leaves. Cuttings should be taken only from plants that are healthy.

To take a tip cutting, cut off the growing tip and a 5–10cm (2–4in) section of stem using a sharp knife; for a stem cutting, remove a similar length of stem. Push the base of the stem into a pot filled with seed and cutting compost. Cover the pot with a polythene bag supported on a stick frame and keep the compost moist. Keep the temperature at 19–24°C (66–75°F). Some plants can be propagated by laying sections of stem on the surface of the compost. Keep it moist and maintain the temperature within the range given above.

To propagate from a leaf cutting, insert the leaf by its stalk into seed and cutting compost, where it will take root. Some plants, such as *Begonia rex*, can be propagated by pegging a leaf, upperside down, on to the compost. Tiny plantlets will develop, which can be potted when they are large enough to handle.

Offsets
Some plants form offsets, which can be teased apart and potted. Moisten the compost first to make separation easier. When planting cactus offsets do not over-moisten the compost, and wear gloves.

Layering
Layering is used to propagate plants which produce plantlets on the stems or leaves. Allow the plantlets to rest in a pot of seed and cutting compost and they will root. Some plants can be forced to produce plantlets from sections of stem, a process known as air layering. Cut half way into the stem and then up about 5cm (2in). Partly open the wound, dust it with rooting powder, and pack moss between and around the cut. Wrap polythene around the moss and wait a few weeks until roots fill the area. Remove and pot the plantlet.

Dip tip cuttings in rooting powder and push halfway into the compost. Cover with a polythene bag.

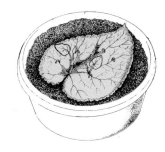

To propagate Begonia rex, peg a whole leaf, with the veins cut, on compost or cut a leaf into sections and lay them on compost.

Chlorophytum plantlets can be pegged into separate pots and when they start growing the stems can be cut.

Using Plants Indoors

Tradescantias and Chlorophytums are particularly effective when trailed from furniture such as this corner cabinet.

The following sections offer advice on what to look for when purchasing plants as well as some notes on the locations in which they can be used indoors.

Buying plants
When buying plants, make sure they have been well cared for by the retailer. Check that the growth is strong and sturdy; that no leaves are dirty, brown, damaged or deformed; and that there are no signs of pests or diseases. With flowering plants, ensure that one or two flowers are open and in good condition and that there are enough unopened buds to guarantee a reasonable flowering period. When buying plants in winter have them wrapped up before taking them outside, to avoid any shock.

Using plants
Position plants according to their temperature and light requirements. Place a saucer under the pot and never put plants on electrical items as you may suffer electrocution from water spillages. Watch out for plant pests as they can deposit excrement on furniture. Keep poisonous plants and plants with sharp leaves or spines out of the way of people, especially children, and pets.

Windowsills
This position is likely to offer the most light, often with direct sunlight if the window does not face north. Net curtains provide soft shade if needed. In winter, window temperatures can drop sharply at night so move plants into the body of the room overnight.

Lounges and dining rooms
The more exotic and bold plants are worth using here, as feature plants. Unless conditions are carefully controlled, though, these rooms can be too warm and dry for some plants.

Kitchens and bathrooms
These rooms normally offer an increased level of humidity and warmth. Plants that need watering regularly are also less likely to be neglected where there is easy access to water.

Bedrooms
These are usually slightly cooler rooms and may suit some of the more hardy varieties.

Offices
Avoid using delicate plants in offices unless you can afford the time to care for them properly. Plants that require constant warmth may suffer in offices during winter nights and weekends when the heating is off. If you plan to use plants in office receptions, ensure there are no draughts from frequently opened outside doors.

Conservatories

The practicalities of constructing a conservatory are beyond the scope of this book but it is possible to give some general guidelines on planning or choosing a conservatory and on using plants within it.

Conservatory essentials
It is vital to decide if the conservatory is to be used mainly for growing plants or if it is to form another living room in which plants merely provide decoration. This decision will dictate the types of plants that can be grown as the needs of plants and people rarely coincide.

When constructing the conservatory make sure you adhere to local planning and building regulations. The conservatory should include a tap and some means of heating for winter. Have electricity installed by an approved electrician and ensure it is insulated from damp. Lay rot-resistant flooring, such as tiles, so you can douse it with water to create humidity. Ventilation is essential and there should be openings in the roof, the walls and near the ground. Shade from summer sun is also important and can be provided with blinds or screens or by training vines and other sun-resistant plants up the wall and along the ceiling.

Using plants in the conservatory
Most plants that can be grown indoors are also suitable for the conservatory. However, it is best to use the larger, more exotic plants that cannot be grown indoors. There are many ways to display plants in the conservatory. They can be trained up a wall or trellis, trailed from ornaments, grown in containers or conservatory beds, or planted around an indoor pool.

Conservatory beds
These are areas of open soil let into the conservatory floor. They provide great scope for attractive displays, and allow plants to reach full size. The beds must be no less than 50cm (18in) deep; the depth can be increased by building up the beds with a wall. Good drainage is vital, and the beds should contain soil-based compost.

This dwarf Azalea, grown as a standard, provides a striking centrepiece in a conservatory display that also includes Lobelias, ivies, Mimulus, Phlox and Stocks.

Foliage Plants

Providing interest all year round, foliage plants form the backbone of the material for use indoors. They have a multitude of leaf shapes, and colours that vary from shades of green to the more vibrant hues of such plants as the Coleus pictured here. Many foliage plants are impressive enough to display on their own and numerous varieties are ideal for group planting.

Acer palmatum

This is one of the best shrubs or small trees for the conservatory. Its attractive foliage makes a good focal point in a grouping of shrubs and other plants and it maintains its interest from spring to autumn. The many cultivars available include *A. p.* 'Atropurpureum', with deep purple leaves, *A. p.* 'Chitoseyam', with bronze-green foliage, and *A. p.* 'Shishio', with pink leaves that become purple with age. *A. p. dissectum*, the cut-leaved Japanese Maple, has very finely divided leaves and is ideal for growing in a large tub. *A. p. d. atropurpureum* and *A. p. d.* 'Garnett' are purple-leaved forms.

COMMON NAME
Japanese Maple

Replace 5cm (2in) of the top compost in spring

Plant type	Foliage shrub or small tree with upright habit
Season of interest	Spring to autumn
Size	To 3m (10ft)
Flower	Small, purple-red, in clusters, produced in early spring
Leaf	Palmate, 5–7 lobed, 5–10cm (2–4in) long, shades of green, bronze, purple, yellow, red
Temperature	Minimum −5°C (23°F)
Aspect/Light	Shade; protect from bright summer sun
Humidity	Moderate
Watering	Keep compost evenly moist from spring to autumn; keep on the drier side in winter
Feeding	Once every two weeks with a flowering plant liquid fertilizer in spring and early summer
Propagation	Named varieties are propagated by grafting; *A. palmatum* may be grown from seed sown in autumn
Potting	Soil-based potting compost
Problems	Leaf scorch in bright summer sunlight
Availability	Commonly available throughout the year
Uses indoors	Feature shrub or small tree for conservatory or greenhouse

Aglaonema crispum 'Silver Queen'

The Aglaonema is ideal for use as an ornamental feature on a table-top, until it outgrows the situation. As it grows larger, the plant can be displayed at ground level. The Aglaonema is susceptible to over-watering and to cold draughts, both of which cause premature yellowing of leaves, followed by untimely loss. Over-watering can also cause leaves to rot at the base and these should be quickly removed with a sharp knife. Following leaf loss, keep the compost a little drier for a while to allow the plant to create fresh root and recover. The flower is insignificant and will wither and rot once it has finished. It is probably best removed with a sharp knife at its base as soon as it begins to fade. Although the plant can be propagated by division, care should be taken not to damage the fleshy foliage.

COMMON NAME
Painted Drop Tongue

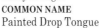

Remove damaged leaves with a sharp knife

Plant type	Foliage plant with single or multi-stemmed erect habit
Season of interest	All year round
Size	30–45cm (12–18in)
Flower	Whitish, arum-like, 5cm (2in), relatively uninteresting
Leaf	20–30cm (8–12in) long, 5–10cm (2–4in) broadly spear-shaped, greyish green; stems fleshy, succulent
Temperature	20–24°C (68–75°F)
Aspect/Light	Moderate, out of direct sun
Humidity	Average
Watering	Evenly moisten compost in spring and summer, allowing to partially dry out between waterings; keep drier in autumn and winter
Feeding	Once every three to four weeks in spring and summer with houseplant fertilizer
Propagation	Divide plant into small clumps mid spring to early summer; sow seeds at 24°C (75°F); lay stem cuttings, 4–5cm (1½in–2in), on surface at same temperature
Potting	Houseplant potting compost
Problems	Mealy bug, root mealy bug, red spider mite
Availability	Commonly available throughout year
Uses indoors	Best as table-top plant in body of room such as lounge or dining room
Other varieties	*A. commutatum* – silver grey

Araucaria heterophylla

The Araucaria is a superb plant for the enthusiast who likes a plant of regular geometrical shape. However, the radiating growth will only be achieved by providing the plant with even light and sufficient space to grow and develop. Failure to do so will result in growth that is somewhat lopsided, which almost ruins the effect of the plant. This species is closely related to the Monkey Puzzle Tree, which grows in gardens, but it is not hardy outside. However, it does share some similar characteristics in that the needles become sharp as they mature. As the plant becomes older the needles tend to drop off, as do the branches, creating a mess on the floor. The plant is best cleaned by using a pressure water mister to wash the dust off, thus allowing the natural sheen to show through.

COMMON NAME
Norfolk Island Pine

Plant type	Foliage plant with radiating branches on evenly shaped erect habit
Season of interest	All year round
Size	1–3m (3–10ft)
Flower	None
Leaf	Green needles, 0.5–1cm ($\frac{1}{4}$in–$\frac{1}{3}$in), which become harder and sharper as they mature, on branches 30–60cm (12–24in)
Temperature	10–20°C (50–68°F)
Aspect/Light	Moderate to reasonably bright, but dislikes prolonged exposure to direct sunlight
Humidity	Moderate
Watering	Evenly moisten compost in spring and summer; keep on the dry side in autumn and winter
Feeding	Once every three to four weeks with houseplant fertilizer in spring and summer
Propagation	Sow seeds in pans at 18–20°C (65–68°F) from mid spring to early summer in seed and cutting compost
Potting	Houseplant potting compost
Problems	Mealy bug, root mealy bug, premature loss of lower leaves
Availability	Occasionally available throughout year
Uses indoors	Floor-standing feature plant for lounge, dining room or conservatory; can be used as Christmas tree

Spray the foliage to clean off dust

Asparagus setaceus

Although it has the common name of Asparagus Fern, this plant is not even related to ferns and should not be classified as such. It is in fact from the lily family, a point which surprises many. It is a useful plant for display throughout the home and is relatively easy to grow. Apart from being suitable for a traditional pot or container, the Asparagus Fern also makes a good subject for a hanging pot or hanging basket. Not only is it suitable for use as an indoor plant, either singly or in association with other plants, but it also provides interesting foliage for cut flower arrangements. The Asparagus dislikes a warm and dry atmosphere as the foliage can rapidly dehydrate with resultant desiccation and browning of the leaf tissue.

COMMON NAME
Asparagus Fern

Plant type	Foliage plant with upright, compact habit
Season of interest	All year round
Size	30–90cm (12–36in)
Flower	Insignificant; sometimes followed by small red berries, produced spring/summer
Leaf	Tiny, green, needle-like, on branchlets
Temperature	13–20°C (55–68°F)
Aspect/Light	Well-lit situation out of direct sunlight
Humidity	Moderate to high
Watering	Keep compost evenly moist in spring and summer; water less in autumn and winter but avoid drying out
Feeding	Once every two weeks with half strength houseplant fertilizer in spring and summer
Propagation	Sow seeds at 21°C (70°F) in seed and cutting compost in spring; separate in mid spring to mid summer using houseplant potting compost
Potting	Houseplant potting compost
Problems	Dehydration due to dry atmosphere
Availability	Commonly available throughout year
Uses indoors	Good plant for special planter and cultivation in most rooms except hot, dry situations; ideal for cloakroom, bathroom or kitchen where well lit
Other varieties	A. densiflorus 'Myers' – erect, bushy fronds A. d. 'Sprengeri' – hanging stems

Foliage may be removed for floral arrangement

Aspidistra elatior

Well-known for its toughness and durability, the Aspidistra was given its common name of Cast-iron Plant by the Victorians. They valued its ability to tolerate gas, a recent introduction to homes that killed many other indoor plants grown at the time. With the current fashion for some of the older styles of interior furnishing and decoration, the Aspidistra is enjoying a moderate comeback in popularity. It makes an ideal subject for less well-lit positions, although the key to presenting and displaying the plant well lies in finding the right type of container or pot. For a little more colour the variegated form, *A. e.* 'Variegata', can be grown, but this plant requires more light to promote the variegation.

COMMON NAME
Cast-iron Plant

Clean the foliage with a soft, damp cloth

Plant type	Foliage plant with somewhat loose, untidy habit
Season of interest	All year round
Size	30–60cm (12–24in)
Flower	Uninteresting, purple, at base of plant in late summer
Leaf	Broad, slightly ribbed, spear-shaped, 30–45cm (12–18in) long, 7.5–10cm (3–4in) wide
Temperature	10–20°C (50–68°F)
Aspect/Light	Low to moderate light
Humidity	Tolerant of moderately dry atmosphere
Watering	Evenly moisten compost all year round, allowing to get on the dry side before re-watering
Feeding	Once every four weeks with houseplant fertilizer in spring and summer
Propagation	Separate rhizomes mid spring to early summer and pot them singly or in groups at 18–20°C (65–68°F) in houseplant potting compost
Potting	Houseplant potting compost
Problems	Mealy bug, root mealy bug
Availability	Occasionally available throughout the year
Uses indoors	Good plant for relatively poorly lit position on table, desk or in north facing window; display plant in unusual pot to make best of both plant and pot
Other varieties	*A. e.* 'Variegata' – cream and green variegated foliage

Aucuba japonica 'Variegata'

The Aucuba is a good example of an indoor/outdoor plant. It can be grown for two to three years inside before it becomes too large and unmanageable as a houseplant, and then planted outside in the garden. If the plant is to be taken outside during the autumn and winter months, it may first need to be hardened off. If possible, it is better to move it outside in the spring or summer when there is little or no danger of frosts. As an indoor plant the Aucuba is a fairly tough subject which can tolerate fairly cool and draughty positions such as beside front or back doors or in porches. The attractive, variegated foliage makes it suitable for display either on its own or as part of a mixed grouping.

COMMON NAMES
Japanese Laurel, Gold-dust Plant or Tree

The Aucuba can be propagated from tip cuttings

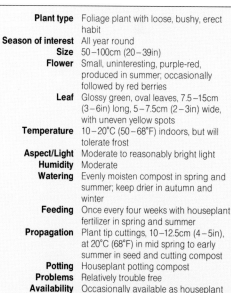

Plant type	Foliage plant with loose, bushy, erect habit
Season of interest	All year round
Size	50–100cm (20–39in)
Flower	Small, uninteresting, purple-red, produced in summer; occasionally followed by red berries
Leaf	Glossy green, oval leaves, 7.5–15cm (3–6in) long, 5–7.5cm (2–3in) wide, with uneven yellow spots
Temperature	10–20°C (50–68°F) indoors, but will tolerate frost
Aspect/Light	Moderate to reasonably bright light
Humidity	Moderate
Watering	Evenly moisten compost in spring and summer; keep drier in autumn and winter
Feeding	Once every four weeks with houseplant fertilizer in spring and summer
Propagation	Plant tip cuttings, 10–12.5cm (4–5in), at 20°C (68°F) in mid spring to early summer in seed and cutting compost
Potting	Houseplant potting compost
Problems	Relatively trouble free
Availability	Occasionally available as houseplant throughout year
Uses indoors	Useful plant for position that can suffer draughts, such as close to front door or possibly in a porch
Other varieties	*A. j.* 'Crotonifolia' – yellow-cream with white blotches

Begonia boweri

This Begonia is difficult to classify satisfactorily as a specific type of houseplant. The heart-shaped, mottled leaves are attractive and provide interest throughout the year. For this reason it is described here as a foliage plant. However, unlike many other foliage plants, it also has very attractive, pink flowers. Although small, they are produced in sufficient number to compensate. The low-growing habit of the plant and rather loose way that the leaves are produced can make it look a little untidy after a while, so an occasional trim is recommended to maintain the shape. The Begonia is a good plant for using in groups, either of several specimens in a small display or with other plants that it will complement.

COMMON NAME
Eyelash Begonia

Plant type	Foliage plant with rather straggly, loose growth
Season of interest	All year round
Size	10–20cm (4–8in)
Flower	Often plentiful, pale pink but are insufficient to consider it as a flowering plant
Leaf	Attractive mid green leaves with dark mottling, heart-shaped, 4–5cm (1½–2in)
Temperature	13–20°C (55–68°F)
Aspect/Light	Reasonably bright condition, out of direct sun with some shade
Humidity	Moderate
Watering	Keep compost moderately moist throughout year
Feeding	Houseplant fertilizer once every two to four weeks in spring and summer
Propagation	Plant 5cm (2in) sections of rhizome with a number of leaves, or leaf cuttings, at 20°C (68°F) in spring using seed and cutting compost
Potting	Houseplant potting compost
Problems	No major problems
Availability	Occasionally available throughout year
Uses indoors	Attractive plant for bathroom, cloakroom or kitchen windowsill or nearby, provided some shade is available

Associated planting can make better use of the plant

Begonia masoniana

The foliage of this Begonia is most curious, being extremely crinkled and pitted, and bearing a dark brown pattern suggestive of the Iron Cross – hence the common name. An ideal plant for grouping or for a container display, it is a little less tolerant of windowsill cultivation. Not only is it more susceptible to root rot caused by over-watering, often coupled with lower temperatures, but the green pigment can fade if it is exposed to too much light. The crinkled leaves can become dusty and should be gently rinsed with tepid water. Shake off any excess moisture and leave the plant to dry well away from sunlight.

COMMON NAME
Iron Cross Begonia

Plant type	Foliage plant with compact and somewhat horizontal growth
Season of interest	All year round
Size	10–20cm (4–8in)
Flower	Infrequent, greenish, insignificant, 0.6cm (¼in)
Leaf	Unusual, roughly heart-shaped, very crinkled with slight serration; green with dark brown 'Iron Cross' pattern, 7.5–12.5cm (3–5in)
Temperature	18–20°C (65–68°F)
Aspect/Light	Moderate light with some shade
Humidity	Average to high
Watering	Keep compost moderately moist in spring and summer; keep on dry side in autumn and winter
Feeding	Once every two weeks with half strength houseplant fertilizer in spring and summer
Propagation	5cm (2in) sections of rhizome with leaves, or leaf cuttings, at 21°C (70°F) in spring or summer in houseplant potting compost
Potting	Houseplant potting compost
Problems	Root rot, leggy growth, bleaching of leaves in too much light
Availability	Occasionally available, particularly in spring or summer
Uses indoors	Table display or in bowl or planter

Remove dust from the leaves with a spray of tepid water

Begonia rex hybrids

Available in an enormous range of colours and patterns, this Begonia is one of the most popular indoor plants. The brightest colours and boldest patterns occur on the upper leaf surfaces, so the plant needs to be displayed where the foliage can be seen from above. It can be used effectively on its own and will also complement plants of a more subtle tone such as *Ficus pumila*, the Creeping Fig, which is a plain green, small-leaved trailing plant. Sadly, this Begonia is particularly susceptible to mildew and a close inspection for the disease needs to be made regularly. Mildew starts as small, discoloured spots on the leaves, so it is easy to falsely diagnose leaf scorch before the white blotches appear, by which time the damage potential is considerably greater.

COMMON NAMES
Fan Plant, King Begonia

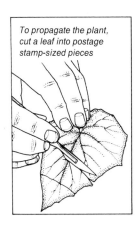
To propagate the plant, cut a leaf into postage stamp-sized pieces

Plant type	Foliage plant with compact and somewhat horizontal growth
Season of interest	All year round
Size	10–25cm (4–10in)
Flower	Small, white to pale pink, insignificant, 1.3cm (½in)
Leaf	Roughly heart-shaped with crinkled edge, wide range of patterns and colours (silver, pink, purple, red and green), with small hairs on underside and on leaf stalks, 7.5–25cm (3–10in)
Temperature	13–20°C (55–68°F)
Aspect/Light	Reasonably bright with some shade
Humidity	Average to high
Watering	Keep compost moderately moist throughout year
Feeding	Once every two to four weeks with houseplant fertilizer in spring and summer
Propagation	Lay leaf cuttings on surface of seed and cutting compost or peat and sand mix; or cut the leaf into postage stamp-sized pieces and treat similarly in spring and summer at 21°C (70°F)
Potting	Houseplant potting compost
Problems	Mildew, mealy bug, root mealy bug, botrytis, leggy growth in time
Availability	Freely available throughout the year
Uses indoors	Excellent plant for table or slightly shaded windowsill; good for plant arrangements and bowls

Brassaia actinophylla

The Brassaia is quite similar to *Heptapleurum arboricola*. However, unlike that species, which produces a relatively compact 'tower' of foliage, this plant has a far more open habit, requiring considerably more floor space. The plant creates a very bold and striking effect, especially when artificial light plays on the foliage. The Brassaia needs constant inspection for pests and diseases, as it is particularly prone to attack by aphid and red spider mite. Aphid soon severely damage and deform the young leaves, spoiling the balance of the plant. Red spider mites cause yellowing and cupping of the older foliage, resulting in premature leaf loss. This plant was formerly known by the latin name *Schefflera actinophylla*.

COMMON NAMES
Umbrella Plant, Umbrella Tree

Provide a stake to ensure vertical growth

Plant type	Foliage plant with climbing habit
Season of interest	All year round
Size	150–250cm (59–98in)
Flower	None indoors
Leaf	7.5–25cm (3–10in) long, 5–10cm (2–4in) wide, green leaflets, with around five on young leaves and seven to fifteen on mature plants
Temperature	15–20°C (59–68°F)
Aspect/Light	Well-lit situation, out of direct sunlight
Humidity	Moderate
Watering	Evenly but barely moisten compost in spring and summer, allowing to dry a little between waterings; water just enough to prevent drying out in autumn and winter
Feeding	Once every two to four weeks with houseplant fertilizer spring and summer
Propagation	Plant 7.5–10cm (3–4in) tip or stem cuttings in seed and cutting compost at 21–24°C (70–75°F) in spring; sow seed at 20°C (68°F) at same time of year
Potting	Houseplant potting compost
Problems	Aphid, red spider mite, mealy bug, root mealy bug, leaf loss from over-watering or temperature fluctuations
Availability	Commonly available throughout year
Uses indoors	Feature plant best displayed on floor in lounge, dining room, or office

Caladium hortulanum hybrids

The Caladium is a quite extraordinary plant and worth persevering with, providing you are prepared to cosset it with high humidity and a constant warm temperature. Caladiums are particularly prone to draughts, which can cause the total collapse of the plant. An unusual characteristic is the waxy foliage, which has an inherent ability to shed water very effectively. This makes aphid control difficult with a wet spray and a duster can be more effective. After the summer, the foliage begins to die down and the tuber will need to be stored over the dormant autumn and winter period. Store the tuber at about 15°C (60°F) in dry peat. Growth can be restarted in late spring or early summer by potting into a 13cm (5in) pot at 21°C (70°F) in houseplant potting compost that is kept moderately moist.

COMMON NAME
Angels Wings

Plant type	Foliage plant with erect, fleshy stems
Season of interest	Late spring to summer; dormant for over half of year
Size	25–38cm (10–15in)
Flower	Arum-like, 5–7.5cm (2–3in), greenish-white spathe around whitish spadix
Leaf	Highly ornate, heart-shaped, 20–30cm (8–12in), waxy, either translucent white with green veins or with variations of crimson, pink, white and green patterning
Temperature	20–21°C (68–70°F)
Aspect/Light	Well-lit situation out of direct sunlight
Humidity	High
Watering	Keep compost evenly moist in spring and summer; keep tuber dry during dormancy
Feeding	Once every two to four weeks with half strength houseplant fertilizer in summer
Propagation	Separate young tubers in early spring and pot in houseplant potting compost at 21°C (70°F)
Potting	Houseplant potting compost
Problems	Aphid, collapse of foliage due to draughts or cold
Availability	Occasionally available in summer
Uses indoors	Feature plant for display in summer on table close to sunny window

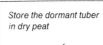
Store the dormant tuber in dry peat

Calathea zebrina

A very attractive foliage plant with unusual coloration, varying from the green pigment when viewed from above, to the distinctly purple-coloured leaves and stems when viewed from below. Unfortunately, the plant is very susceptible to a dry atmosphere and prefers a high level of humidity. The thin leaves, which are borne in a horizontal manner, quickly lose water by transpiration and will dehydrate, resulting in brown edges and even leaf loss. The plant should therefore be placed in a situation that is sympathetic to its needs, or grouped with other plants to create a humid microclimate.

COMMON NAME
Zebra Plant

Plant type	Foliage plant with leaves borne horizontally on erect stems
Season of interest	All year round
Size	20–40cm (8–16in)
Flower	Insignificant, borne on erect stems amongst foliage
Leaf	Oval leaves, 15–20cm (6–8in) long, 5–7.5cm (2–3in) wide with unusual patterning of bold green blotches and veins above, purple below
Temperature	18–21°C (65–70°F)
Aspect/Light	Moderate light well away from brightly lit situation
Humidity	High
Watering	Keep compost moist throughout year
Feeding	Once every two to four weeks with houseplant fertilizer in spring and summer
Propagation	Tease apart clumps and plant separately from mid spring to early summer at 21°C (70°F) in houseplant potting compost
Potting	Houseplant potting compost
Problems	Red spider mite, mealy bug, root mealy bug, yellowing of leaves due to draughts or over-watering
Availability	Often available throughout the year
Uses indoors	Good for display on its own or in group
Other varieties	C. makoyana – more subtle green patterning C. ornata – green and pink striped

Improve humidity by standing the plant on a tray of moist pebbles

Carex morrowii 'Variegata'

As its common name of Japanese Sedge suggests, the Carex is in fact a grass. The delicate, variegated leaves make it an excellent foil for other, bolder plants, either in a terrarium or as part of a mixed bowl arrangement. Air movement through the foliage can also create an interesting effect, especially when coupled with light. The plant is a fairly easy species to cultivate, provided the humidity is kept at quite a high level, otherwise the leaves will turn brown at the tips and edges. This problem is accentuated if the plant is grown at too high a temperature.

COMMON NAME
Japanese Sedge

To propagate the plant, cut clumps apart with a sharp knife

Plant type	Ornamental grass with erect variegated foliage
Season of interest	All year round
Size	25–30cm (10–12in)
Flower	Insignificant, greenish buff, infrequent
Leaf	Fine, erect, 20–30cm (8–12in), cream and green variegated, arching when longer
Temperature	15–21°C (60–70°F)
Aspect/Light	Well-lit situation out of direct sunlight
Humidity	Moderate to high
Watering	Keep compost evenly moist throughout year, but slightly drier in winter
Feeding	Once every four weeks with houseplant fertilizer in spring and summer
Propagation	Separate clumps with sharp knife and pot separately in houseplant potting compost at 20°C (68°F) from mid spring to mid summer
Potting	Houseplant potting compost
Problems	Red spider mite, browning of leaf tips and edges
Availability	Occasionally available throughout the year
Uses indoors	On windowsill, partly shaded by curtain or position close by; useful foil for other plants

Chlorophytum comosum 'Vittatum'

The Chlorophytum is one of the most common and popular houseplants, and is quite tolerant of a variety of conditions. It is often used in planted arrangements, but due to its vigour it is probably best not planted in constrained objects such as terrariums and bottle gardens, as it will quickly outgrow them. With its characteristic trailing stems and plantlets, the Chlorophytum is particularly good as a hanging plant in a basket or pot. To maintain the plant's appearance, trim off brown leaf tips with sharp scissors, taking care to leave a small area of dead tissue.

COMMON NAMES
St Bernard's Lily, Spider Plant

The plant can be propagated from plantlets produced on the trailing stems

Plant type	Foliage plant with divergent habit and trailing stems producing plantlets
Season of interest	All year round
Size	20–40cm (8–16in)
Flower	Tiny, white, on ends of long trailing stems, produced in spring and summer
Leaf	Grass-like, cascading in splayed fashion, 46–61cm (18–24in), succulent, green and white striped
Temperature	10–18°C (50–65°F)
Aspect/Light	Well-lit situation, out of direct sunlight
Humidity	Moderate
Watering	Keep compost evenly moist in spring and summer; keep drier in autumn and winter
Feeding	Once every two to four weeks with houseplant fertilizer in spring and summer
Propagation	Root plantlets in houseplant potting compost or water in spring and summer at 18–20°C (65–68°F)
Potting	Houseplant potting compost
Problems	Aphid, leaf scorch with too much sun, browning of tips in dry air
Availability	Commonly available throughout year
Uses indoors	Wide range of uses, especially on windowsills or in hanging baskets
Other varieties	C. c. 'Picturatum' – green leaves with yellow stripe C. c. 'Variegatum' – green-edged white leaves

Cissus antarctica

A versatile foliage plant with a climbing habit, although loose stems can sometimes trail from the pot as well. The Cissus requires some means of support in the form of a cane or several canes, or some other type of frame, to maintain a balanced appearance. Trimming with sharp scissors or secateurs will help to keep the plant in check, otherwise the foliage can become rather straggly. When positioning the Cissus, great care must be taken to ensure that it is provided with the correct amount of light. Too much light will cause the foliage to become rather hard and yellow; too little will result in foliage that is weak and etiolated. Place it near a window but not in the path of direct sunlight.

COMMON NAME
Kangaroo Vine

Plant type	Foliage climbing plant
Season of interest	All year round
Size	100–200cm (39–78in) high, 30–60cm (12–24in) wide
Flower	None
Leaf	Roughly heart-shaped, 7.5–10cm (3–4in) long, serrated, green
Temperature	15–20°C (59–68°F)
Aspect/Light	Moderate, but dislikes direct sunlight
Humidity	Moderate
Watering	Evenly but barely moisten compost throughout year, allowing to get on the dry side before re-watering
Feeding	Once every two to four weeks with houseplant fertilizer in spring and summer
Propagation	Plant tip cuttings, 7.5–12.5cm (3–5in) in early spring to early summer in seed and cutting compost at 18–20°C (65–68°F)
Potting	Houseplant potting compost
Problems	Red spider mite, mealy bug, root mealy bug, root loss if over-watered
Availability	Widely available throughout year
Uses indoors	Can be used in almost any room on table; larger specimens can stand on floor; useful specimen plant in office
Other varieties	*C. discolor* – green, silver and red foliage

Wayward shoots can be trimmed with sharp scissors

Cissus rhombifolia

This Cissus is particularly good for filling a space in a corner where a column of foliage is required. With its rich green leaves, the plant can provide an excellent background or foil for the display of other plants, and can also be displayed in its own right. It is quite adaptable and can tolerate a range of conditions in the home or office. However, a too brightly lit position can turn the rich green leaves a sickly yellowish green as the plant compensates for the excessive light by producing less chlorophyll. To gain the best from the plant, position it in a moderately lit or even slightly shaded position. However, avoid too much shade as the growth will become thin and etiolated. This plant was formerly known as *Rhoicissus rhomboidea*.

COMMON NAME
Grape Ivy

Plant type	Foliage plant with climbing and semi-trailing habit
Season of interest	All year round
Size	100–200cm (39–78in) high, 30–60cm (12–24in) wide
Flower	None
Leaf	Made up of 3 leaflets with serrated edges, 5–6cm (2–2½in), dark green
Temperature	15–20°C (59–68°F)
Aspect/Light	Moderate light, away from direct sun
Humidity	Moderate
Watering	Evenly moisten compost in spring and summer, taking care not to over-water and allowing to dry a little before re-watering; keep on drier side in autumn and winter
Feeding	Once every two to three weeks with houseplant fertilizer in spring and summer
Propagation	Plant 7.5–12.5cm (3–5in) tip cuttings in seed and cutting compost at 18–20°C (65–68°F) from early spring to early summer
Potting	Houseplant potting compost
Problems	Mealy bug, yellowing with too much sun
Availability	Commonly available throughout year
Uses indoors	Useful in mixed planting or on table-top or floor in most rooms
Other varieties	*C. r.* 'Ellen Danica' – larger, rounder leaves with deeper serrations

Trim the plant to maintain a compact shape

Cleyera japonica

The Cleyera is an uncommon foliage plant and an attractive plant for either the house or the conservatory. *C. japonica* itself has glossy dark leaves, but an even more desirable form is *C. j. variegata*, which has variegated leaves of pale and dark green, edged with yellow. Young leaves may also have a pinkish tinge around the edges. The Cleyera is suitable for cultivation in a pot or tub. It requires little pruning, though the tips of the leaves can be removed to promote bushy growth. Small white flowers may appear in early summer. Leaves should be mist-sprayed regularly to discourage red spider mite.

COMMON NAME
Japanese Cleyera

Cut back young plants in early spring to encourage a bushy habit

Plant type	Foliage plant with bushy habit
Season of interest	All year round
Size	60–75cm (24–30in)
Flower	Small, white, not always produced
Leaf	7–5cm (3in) long, oval, pointed, green or variegated green and yellow
Temperature	−3–20°C (26–68°F)
Humidity	Moderate
Watering	Evenly moisten compost at all times
Feeding	Every two to three weeks with houseplant fertilizer in spring and early summer
Propagation	Plant 7.5–10cm (3–4in) tip cuttings in seed and cutting compost in early spring at 7–10°C (45–50°F)
Potting	Houseplant potting compost
Problems	Red spider mite
Availability	Quite commonly available throughout the year
Uses indoors	As a container grown evergreen for conservatories and greenhouses

Codiaeum variegatum pictum

An unusual plant with brightly coloured pigments that intensify during the summer, when the leaves take on a greater proportion of yellow, orange, pink and red. However, as the light decreases in the autumn and winter, the bright colours tend to fade and the plant becomes rather more green. The Codiaeum is very susceptible to changes in temperature, which can cause rapid leaf drop. The problem is especially acute during the autumn, winter and early spring. For this reason it is essential to provide the plant with as near a constant temperature as possible. Although it likes bright light, it should be moved away from the window in the winter months to avoid exposure to cold.

COMMON NAMES
Croton, Joseph's Coat

The Codiaeum can be propagated from tip cuttings

Plant type	Foliage plant with bushy habit
Season of interest	All year round
Size	30–90cm (12–36in)
Flower	Unusual, insignificant, white, produced on spike in late spring/summer
Leaf	Broadly serrated oval, 10–15cm (4–6in) long, 2.5–7.5cm (1–3in) wide, with variable shape and pattern of bold colours ranging from green to yellow, orange and crimson
Temperature	18–21°C (65–70°F)
Aspect/Light	Full light with exposure to direct sun
Humidity	Moderate
Watering	Evenly moisten compost in spring and summer, allowing to dry a little before re-watering; keep on drier side in autumn and winter
Feeding	Once every two to four weeks in spring and summer with houseplant fertilizer
Propagation	Plant tip cuttings, 10–15cm (4–6in), from late spring to summer in seed and cutting compost at 21–24°C (70–75°F)
Potting	Houseplant potting compost
Problems	Red spider mite, mealy bug, root mealy bug, leaf loss with low temperatures
Availability	Available through the year, but more common in spring and summer
Uses indoors	Specimen feature plant for brightly lit position in lounge or dining room; useful office plant

Coffea arabica

An attractive plant with bold glossy green foliage. Once it has grown to maturity and is over four years old, and provided cultural conditions are right, it is possible that in late summer the plant might flower. The white flowers are star-like and enhanced by their fragrant scent. With luck, they may give rise to the production of fruit. These are green at first, but then turn red before finally ripening to darker brown 'coffee beans'. However, the production of these beans on an indoor specimen is such an unlikely event that it would be unwise to choose the plant for this purpose alone. The Coffea can grow quite large, requiring considerable space. Older plants are therefore best displayed on the floor.

COMMON NAMES
Coffee Plant, Arabian Coffee Plant

Plant type	Foliage plant with bushy, shrubby habit
Season of interest	All year round, with extra summer interest when in flower
Size	100–150cm (39–59in)
Flower	Star-shaped, white, fragrant, produced in late summer; rarely followed by green fruits that turn red, then brown
Leaf	Oval, ribbed, 10–15cm (4–6in) long, 2.5–5cm (1–2in) wide, shiny, green
Temperature	18–21°C (65–70°F)
Aspect/Light	Reasonable light, but away from direct sunlight
Humidity	Reasonable to high; dislikes a dry atmosphere
Watering	Evenly moisten compost in spring and summer, taking care not to over-water; keep on drier side in autumn and winter
Feeding	Once every two to four weeks with houseplant fertilizer in spring and summer
Propagation	Sow seed in seed and cutting compost in spring at 24°C (75°F)
Potting	Houseplant potting compost
Problems	Scale insect
Availability	Occasionally available throughout year
Uses indoors	Floor standing plant in lounge or dining room close to a window

The plant can be grown as a standard by removing the side shoots

Coleus blumei

This Coleus is one of the most popular and common of indoor plants. It is suitable for using in almost any location where there is direct sunlight to brighten the colour pigments in the leaves. The plant is also a very easy species to grow and can be shaped very simply by pinching out the terminal shoots. These same shoots provide ideal propagation material when they are large enough, and can be fun to root in water, where the roots can be watched developing. The small flowers are rather disappointing and may be cut off if not wanted. After the first season of growth, the Coleus becomes rather leggy, so it is best treated as an annual to be discarded and renewed each year. Propagate new plants from the terminal shoots.

COMMON NAMES
Flame Nettle, Painted Nettle

Plant type	Foliage plant with bushy habit
Season of interest	All year round
Size	30–60cm (12–24in)
Flower	Insignificant, blue, amongst foliage, produced in late spring/summer
Leaf	Pointed, oval, 5–7.5cm (2–3in), with variable coloration and bold patterning, ranging from white to pink, orange, red and green
Temperature	15–18°C (60–65°F)
Aspect/Light	Full light, some direct sunlight
Humidity	Reasonable, but requires more humidity as temperature increases
Watering	Evenly moisten compost throughout year
Feeding	Houseplant fertilizer once every two weeks in spring and summer
Propagation	Plant tip cuttings, 5–7.5cm (2–3in), from mid summer to autumn in seed and cutting compost or in water at 18–20°C (65–68°F)
Potting	Houseplant potting compost
Problems	Red spider mite, legginess as plant gets older
Availability	Commonly available in spring and early summer
Uses indoors	Good plant for windowsill, conservatory, greenhouse or porch

Pinching out the terminal shoots helps to improve bushiness

Cordyline terminalis

An attractively coloured, large-leaved plant, which was formerly known as *Dracaena terminalis*. Like other highly coloured foliage plants, the Cordyline produces its pretty cerise-pink new leaves in the mid to late spring and summer when light intensities are higher. However, direct sunlight will scorch and disfigure the plant. As light intensities reduce in the autumn and winter, any emerging leaves are likely to be much more green in coloration. The thin leaves are also very sensitive to a dry atmosphere and it is important to keep the humidity high, otherwise leaf tips and edges will quickly turn brown and leaf loss may also occur. For a more diminutive variety, it may be worth trying *C. t.* 'Rededge', although this too is just as susceptible to the same problems.

COMMON NAMES
Flaming Dragon Tree, Tree of Kings

Gently wipe the leaves with a soft, damp cloth to remove dust

Plant type	Foliage plant with erect stem and bushy growth
Season of interest	All year round
Size	30–90cm (12–36in)
Flower	Uninteresting spike infrequently produced on mature plants in spring/summer
Leaf	Spear-shaped, 30–45cm (12–18in) long, 5–7.5cm (2–3in) wide, green and pink (vivid pink on new leaves)
Temperature	20–21°C (68–70°F)
Aspect/Light	Moderate to reasonable light, away from direct sunlight
Humidity	High
Watering	Evenly moisten compost throughout year, taking care not to over-water and allowing to dry a little before re-watering
Feeding	Once every two weeks with houseplant fertilizer in spring and summer
Propagation	Plant 10–15cm (4–6in) tip cuttings, or 5–7.5cm (2–3in) sections of stem in seed and cutting compost at 21°C (70°F) in late spring
Potting	Houseplant potting compost
Problems	Red spider mite, mealy bug, browning of tips and edges with dry atmosphere
Availability	Widely available throughout the year
Uses indoors	Very useful specimen plant
Other varieties	*C. t.* 'Rededge' – smaller; red and green striped

Cupressus macrocarpa

A conifer may seem like an unusual choice for an indoor plant, but *C. macrocarpa*, the Monterey Cypress, is one of several Cupressus species which can be successfully grown in the conservatory when young. It has bright green, frond-like foliage and a graceful habit of growth; the variety *C. m.* 'Goldcrest' is a particularly attractive golden yellow colour. Mature specimens will reach a height of 18m (60ft) or more as garden trees, but the size of conservatory-grown plants can be controlled by pruning in spring. Cypresses may either be planted in the conservatory border or grown in a pot or tub. Effective in group plantings, they can also be used as a backing to flowering plants.

COMMON NAME
Monterey Cypress

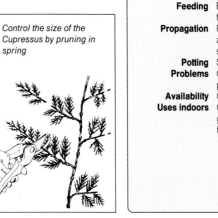

Control the size of the Cupressus by pruning in spring

Plant type	Foliage plant with erect habit
Season of interest	All year round
Size	180cm (72in) if grown in a pot, if not double or more
Flower	Insignificant
Leaf	Frond-like flattened spray, green or gold
Temperature	−6–20°C (21–68°F)
Aspect/Light	Well-lit situation shaded from direct sunlight
Humidity	Moderate
Watering	Evenly moisten compost from spring to autumn; keep drier in winter
Feeding	Every two weeks with houseplant fertilizer from mid spring to mid summer
Propagation	Plant 10cm (4in) stem cuttings in seed and cutting compost at 12°C (55°F) in spring
Potting	Soil-based potting compost
Problems	Overall size which can be controlled by pruning
Availability	Commonly available all year round
Uses indoors	Conservatory or greenhouse plant grown in pot or border; good backing for mixed planting

Cycas revoluta

Although it has the common name of Sago Palm, the Cycas is not a species of palm at all and is only palm-like in appearance. It is one of the most primitive plants, dating back many millions of years. It is thought to be the food plant of dinosaurs, and the toughness of the leaves might be one reason why the dinosaur became extinct! The Cycas is extremely slow-growing, putting out just one new leaf each year. Eventually it forms an attractive rosette of arching plumes. Because of its lack of vigour and slow root action and development, this plant is very susceptible to over-watering, which causes the leaves to turn yellow. These should be removed with a sharp knife.

COMMON NAME
Sago Palm

Plant type	Foliage plant with radiating plumes of semi-erect foliage
Season of interest	All year round
Size	30–90cm (12–36in)
Flower	None as houseplant
Leaf	Tough leaflets, 5–15cm (2–6in) long, green, borne on stems 15–90cm (6–36in) long, forming feather-like appearance, radiating from central cone
Temperature	15–21°C (60–70°F)
Aspect/Light	Brightly lit situation
Humidity	Moderate
Watering	Evenly moisten compost in spring and summer; keep on dry side when dormant in autumn and winter
Feeding	Once a month with houseplant fertilizer in spring and summer
Propagation	Sow seeds at 21–24°C (70–75°F) in seed and cutting compost in late spring to early summer; germination and growth very slow and uneven
Potting	Houseplant potting compost
Problems	Mealy bug, scale insect, leaf yellowing with over-watering
Availability	Occasionally available throughout year
Uses indoors	Table-top next to bright window or in heated conservatory

Remove brown or damaged leaves with a sharp knife

Cyperus alternifolius

The Cyperus forms umbrella-like rosettes of leaves arching out from the top of a rigid, slender stem. In its natural environment the plant grows in marshes, so when cultivated indoors it must be stood in a saucer of water. If it is not kept constantly moist it will quickly die. After a while, the Cyperus can appear rather leggy and the top-heavy fronds can easily fall over, so support the foliage with stakes and ties. The more compact *C. a.* 'Gracilis' is probably better as a houseplant, as the taller variety requires considerably more space. 'Variegatus' is a little more colourful due to the variegated bracts.

COMMON NAME
Dwarf Umbrella Palm

Plant type	Ornamental foliage grass with palm-like fronds on erect stems
Season of interest	All year round
Size	30–120cm (12–48in)
Flower	Insignificant, infrequent, grass-like, buff, produced in spring/summer
Leaf	Thin green bracts, 10–30cm (4–12in), in clusters around erect stem
Temperature	15–20°C (60–68°F)
Aspect/Light	Well-lit situation
Humidity	Moderate to high
Watering	Keep compost constantly moist throughout year; prefers to stand in water
Feeding	Once a month with houseplant fertilizer in spring and summer
Propagation	Separate clump and pot into usual compost; place head with bracts cut back by about a third to a half in water or seed and cutting compost in spring or early summer at 20–22°C (68–72°F)
Potting	Houseplant potting compost
Problems	No real problems, unless plant is allowed to dry out
Availability	Occasionally available, but not a very popular houseplant
Uses indoors	Close to window; effective standing in an indoor pond
Other varieties	*C. a.* 'Gracilis' – more compact, growing up to 60cm (24in) *C. a.* 'Variegatus' – variegated bracts

Provide constant moisture by standing the plant in a saucer of water

Cyperus papyrus

Several species of Cyperus may be grown indoors but *C. papyrus* is the most suitable as a conservatory plant. This is the Papyrus from which the ancient Egyptians made paper, and is also the 'bulrush' of the bible used for making Moses' cradle. Its striking appearance – smooth green stems topped by a spectacular tuft of long, thread-like leaves – makes it a very desirable plant. It is not easy to grow as it needs warmth and plenty of moisture, and the roots must never be allowed to dry out. One of the most suitable positions for the Papyrus is beside an indoor pool, although not actually in the water.

COMMON NAME
Papyrus

Provide the roots with moisture by standing the pot in a saucer of water

Plant type	Foliage plant with upright habit
Season	All year round
Size	120–240 cm (48–96in)
Flower	Small brown tufts
Leaf	Long, thread-like, 10–25cm (4–10in) green, borne in a tuft
Temperature	16–21°C (61–70°F)
Aspect/Light	Well-lit situation, shaded from full sun
Humidity	High
Watering	Water copiously all year round and keep root ball moist at all times, but do not allow the stems to stand in water
Feeding	Every 4 weeks with houseplant fertilizer from mid spring to mid summer
Propagation	By division in spring
Potting	Peat-based potting compost
Availability	Quite commonly available throughout the year
Uses indoors	Decorative water feature in very humid conditions

Dieffenbachia amoena

A boldly variegated plant that can create quite a dramatic display in the home. However, it should be positioned and handled with care as the sap is very poisonous. The Dieffenbachia tends to lose its lower leaves, which first become yellow and then turn a soft mushy brown. Before this occurs, any fading leaves should be removed with a sharp knife. Wear protective gloves, as the sap can cause chronic inflammation. Where the atmosphere is drier, the fading leaf may simply dehydrate, but it should still be cleanly cut off to prevent any rot from spreading. When the plant becomes top heavy, with a long, bare stem, it may be worth cutting it back. The material removed can be used for propagation and the stump should produce new shoots in time.

COMMON NAMES
Dumb Cane, Leopard Lily

The plant can be propagated by laying sections of stem on the surface of the compost

Plant type	Foliage plant with shrubby growth
Season of interest	All year round
Size	100–150cm (39–59in)
Flower	Arum-like, 5–7.5cm (2–3in), greenish white; produced in spring/summer
Leaf	Oval, 20–45cm (8–18in) long, 10–20cm (4–8in) wide, boldly variegated
Temperature	19–21°C (66–70°F)
Aspect/Light	Well-lit situation, out of direct sunlight
Humidity	High
Watering	Evenly moisten compost in spring and summer, allow to dry a little in autumn and winter
Feeding	Once every two to three weeks with houseplant fertilizer in spring and summer
Propagation	Plant 10–12.5cm (4–5in) tip cuttings in or lay 7.5cm (3in) sections of stem on seed and cutting compost in mid spring to early summer at 22–24°C (72–75°F)
Potting	Houseplant potting compost
Problems	Mealy bug, root mealy bug, red spider mite, stem rot and leaf yellowing due to draughts, cold or over-watering
Availability	Commonly available throughout year
Uses indoors	Close to window on table or floor, but take care with positioning as it is very poisonous
Other varieties	*D. exotica* – green and white
D. picta – greenish yellow
D. 'Tropic Snow' – white

Dionaea muscipula

The Dionaea is an extraordinary plant that particularly appeals to children. The fierce-looking, jaw-like leaf pads form an open 'mouth' which gapes to attract any insect that passes by. The jaw is activated by trigger hairs. If these are brushed by an insect on the leaf pad, two pads close and the spine-like extensions intermesh. The jaws then close around the doomed insect, which is digested by chemicals. It may be worth placing a jam or bell jar over the plant to improve the humidity, although this will have to be removed from time to time so the plant can catch insects.

COMMON NAME
Venus Fly Trap

Plant type	Prostrate novelty foliage plant
Season of interest	Spring and summer
Size	4–10cm (1½–4in)
Flower	Uninspiring, white, produced in early summer
Leaf	Elongated, split into two opposing pads, hinged at base with tooth-like extensions around edge, green
Temperature	19–21°C (66–70°F)
Aspect/Light	Moderate to well-lit situation
Humidity	High
Watering	Keep compost constantly moist in spring and summer; keep on drier side when dormant; prefers rain-water
Feeding	Once every month with half strength houseplant fertilizer in spring and summer
Propagation	Separate root; sow seed in seed and cutting compost from late spring to early summer at 20–21°C (68–70°F)
Potting	Even mixture of sphagnum moss peat, sphagnum moss and leaf mould
Problems	No real problems
Availability	Quite commonly available throughout year, even when dormant; most common in spring and summer when in growth
Uses indoors	Appealing novelty plant for windowsill or situation close to window

A bell jar or inverted jam jar can improve humidity

Dizygotheca elegantissima

This delicate-leaved plant looks effective when silhouetted against a plain wall or spotlit to produce interesting shadow effects, although the light should not be placed too close to the plant. It is perhaps better grown as a multi-stemmed plant, with several plants of the same type in the same pot to provide a more condensed and compact effect. Care must be taken to ensure that it is protected from draughts and temperature fluctuations, as these will cause the leaflets to be shed very rapidly. Scale insects can also be a problem, especially as they camouflage themselves well on the dark stems. The Dizygotheca is sometimes sold as a plant for bottle gardens and bowl arrangements, but is best displayed as a feature plant.

COMMON NAMES
Finger Aralia, Spider Plant

Plant type	Foliage plant with erect habit
Season of interest	All year round
Size	100–150cm (39–59in)
Flower	None as indoor plant
Leaf	Leaflets, 7.5–10cm (3–4in), 7–10 per leaf stem, radiating from centre, broadly serrated, bronze-purple green
Temperature	18–21°C (65–70°F)
Aspect/Light	Well-lit situation out of direct sun
Humidity	High
Watering	Evenly moisten compost throughout year, taking care not to over-water and allowing to dry a little before re-watering
Feeding	Once every two to four weeks with houseplant fertilizer in spring and summer
Propagation	Difficult, but sow seed at 21°C (70°F) in seed and cutting compost
Potting	Houseplant potting compost
Problems	Red spider mite, mealy bug, root mealy bug, scale insect, aphid, premature lower leaf drop
Availability	Occasionally available in spring and summer
Uses indoors	Feature plant on table or furniture relatively close to window away from draughts; effective office plant

Spotlighting can produce a striking effect

Dracaena deremensis

An excellent plant for a lounge, dining room, or wherever it can be showed off to good effect, this Dracaena provides many years of pleasure. The plant can grow to quite a size so is best displayed at floor level. As it gets older, the leaf edges and tips turn brown and the lower leaves are shed, but the palm-like appearance that results is not displeasing. If, however, this is not to your taste, try cutting the plant back to encourage it to break into leaf further down the stem. The material that is pruned off is useful for propagation. Damaged or dead leaves can be trimmed back with a sharp pair of scissors, taking care to leave a small area of dead tissue, or removed altogether at the base of the leaf with a sharp knife.

COMMON NAME
Striped Dracaena

Cut back leggy plants to promote new growth

Plant type	Ornamental foliage plant with erect habit
Season of interest	All year round
Size	150–250cm (59–98in)
Flower	Rarely produced indoors, in spring/summer
Leaf	30–45cm (12–18in) long, 5cm (2in) wide, green and white striped
Temperature	18–21°C (64–70°F)
Aspect/Light	Well-lit situation out of direct sunlight
Humidity	Moderate
Watering	Evenly moisten compost in spring and summer, allowing to dry a little before re-watering; keep on drier side in autumn and winter
Feeding	Houseplant fertilizer once every two to four weeks in spring and summer
Propagation	Plant 10–15cm (4–6in) tip cuttings or 5–7.5cm (2–3in) stem cuttings in seed and cutting compost from late spring to summer at 24°C (75°F)
Potting	Houseplant potting compost
Problems	Mealy bug, root mealy bug
Availability	Occasionally available throughout year
Uses indoors	Good specimen plant to be grown at floor level in lounge, dining room, bedroom or office
Other varieties	D. fragrans – broader, variegated foliage

Dracaena marginata

A graceful, palm-like plant. Oddly enough, it becomes more attractive as the lower leaves are shed to produce a crown of shiny foliage atop a woody, often twisted stem. Care should be taken with the positioning of this Dracaena, as any damage to the foliage will cause the subsequent growth to be deformed for a while. If damage does occur, the plant should either be left to grow through it or cut off below the damaged area with sharp secateurs. This will encourage it to produce up to three side-shoots. Plants that become too large can be treated similarly. The sections of stem removed are suitable for propagating, but it is advisable to mark them with a felt tip pen to indicate which is the right way up.

COMMON NAMES
Silhouette Plant, Striped Dragon Tree

Prune off damage to the terminal shoot

Plant type	Ornamental foliage plant with erect habit
Season of interest	All year round
Size	100–200cm (39–78in)
Flower	None usually as indoor plant
Leaf	Narrow, 30–45cm (12–18in) long, 1.5cm ($\frac{1}{2}$in) wide, tapering to fine point, produced in tight rosette, green
Temperature	15–21°C (59–70°F)
Aspect/Light	Slightly shady or reasonably well-lit situation
Humidity	Moderate
Watering	Barely moisten compost in spring and summer; keep on dry side in autumn and winter
Feeding	Once every two to four weeks with houseplant fertilizer in spring and summer
Propagation	Plant 10–15cm (4–6in) tip cuttings or 5–7.5cm (2–3in) stem cuttings in seed and cutting compost from late spring to summer at 24°C (75°F)
Potting	Houseplant potting compost
Problems	Mealy bug, root mealy bug, premature lower leaf loss
Availability	Commonly available throughout year
Uses indoors	Ideal plant for many situations around the home or in an office; good as floor-standing specimen plant
Other varieties	D. m. 'Tricolor' – pinkish-cream variegation; more delicate

Dracaena sanderana

An attractive plant with broad, cream and green variegated leaves. It must be provided with a fair level of humidity, otherwise the lower leaves will be shed quite freely, making it look rather absurd. In this respect, the species differs from other Dracaena, in which leaf loss can actually improve the appearance. If it does shed its leaves, the stem can be trimmed back to encourage the production of side shoots. However, this plant looks better when the stem is allowed to grow unimpeded. Provide the plant with a stake to encourage erect growth. Take care not to over-water the compost as this can cause premature yellowing of the leaves.

COMMON NAMES
Belgian Evergreen, Ribbon Plant

Plant type	Ornamental foliage plant with erect habit
Season of interest	All year round
Size	60–90cm (12–36in)
Flower	None usually as houseplant
Leaf	7.5–15cm (3–6in) long, 2.5cm (1in) wide, green with cream border
Temperature	18–21°C (64–70°F)
Aspect/Light	Well-lit situation, out of direct sunlight
Humidity	Moderate to high
Watering	Evenly moisten compost in spring and summer, taking care not to over-water, and allowing to get on the dry side before re-watering; keep on drier side in autumn and winter
Feeding	Once every two to four weeks with houseplant fertilizer in spring and summer
Propagation	Plant 10–15cm (4–6in) tip cuttings, or 5–7.5cm (2–3in) stem cuttings in seed and cutting compost in late spring to early summer at 24°C (75°F)
Potting	Houseplant potting compost
Problems	Red spider mite, mealy bug, root mealy bug, premature leaf yellowing when too wet
Availability	Commonly available throughout year
Uses indoors	Useful for limited life in bowl or trough; or as floor standing specimen plant in lounge, dining room or bedroom; good for mixed planting in office

A stake will help to promote erect growth

Epipremnum aureum

An effective climbing and trailing plant best suited to a situation where it can be given sufficient space for the fleshy foliage to grow relatively unimpeded. The Epipremnum can be grown either as a trailing plant, in a hanging pot or basket, or as a climbing plant, trained up a moss pole. The pole should be kept moist to encourage the plant to root on to it. Take care with watering, as root failure can occur if the plant is over-watered. Furthermore, all of the varieties are susceptible to draughts, especially *E. a.* 'Marble Queen'. Variegation in the foliage can be adversely affected by placing the plant in too shaded a situation, which will cause the colours to revert to green. This plant was formerly known by the Latin name *Scindapsus aureum*.

COMMON NAME
Devil's Ivy

Plant type	Ornamental foliage plant with climbing and trailing habit
Season of interest	All year round
Size	100–200cm (39–78in)
Flower	None
Leaf	Heart-shaped, 10–15cm (4–6in), fleshy, green and yellow variegated
Temperature	18–22°C (64–72°F)
Aspect/Light	Moderately lit to well-lit situation away from direct sun
Humidity	Moderate to high
Watering	Evenly moisten compost in spring and summer, taking care not to over-water, and allowing to get on the dry side before re-watering; keep on dry side in autumn and winter
Feeding	Once every two to four weeks with houseplant fertilizer in spring and summer
Propagation	Plant 7.5–10cm (3–4in) tip cuttings in seed and cutting compost from late spring to early summer at 21–24°C (70–75°F)
Potting	Houseplant potting compost
Problems	Root rot due to over-watering
Availability	Quite commonly available throughout year
Uses indoors	Useful in any room where there are no draughts and the temperature is even
Other varieties	*E. a.* 'Golden Queen' – yellow *E. a.* 'Marble Queen' – white and green

Use wire clips to anchor the plant to a moss pole

Eriobotrya japonica

Eriobotrya japonica, the Japanese Loquat, is a small tree, which produces edible yellow fruit in warm climates. When grown indoors it is unlikely to produce either flowers or fruit, but large, deeply veined leaves are enough to justify its inclusion in the conservatory as a handsome specimen tree. Young leaves are also covered with a fuzz of silvery hairs, but this disappears with age. Eriobotryas are easy to grow from their stones which may be obtained from nurserymen; or the fruits themselves, which are called loquats. They can also sometimes be found on sale in greengrocers.

COMMON NAME
Japanese Loquat

Use this plant to shade smaller plants, such as the Arum Lily

Plant type	Foliage tree with upright habit
Season of interest	All year round
Size	240cm (96in) when grown in a pot, if not double
Flower	None if grown indoor
Leaf	15–25cm (6–10in); mid-green, new leaves covered with silvery hairs; toothed, deeply veined
Temperature	−2–20°C(28–68°F)
Aspect/Light	Well-lit situation with some exposure to sunlight
Humidity	Moderate
Watering	Keep compost evenly moist from spring to autumn; keep on the dry side in winter
Feeding	Once every two weeks with liquid fertilizer from spring to mid summer
Propagation	Propagate from seed (stone), which should be soaked for 24 hours before sowing at 10°C (50°F) in seed and cutting compost
Potting	Houseplant potting compost
Problems	Loss of lower leaves
Availability	Fairly commonly available throughout the year
Uses indoors	Conservatory or greenhouse plant

Euonymus fortunei

The Euonymus is quite a hardy species, provided that it is not over-watered. The leaf colour is not very stable and easily reverts to green, particularly with lack of light. When green shoots are produced these are best removed before the plant starts to look uninteresting. The plant is suitable for cooler locations, such as a porch. It can also be grown outside, where it is quite hardy and tolerates low temperatures and a certain amount of neglect. During the spring and summer, when it is actively growing, the plant should be inspected regularly, as it is quite prone to a number of pests and diseases. A related species, *E. japonicus*, is available in a number of varieties, with green, yellow and white variegation.

Reverted foliage should be pruned out

Plant type	Ornamental foliage with shrubby habit
Season of interest	All year round
Size	30–200cm (12–78in)
Flower	None indoors
Leaf	Oval, 2.5–4cm (1–1½in), variegated green
Temperature	10–18°C (50–64°F)
Aspect/Light	Well-lit situation
Humidity	Moderate
Watering	Evenly moisten compost in spring and summer; keep on dry side in autumn and winter
Feeding	Once every two weeks with houseplant fertilizer in spring and summer
Propagation	Plant 7.5cm (3in) tip cuttings in mid spring to early summer in seed and cutting compost at 21°C (70°F)
Potting	Houseplant potting compost
Problems	Red spider mite, tortrix moth caterpillar, mildew, scale insect, mealy bug, aphid
Availability	Commonly available throughout year
Uses indoors	Good plant for cool, well-lit room such as porch or conservatory; can be grown in container outside
Other varieties	*E. japonicus* 'Albomarginata' – green and yellow variegation *E. j.* 'Mediopicta' – yellow centre to leaf *E. j.* 'Microphylla Variegatus' – smaller, white-bordered leaves

Fatshedera lizei

The Fatshedera is a useful foliage plant of erect habit that can be quite tolerant of a variety of conditions. It is, however, very susceptible to over-watering and will suffer rapid root loss and wilt if it is kept too wet. It is therefore wise to allow the compost to dry out a little between waterings. The Fatshedera's erect growth is not very rigid and requires support from a cane or framework; alternatively, it can be trained to grow up a trellis. To create a more massed effect put several specimens together in the same pot. The variegated form of Fatshedera, *F. l.* 'Variegata', is slower-growing, which tends to make it even more susceptible to over-watering.

COMMON NAMES
Ivy Tree, Botanical Wonder, Tree Ivy

Plant type	Foliage plant with erect semi-climbing habit
Season of interest	All year round
Size	100–300cm (39–117in)
Flower	None
Leaf	Maple-leaf shape with five lobes, 7.5–15cm (3–6in), green
Temperature	15–20°C (60–68°F)
Aspect/Light	Moderate to bright light
Humidity	Moderate
Watering	Evenly moisten compost in spring and summer, taking care not to over-water and allowing to get on the dry side before re-watering; keep drier in autumn and winter
Feeding	Once every two to four weeks in spring and summer
Propagation	Plant 7.5–10cm (3–4in) tip cuttings in seed and cutting compost at 18–20°C (65–68°F)
Potting	Houseplant potting compost
Problems	Aphid, red spider mite, mealy bug, root rot from over-watering
Availability	Commonly available throughout year
Uses indoors	Suitable for most well-lit rooms, including conservatories
Other varieties	*F. l.* 'Variegata' – green and white leaves; more delicate; slower-growing

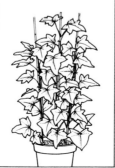

Put several plants in one pot for a better effect

Ficus benjamina

This Ficus is a magnificent plant that provides an impressive display of gently weeping foliage. Not as hardy as many other members of the fig family, it tends to be more susceptible to root problems, normally caused by over-watering, and is very sensitive to temperature changes. Such problems inevitably result in the plant dropping its leaves, almost overnight. Draughts have a similar effect and should be avoided. The plant prefers to be grown in the body of a room, where the temperature is more constant, although it does like a well-lit position. Avoid excessive sun as this will cause yellowing or scorching of the foliage. Young plants may need some support to ensure that they grow as erect as possible, although eventually they should be self-supporting. Occasional trimming can help to maintain the plant's balance.

COMMON NAME
Weeping Fig

Plant type	Foliage plant with erect and slightly weeping habit
Season of interest	All year round
Size	100–400cm (39–156in)
Flower	None
Leaf	Oval, pointed, 5–7.5cm (2–3in) long, 4–5cm (1½–2in) wide, green
Temperature	15–20°C (60–68°F)
Aspect/Light	Moderate to well-lit situation
Humidity	Moderate to high
Watering	Evenly moisten compost spring and summer, allowing to get on drier side before re-watering; water less in autumn and winter
Feeding	Once every two to four weeks with houseplant fertilizer from May to September
Propagation	Plant 7.5–10cm (3–4in) tip cuttings in seed and cutting compost in mid spring to early summer at 21–24°C (70–75°F)
Potting	Houseplant potting compost
Problems	Red spider mite, mealy bug, root mealy bug, scale insect; rapid leaf loss resulting from over-watering or low temperature
Availability	Commonly available throughout year
Uses indoors	Specimen plant to display on floor or low table in most rooms, including conservatories
Other varieties	*F. b. nuda* – thinner foliage; *F. b.* 'Variegata' – variegated foliage

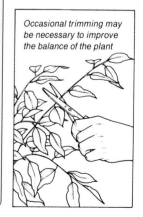

Occasional trimming may be necessary to improve the balance of the plant

Ficus elastica 'Robusta'

A combination of bold foliage and great adaptability makes this Ficus an extremely popular indoor plant. In its natural habitat, it grows as a tree, and even indoors it can attain well over two metres (six feet) if space permits. The plant is susceptible to over-watering, which can lead to premature leaf loss and cause the remaining top leaves to droop. Cleaning and polishing of the foliage is quite a passion with some people, who seek to embellish the leaves with an artificial glossy lustre. This is quite unnecessary, and the leaves should be only gently cleaned to remove grime and dust. Occasionally, this species experiences difficulty in breaking out of dormancy, with the terminal shoot becoming hard and stunted. If this continues, remove the blind shoot to help promote the production of side shoots.

COMMON NAME
Rubber Plant

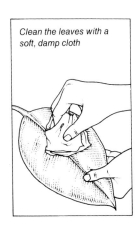

Clean the leaves with a soft, damp cloth

Plant type	Foliage plant with bold erect habit
Season of interest	All year round
Size	100–400cm (39–156in)
Flower	None
Leaf	15–25cm (6–10in) long, 10–15cm (4–6in) wide, oval, leathery, green
Temperature	13–20°C (55–68°F)
Aspect/Light	Medium to full light with a little shade from direct sun
Humidity	Moderate
Watering	Evenly moisten compost in spring and summer, allowing to almost dry out before re-watering; water less in autumn and winter dormancy
Feeding	Once every two to three weeks with houseplant fertilizer in spring and summer
Propagation	Plant 10–15cm (4–6in) tip cuttings, or 5–6cm (2–2½in) stem cuttings with leaf in seed and cutting compost from spring to mid summer at 27°C (80°F)
Potting	Houseplant potting compost
Problems	Aphid, red spider mite, mealy bug, scale insect, leaf loss from over-watering
Availability	Very common throughout year
Uses indoors	Specimen plant for indoor or conservatory use; adaptable
Other varieties	F. e. 'Black Prince' – dark green foliage F. e. 'Decora' – more drooping leaves

Ficus pumila

This Ficus is a delicate trailing and climbing plant, which looks particularly good growing up a moss pole. The heart-shaped leaves gently curl around the support, whilst the aerial roots help to anchor the climbing stem. The plant makes an ideal subject for a hanging basket, bottle garden, terrarium, trough, bowl or trellis. It is happy growing at lower light intensities, so is suitable for many locations. However, this plant cannot tolerate drying out. It has thin leaves, which lose water rapidly, and once it wilts the chances of recovery are poor. The compost must therefore be kept evenly moist at all times.

COMMON NAME
Creeping Fig

When planting stem cuttings, take care to insert them the correct way up

Plant type	Foliage plant with climbing, creeping and trailing habit
Season of interest	All year round
Size	30–300cm (12–117in)
Flower	None
Leaf	Heart-shaped, 1.25–2.5cm (½–1in), slightly crinkled, mid green
Temperature	15–20°C (60–68°F)
Aspect/Light	Moderate to lightly shaded situation
Humidity	Moderate to high
Watering	Keep compost evenly moist throughout year; do not allow to dry out
Feeding	Once every two to four weeks in spring and summer
Propagation	Plant 7.5–10cm (3–4in) tip or stem cuttings with lower leaves removed in seed and cutting compost in spring to early autumn at 18–20°C (65–68°F)
Potting	Houseplant potting compost
Problems	Red spider mite, dehydration of foliage and loss of plant if allowed to dry out
Availability	Commonly available throughout year
Uses indoors	Good plant for lightly shaded position in body of most rooms, including conservatories and offices; can be grown as climber up a moss pole or as trailer
Other varieties	F. p. 'Variegata' – cream variegation

Fittonia verschaffeltii

This pretty plant is delicate and dislikes draughts, temperature fluctuation, dry air and neglect. As it requires quite a lot of care, it is an ideal subject to be grown in a protected environment, such as a terrarium or bottle garden, where there are no draughts and the level of humidity is likely to be high. The plant is also susceptible to damage by slugs and snails. A tiny slug or snail can hide in the surface of the compost during the day and come out at night to feed. Take care that the plant and compost are free of the pests and that any plants grown in association with it are similarly clean.

COMMON NAME
Snakeskin Plant

Plant type	Foliage plant with semi-prostrate habit
Season of interest	All year round
Size	15–20cm (6–8in)
Flower	Uninteresting spike, produced in spring/summer
Leaf	Rounded, oval, 5–7.5cm (2–3in), green with pink veins
Temperature	18–21°C (65–70°F)
Aspect/Light	Moderate light to light shade
Humidity	High
Watering	Evenly moisten compost throughout year
Feeding	Once every two to three weeks with half strength houseplant fertilizer in spring and summer
Propagation	Plant 7.5–9cm (3–3½in) cuttings with at least two pairs of leaves in seed and cutting compost at 20–21°C (68–70°F) during mid spring to early summer
Potting	Houseplant potting compost
Problems	Slug, snail, shrivelling leaves caused by dry atmosphere
Availability	Fairly commonly available throughout year
Uses indoors	Good plant for bottle garden, bowl or terrarium

Group planting can help the plant to grow better

Fittonia verschaffeltii argyroneura 'Nana'

This diminutive Fittonia is actually much easier to keep than the larger leaved variety *F. verschaffeltii*, although it cannot be neglected by any means. It is a pretty little subject, with a relatively compact and prostrate habit that is at its best when the plant is young, as the growth can tend to be somewhat straggly in time. For this reason it is perhaps best to regularly renew the plant from cuttings obtained by pinching off the growing tips. The plant is suitable for a variety of situations and uses, including bottle gardens, bowl arrangements and terrariums. These enclosed environments will help to provide it with the fairly high level of humidity required – once the plant is allowed to dry out it quickly wilts and dehydrates, and rarely recovers.

COMMON NAME
Little Snakeskin Plant

Plant type	Foliage plant with prostrate habit
Season of interest	All year round
Size	7.5–10cm (3–4in)
Flower	Uninteresting, green spike, produced in spring/summer
Leaf	Oval, 2.5cm (1in), pale green with white veins
Temperature	15–20°C (60–68°F)
Aspect/Light	Moderate light to lightly shaded
Humidity	Moderate to high
Watering	Keep compost evenly moist throughout year; do not allow to dry out
Feeding	Once every two to four weeks with half strength houseplant fertilizer in spring and summer
Propagation	Plant 7.5cm (3in) tip cuttings with at least three pairs of leaves in seed and cutting compost from mid spring to early autumn at 18–20°C (65–68°F)
Potting	Houseplant potting compost
Problems	Slug, snail, dehydration from lack of water
Availability	Commonly available throughout year
Uses indoors	Good plant for bowl, bottle garden or terrarium

Pinching out the tips on wayward stems helps to keep the plant compact

Grevillea robusta

An attractive plant with ornamental, fern-like foliage, which has a brownish tinge and a slightly downy texture when young. The Grevillea is quite hardy and can be grown easily in a range of conditions. It does, however, prefer to be kept on the cool side, as higher temperatures cause lower humidity, which can lead to dehydration of the leaves. The Grevillea is therefore ideally suited to a porch. In its natural habitat this plant is a vigorous tree, so indoor specimens need to be kept in check. Unbalanced or wayward growth should be carefully trimmed off with a sharp pair of secateurs. It is also essential to maintain an erect habit, and it may be necessary to use a stake for this purpose.

COMMON NAME
Silk Oak

A stake will keep the plant erect

Plant type	Foliage plant with erect habit
Season of interest	All year round
Size	100–350cm (39–137in)
Flower	None indoors
Leaf	Fern-like, 20–40cm (8–16in), green with slight brown coloration when young
Temperature	10–18°C (50–65°F)
Aspect/Light	Moderate to full light
Humidity	Moderate
Watering	Evenly moisten compost in spring and summer, allowing to dry a little before re-watering; water less in autumn and winter
Feeding	Once every two to three weeks with houseplant fertilizer in spring and summer, when growing actively
Propagation	Sow seed at 15°C (60°F) in seed and cutting compost in spring
Potting	Houseplant potting compost
Problems	Dehydration from warm, dry atmosphere
Availability	Occasionally available, especially in spring and summer
Uses indoors	Feature plant for cool, well-lit room such as porch or conservatory

Gynura sarmentosa

The leaves of the Gynura have an unusual purple-velvet sheen, which creates interesting visual effects when the foliage is moved. It is usually seen as a relatively compact and low growing plant, but can also trail or climb. It will, however, require tying to the support frame or cane, otherwise it can easily sag. The Gynura should be grown only as a foliage plant and any emerging flowers should quickly be removed. The flowers are unattractive in appearance and have a revolting smell that will fill the room where the plant is kept. After watering the plant, take care to remove any water droplets from the hairy leaves as they can magnify the rays of the sun and cause the leaves to be scorched.

COMMON NAMES
Velvet Plant, Purple Passion Vine, Violet Nettle, Purple Nettle

Remove emerging flowers to avoid their unpleasant smell

Plant type	Foliage plant with loose trailing and semi-climbing habit
Season of interest	All year round
Size	30–100cm (12–39in)
Flower	Indistinct, orange-yellow, 1cm ($\frac{1}{2}$in), with an unpleasant smell, produced in late spring/summer
Leaf	Triangular, slightly serrated, 6.5–10cm ($2\frac{1}{2}$–4in), fleshy, dark green with attractive purple hairs
Temperature	13–18°C (55–65°F)
Aspect/Light	Full light
Humidity	High
Watering	Barely moisten compost in spring and summer allowing to dry a little between waterings; keep drier in autumn and winter
Feeding	Half strength houseplant fertilizer once every four weeks throughout year
Propagation	Plant 7.5–10cm (3–4in) tip cuttings in seed and cutting compost at 18–20°C (65–68°F) from early spring to late autumn (mid spring to early summer gives best results)
Potting	Houseplant potting compost
Problems	Aphid, mealy bug
Availability	Occasionally available throughout year
Uses indoors	As novelty windowsill plant or as climber grown close to window

Hedera canariensis 'Variegata'

This boldly variegated and large-leaved ivy can be used effectively in a very wide range of situations, although it does not like hot, dry conditions. Apart from dehydration due to a dry atmosphere, it is particularly susceptible to attack by red spider mite, a pest that thrives under such conditions. The plant is best grown in a room with a moderate temperature and full light, and is ideal for a porch. It can also grow quite well outside, although it does not like a very exposed situation. Although the plant is occasionally grown in a mixed arrangement, it is best planted either on its own or with two or three plants of the same variety to create a more dense effect. Wire ties or rings and a bamboo cane should be used to provide support, and the plant should be trimmed occasionally with vine scissors to keep it tidy.

COMMON NAME
Canary Island Ivy

Plant type	Foliage plant with vigorous climbing and trailing habit
Season of interest	All year round
Size	100–400cm (39–156in)
Flower	None
Leaf	Unevenly shaped, cupped, 7.5–10cm (3–4in), boldly variegated cream, white and green with red leaf stems
Temperature	7–18°C (45–65°F)
Aspect/Light	Full light
Humidity	Moderate
Watering	Evenly moisten compost in spring and summer, allowing to dry out a little between waterings; keep on drier side in autumn and winter
Feeding	Once every two to three weeks with houseplant fertilizer in spring and summer
Propagation	Plant 10–12.5cm (4–5in) tip or stem cuttings in seed and cutting or potting compost at 18–20°C (65–68°F) from mid spring to late summer
Potting	Houseplant potting compost
Problems	Red spider mite, aphid, mealy bug, root mealy bug
Availability	Commonly available throughout year
Uses indoors	Can be used in mixed plantings when small, then as specimen plant when larger; best in cool, light room such as well-ventilated porch, office foyer or conservatory

Wire rings can help to give effective support

Hedera helix 'Goldchild'

The ivy was one of the first houseplants to become popular and it continues to be so. However, the plant's indoor environment has become increasingly inhospitable over the years with the use of central heating. The warm, dry atmosphere causes the leaves to become brown, dehydrated and often to fall prematurely. Getting the balance right with watering can also be difficult and it is very easy to over-water the plant, causing root rot. It may seem that the ivy would always prefer the conditions found outside. However, by careful selection of the right location the growth produced indoors can be superior, with brighter and more lush foliage than that seen in outdoor ivies. The plant can grow as a trailing or prostrate subject as well as being trained as a climber, using a cane or stake and wire rings for support.

COMMON NAME
English Ivy

Plant type	Foliage plant with climbing and trailing habit
Season of interest	All year round
Size	10–15cm (4–6in) trailing, 100–300cm (39–117in) with support
Flower	None
Leaf	Three- to five-lobed, 2.5–4cm (1–1½in), yellow and green variegated
Temperature	7–18°C (45–65°F)
Aspect/Light	Full light
Humidity	Moderate
Watering	Evenly moisten compost in spring and summer, allowing to dry out a little before re-watering; keep drier in autumn and winter
Feeding	Once every two to three weeks with houseplant fertilizer in spring and summer
Propagation	Plant 10cm (4in) tip cuttings in seed and cutting or potting compost at 18–20°C (65–68°F) in mid spring to late summer
Potting	Houseplant potting compost
Problems	Red spider mite, aphid, mealy bug, root mealy bug, fungal leaf spot, bacterial leaf spot, root rot
Availability	Commonly available throughout year
Uses indoors	Cool, light position on windowsill in kitchen, bathroom, cloakroom or well-ventilated porch; good for conservatory

Trim untidy growth to create a better shape

Heptapleurum arboricola

The Heptapleurum is a useful foliage plant that can grow quite tall and statuesque, without taking up too much room widthways. Also, it does not tend to look as straggly as some plants do. The relatively compact foliage, consisting of leaflets held in a ray formation on semi-erect leaf stalks, helps to produce a plant of almost columnar habit. The effect can be enhanced by growing more than one plant in a pot, but generally a single plant grown well can suffice. A more compact, variegated form, *H. a.* 'Geisha Girl', is very useful for its tidier habit and appealing rounded leaves. All Heptapleurum species can be somewhat 'whippy', as they have supple stems that flex and bend easily. It may therefore be prudent to use a stake to ensure that the stem grows vertically.
COMMON NAME
Parasol Plant

A stake helps to maintain erect growth

Plant type	Foliage plant with erect habit
Season of interest	All year round
Size	100–250cm (39–98in)
Flower	None
Leaf	Seven to ten leaflets, 7.5–10cm (3–4in), green, radiating evenly around leaf stem
Temperature	18–21°C (65–70°F)
Aspect/Light	Well-lit situation
Humidity	Moderate
Watering	Evenly but barely moisten compost in spring and summer, allowing to dry a little before re-watering; keep on drier side in autumn and winter
Feeding	Once every two weeks with houseplant fertilizer in spring and summer
Propagation	Plant 7.5–10cm (3–4in) tip and stem cuttings in seed and cutting compost at 21°C (70°F) in mid to late spring
Potting	Houseplant potting compost
Problems	Red spider mite, aphid, mealy bug, root mealy bug, leaf loss from over-watering or draughts
Availability	Commonly available throughout year
Uses indoors	Specimen plant on table when small, or on floor when larger in lounge, dining room, bedroom or office
Other varieties	*H. a.* 'Geisha Girl' – compact habit; more rounded green leaves *H. a.* 'Variegata' – yellow and green variegation

Hypoestes phyllostachya

An attractive plant with unusual, pink-spotted leaves. The Hypoestes is often described as a hardy, easy-to-grow plant, but it does require some extra care and attention in order to thrive. In particular it does not like cool conditions and will rapidly fail if the temperature drops below the minimum. Failure to supply the plant with sufficient light will result in the leaves losing much of their bright pink pigmentation in favour of a greener hue. The Hypoestes should be trimmed regularly to prevent it becoming straggly, and is best replaced every year or two with a new plant, which can be created from cuttings taken from the growing tips.
COMMON NAME
Polka-dot Plant

Trim leggy growth to keep the plant compact

Plant type	Foliage plant with loose, bushy habit
Season of interest	All year round
Size	20–30cm (8–12in)
Flower	Uninteresting, mauve, produced in spring/summer
Leaf	Almost oval, 4–5cm (1½–2in) long, 2.5cm (1in) wide, dark green with pink spots
Temperature	18–21°C (65–70°F)
Aspect/Light	Well-lit position with some exposure to sunlight
Humidity	Moderate
Watering	Evenly moisten compost in spring and summer, allowing to dry a little between waterings; keep on drier side in autumn and winter
Feeding	Once every two to three weeks with houseplant fertilizer in spring and summer
Propagation	Plant 7.5–10cm (3–4in) tip cuttings in seed and cutting compost at 20–21°C (68–70°F) in mid spring to early autumn; sow seeds as above
Potting	Houseplant potting compost
Problems	Aphid, lower leaf loss from low temperatures
Availability	Commonly available throughout the year
Uses indoors	Good plant for windowsill, provided some shade is available to shield it from prolonged exposure to sunlight

Kochia scoparia

Although it looks very like a conifer, the Kochia is really a tender bedding plant. Throughout spring and summer, its foliage has a delicate, feathery appearance, and it is very soft to the touch. From late summer through autumn, the foliage turns to vibrant reds, oranges and purples, providing the display from which the plant takes its common name of Burning Bush. It requires a fairly bright situation; shade will encourage it to produce an unattractive, open habit. The Kochia is normally available as a bedding plant in spring. It can be grown in a large container either indoors or in the conservatory. Once the foliage display has finished, at the end of autumn, the plant is normally discarded.

COMMON NAMES
Summer Cypress, Burning Bush

Plant type	Foliage plant with busy habit
Season of interest	Mid summer to late autumn
Size	80–100cm (30–39in)
Flower	Not normally produced indoors
Leaf	Feathery, conifer-like fronds, up to 5cm (2in) long, soft green turning vibrant red, orange and purple in autumn
Temperature	5–20°C (41–68°F)
Aspect/Light	Moderately to fairly bright situation
Humidity	Average
Watering	Keep compost evenly moist from late spring to autumn
Feeding	Once a week with liquid houseplant fertilizer from spring to summer
Propagation	Sow seed in houseplant potting compost at 20–22°C (68–72°F) from mid to late spring
Potting	Houseplant or general potting compost
Problems	Red spider mite, vine weevil, dehydration
Availability	Quite commonly available in spring
Uses indoors	Indoor or conservatory plant

Sow seed in a tray of houseplant potting compost

Laurus nobilis

The elegant Laurus should really be grown alternately indoors and outdoors as the season dictates. During spring and summer the plant will grow quite happily outside, and is particularly good as a specimen plant in a container on a patio or gracing the front of a house. In autumn and winter it prefers a cool to moderately heated indoor situation in full light. Although it can be grown indoors in the spring and summer, the growth can tend to become soft and etiolated. The Laurus is an excellent subject for trimming and training, the most usual shapes being the standard and pyramidal forms. Shaped plants look particularly effective when displayed in matched pairs. Remember, also, that bay leaves can be used in cooking.

COMMON NAMES
Bay Tree, Bay Laurel, Sweet Bay

Plant type	Compact foliage shrub with standard or erect habit
Season of interest	All year round
Size	100–400cm (39–156in)
Flower	Insignificant, pale greenish, produced in spring
Leaf	Oval, pointed, 5–6cm (2–2½in) long, 2–2.5 (¾–1in) wide, tough, green, with pungent smell, especially when crushed
Temperature	10–20°C (50–68°F)
Aspect/Light	Moderate to full light
Humidity	Moderate
Watering	Evenly moisten compost in spring and summer; keep on drier side when dormant in autumn and winter
Feeding	Once a month with houseplant fertilizer in spring and summer
Propagation	Plant 10cm (4in) tip cuttings with bottom leaves removed in seed and cutting compost at 18–20°C (65–68°F) from mid spring to early autumn
Potting	Houseplant potting compost
Problems	Scale insect
Availability	Commonly available as indoor or garden plant throughout year
Uses indoors	Excellent plant for cool, well-lit room or porch or by entrance to office foyer; useful in conservatory or as patio plant

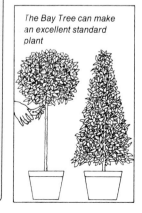

The Bay Tree can make an excellent standard plant

Maranta leuconeura erythroneura

Also known by the latin name *M. tricolor*, this is a highly attractive plant but tends to be rather delicate. Unless it can be provided with a humid, draught-free situation at an even temperature, it may be better to try the easier-to-grow variety, *M. l. kerchoviana*, first. However, if you really are keen to cultivate the plant, then put it in a terrarium or some other partly enclosed container, which will improve the humidity, whilst being adequately ventilated. The humidity can be increased still further by grouping the plant in the container with other low-growing and possibly slightly taller subjects. This Maranta does not benefit much from being misted, as this can cause spotting of the foliage.

COMMON NAMES
Herringbone Plant, Red Herringbone

Planting in a terrarium may help the plant to grow better

Plant type	Foliage plant with semi-prostrate habit
Season of interest	All year round
Size	20–25cm (8–10in)
Flower	Insignificant pale pink flowers on green spike amongst foliage, produced in spring/summer
Leaf	Oval, 10–12.5cm (4–5in) long, 5–6cm (2–2½in) wide, with two-tone green patterning, distinctive red central and lateral ribs, and pink underside
Temperature	18–21°C (65–70°F)
Aspect/Light	Moderate to slight shade
Humidity	High
Watering	Evenly moisten compost in spring and summer; keep slightly drier in autumn and winter
Feeding	Once every two to four weeks with houseplant fertilizer in spring and summer
Propagation	Divide mature plant from mid to late spring; plant 10cm (4in) cuttings in seed and cutting compost at 21°C (70°F) from early to mid summer
Potting	Houseplant potting compost
Problems	Red spider mite, mealy bug, browning of leaves due to dry atmosphere
Availability	Commonly available throughout the year
Uses indoors	Bowl garden or terrarium; prefers draught-free, humid position; can be grouped effectively with other plants

Maranta leuconeura kerchoviana

This Maranta is commonly known by two descriptive names, Rabbit's Tracks and Prayer Plant. The former name describes the unusual markings on the leaves, while the latter refers to the way that the leaves close together during the evening like hands held in a posture of prayer. The unusual, almost sideways growth may require slight staking. Alternatively, the plant can be left to grow sideways and sprawl somewhat. The paper-thin leaves are very sensitive to a dry atmosphere and will quickly dehydrate, resulting in browning of the tips and edges. A high level of humidity is essential and can be promoted by growing the plant in association with other plants.

COMMON NAMES
Rabbit's Tracks, Prayer Plant

Group planting with other plants helps to improve humidity

Plant type	Foliage plant with semi-prostrate habit
Season of interest	All year round
Size	20–25cm (8–10in)
Flower	Insignificant, bluish, on long flower spike amongst foliage, produced in spring/summer
Leaf	Oval, 10–12.5cm (4–5in) long, 5–6cm (2–2½in) wide, papery, mid green with dark green blotches
Temperature	18–21°C (65–70°F)
Aspect/Light	Moderate to light shade
Humidity	High
Watering	Evenly moisten compost in spring and summer; keep slightly drier in autumn and winter
Feeding	Once every two to four weeks with houseplant fertilizer in spring and summer
Propagation	Divide mature plant in mid to late spring; plant 10cm (4in) cuttings in seed and cutting compost at 21°C (70°F) from early to mid summer
Potting	Houseplant potting compost
Problems	Red spider mite, mealy bug, brown edges from dry atmosphere
Availability	Commonly available throughout year
Uses indoors	Good plant for bowl gardens, terrariums or as table-top plant in association with other plants

Mimosa pudica

With its frond-like foliage the Mimosa can make an attractive feature plant, but is grown mainly for its novelty value. When touched or even subjected to a strong draught of air, the leaves will immediately fold and wilt, usually recovering again within about half an hour. This unusual characteristic makes the plant particularly appealing to children, although continual teasing can make the foliage tired and less responsive, and too vigorous stimulation will damage it. The Mimosa can be grown for quite a reasonable period as an indoor plant but it does tend to become rather straggly and untidy quite quickly. For this reason, it is better to grow the plant fresh from seed each year or to obtain new young plants.

COMMON NAME
Sensitive Plant

Plant type	Foliage plant with sparse, erect habit
Season of interest	Spring and summer mostly, but can live longer
Size	20–30cm (8–12in)
Flower	Fluffy, pink, globular, produced in summer
Leaf	Tiny leaflets on frond-like leaf stalk, 5–7.5cm (2–3in), which fold together in pairs, with the leaf stalk drooping, when disturbed or touched
Temperature	18–21°C (65–70°F)
Aspect/Light	Well-lit situation with some exposure to sunlight
Humidity	High
Watering	Evenly moisten compost throughout year, but never make too wet
Feeding	Once every two to four weeks with houseplant fertilizer in spring and summer
Propagation	Sow seeds in early spring in seed and cutting compost at 18–21°C (65–70°F)
Potting	Houseplant potting compost
Problems	Children – who cannot stop teasing the plant!
Availability	Infrequently available in spring and summer
Uses indoors	Windowsill novelty plant or close to window on table or furniture

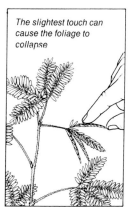

The slightest touch can cause the foliage to collapse

Monstera deliciosa

The Monstera is one of the most popular and distinctive indoor plants. Unlike most other plants it grows sideways in one direction. As it grows the leaves become larger and, if conditions are right, increasingly perforated. When a new leaf unfurls it is rather like watching a cut paper pattern unfolding. At this stage the leaf is very delicate and easily damaged but in a few days it becomes stiffer and takes on the characteristic leathery texture. Failure to provide sufficient humidity results in leaves that have fewer perforations or even no holes at all. Another feature of the plant is its aerial roots, which sometimes dangle uselessly over the side. When this happens, either push them back into the compost or wind them round the stem.

COMMON NAMES
Swiss Cheese Plant, Mexican Breadfruit Plant

Plant type	Foliage plant with lateral growth
Season of interest	All year round
Size	100–400cm (39–156in) spread
Flower	Occasional, greenish white, arum-like spathe on mature plant, followed by development of whitish fruit from spadix, produced at almost any time
Leaf	Heart-shaped when young, developing perforations and cuts, 10–45cm (4–18in) long, 10–45cm (4–18in) wide, leathery, green, on rigid stems
Temperature	18–21°C (65–70°F)
Aspect/Light	Well-lit situation, but out of direct sun
Humidity	Moderate to high
Watering	Evenly moisten compost in spring and summer, allowing to dry a little before re-watering; keep on drier side in autumn and winter
Feeding	Once every two to three weeks with houseplant fertilizer in spring and summer
Propagation	Plant growing point with three leaves supported with cane at 21°C (70°F) in potting compost in mid spring to early summer; sow seeds in seed and cutting compost at 21–24°C (70–75°F)
Potting	Houseplant potting compost
Availability	Commonly available throughout year
Uses indoors	Floor-standing plant in lounge, dining room, office or conservatory

Aerial roots may be wound loosely around the plant

Osmanthus illicifolius variegatus

A slow-growing shrub with hard, prickly evergreen leaves that resemble holly. This is a valuable foliage plant for the conservatory, with variegated leaves that are edged with white or cream and sometimes pink-tinged when young. It prefers cool, well-ventilated conditions, so is more suited to the conservatory than to a centrally-heated room, though it is sometimes grown indoors. Good light is needed, with some sun.

To maintain the bushy growth, pinch out growing tips every 4 months, and pinch out longer growths in spring.

This plant is also known as *O. heterophyllus variegatus*.
COMMON NAME
Variegated Sweet Olive

Shorten the shoot ends in spring to encourage a bushy habit

Plant type	Foliage plant with bushy habit
Season of interest	All year round
Size	Height 90cm (36in), spread 60cm (24in)
Flower	Rarely flowers when grown indoors
Leaf	Spiny, holly-like, 5–7cm (2–2½in) long, glossy mid-green with white or cream variegation
Temperature	–5–13°C (23–55°F)
Aspect/Light	Well-lit situation with some exposure to direct sunlight
Humidity	Moderate
Watering	Evenly moisten compost in spring and summer, allowing to dry out a little before re-watering; keep on dry side in autumn and winter
Feeding	Once every two weeks with liquid fertilizer in spring and early summer
Propagation	Plant 7.5–10cm (3–4in) tip cuttings in seed and cutting compost at 18°C (65°F) in spring
Potting	Soil-based potting compost
Problems	None
Availability	Commonly available throughout the year
Uses indoors	Plant for cool conservatory or greenhouse

Pandanus veitchii

The Pandanus is a bold foliage plant with long, sword-like leaves that are initially erect, but may arch and even bend sharply and break when they become longer. As the plant grows it will start to produce a new stem or 'sucker' at the base of the rosette of leaves. Aerial roots are also produced and these become more visible as the plant matures. The tough, leathery leaves are highly glossy on the upper surface. However, they are also quite sharp and contact with the edges can cause a savage cut. The Pandanus should therefore be positioned well out of the way or grown among other plants, which can act as a buffer or barrier. If space is limited, try to obtain the smaller variety, *P. v.* 'Compacta'.
COMMON NAME
Screw Pine

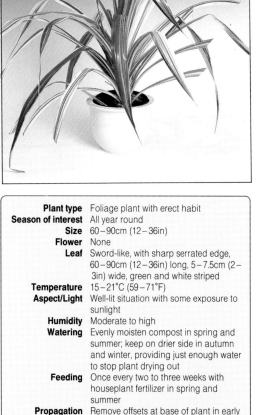

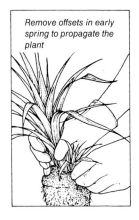

Remove offsets in early spring to propagate the plant

Plant type	Foliage plant with erect habit
Season of interest	All year round
Size	60–90cm (12–36in)
Flower	None
Leaf	Sword-like, with sharp serrated edge, 60–90cm (12–36in) long, 5–7.5cm (2–3in) wide, green and white striped
Temperature	15–21°C (59–71°F)
Aspect/Light	Well-lit situation with some exposure to sunlight
Humidity	Moderate to high
Watering	Evenly moisten compost in spring and summer; keep on drier side in autumn and winter, providing just enough water to stop plant drying out
Feeding	Once every two to three weeks with houseplant fertilizer in spring and summer
Propagation	Remove offsets at base of plant in early spring and pot them in seed and cutting compost at 20–21°C (68–70°F)
Potting	Houseplant potting compost
Problems	Mealy bug, red spider mite
Availability	Commonly available throughout year
Uses indoors	Table-top feature plant in bright situation, but take great care to avoid sharp, saw-like leaf edges
Other varieties	*P.v.* – 'Compacta' – smaller, more compact variety

Pelargonium tomentosum

This Pelargonium produces small, pale blue flowers but the main interest of the plant lies in its aromatic foliage. The peppermint scent is released when the leaves are crushed and also naturally in the late evening, particularly following a hot, sunny day. If space is limited indoors or in the conservatory in summer, Pelargoniums can be grown outside as patio plants and moved back under cover in the early autumn. They will usually maintain their foliage and its scent all year round. This variety is useful as a background to more colourful foliage plants. Other aromatic Pelargoniums include *P. fragrans*, with nutmeg-scented leaves, and *P.* 'Prince of Orange', with orange-scented foliage.

COMMON NAMES
Pelargonium,
Peppermint-scented
Geranium

Plant type	Foliage plant with upright habit
Season of interest	All year round, especially late spring to early autumn
Size	Up to 100cm (39in) in height and spread
Flower	Small, pale blue
Leaf	Hand-shaped and further divided, 5cm (2in) wide, grey-green, peppermint scented
Temperature	0–20°C (32–68°F)
Aspect/Light	Will tolerate light shade but prefers a bright situation, which will also help to release the leaf scent
Humidity	Average
Watering	Keep compost evenly moist in spring and summer; water less in autumn and winter
Feeding	Once every week with liquid houseplant fertilizer from late spring to early autumn
Propagation	Root softwood cuttings in seed and cutting compost at 15–18°C (60–65°F)
Potting	Houseplant or general potting compost
Problems	Vine weevil, mealy bug, red spider mite
Availability	Quite commonly available from spring to summer
Uses indoors	Indoor or conservatory plant

Take cuttings that are three leaf joints long and remove the lower two pairs of leaves

Peperomia caperata

An unusual Peperomia with long, white flower spikes borne above ridged and crinkly leaves. It is a useful subject for a mixed planting and is suitable for growing in a bottle garden. The succulent foliage is capable of retaining water so take care not to provide the plant with too much. Unlike many plants, which initially suffer root loss when over-watered and then wilt, the Peperomia rots from above, and the whole of the top of the plant can simply fall off. It is a good idea to water the plant from below to avoid the crown becoming too wet. Care should be taken when handling the plant, as the foliage can be bruised quite easily, again resulting in disease and loss. If any leaves should become damaged they must be removed with a sharp knife before any rotting occurs.

COMMON NAME
Little Fantasy

Plant type	Foliage plant with compact habit
Season of interest	All year round
Size	10–20cm (4–8in)
Flower	White poker-like flower stalk on pink stem, 10–25cm (4–10in), produced in spring/summer
Leaf	Heart-shaped, puckered, 4cm (1½in), dark green, fleshy, on fleshy pink stems
Temperature	15–20°C (59–68°F)
Aspect/Light	Well-lit situation, but out of direct sun
Humidity	Moderate to high
Watering	Barely moisten compost in spring and summer; keep drier in autumn and winter with just enough to stop compost drying out
Feeding	Once a month with half strength houseplant fertilizer in spring and summer
Propagation	Plant leaf cuttings with 2.5–3cm (1–1¼in) stem in seed and cutting compost at 20°C (68°F) from mid spring to mid summer
Potting	Houseplant potting compost
Problems	Red spider mite, crown rot from careless watering
Availability	Commonly available throughout year
Uses indoors	Good table-top plant, and useful in planters, bowls and bottle gardens
Other varieties	*P.c.* 'Tricolor' – variegated green and white foliage *P. hederifolia* – silver-grey leaves

Remove damaged leaves with a sharp knife

Peperomia magnoliaefolia 'Variegata'

This Peperomia is a hardy plant, capable of tolerating a certain amount of neglect. As the common name of Desert Privet implies, it thrives on barely moist soil conditions and at high light levels. It is better to keep the compost on the dry side – if it is watered too frequently, the root or stem will rot. Failure to provide the plant with sufficient sunlight will make the bold variegation fade quickly and revert to green. The habit of growth will also change and become weak and floppy. Take care to look out for pests, which, surprisingly on such a plant, can be a nuisance. Tortrix moth caterpillars are particularly destructive, as they stick the leaves together and consume the fleshy plant tissue.

COMMON NAME
Desert Privet

Plant type	Foliage plant with low, bushy habit; more open in time
Season of interest	All year round
Size	15–30cm (6–12in)
Flower	Uninteresting, rarely produced, in spring/summer
Leaf	Rounded oval, very fleshy, 5–7.5cm (2–3in), cream, yellow and green variegated
Temperature	15–20°C (59–68°F)
Aspect/Light	Well-lit situation
Humidity	Moderate
Watering	Barely moisten compost in spring and summer; water just enough to prevent drying out in autumn and winter
Feeding	Once a month with half strength houseplant fertilizer in spring and summer
Propagation	Plant 7.5cm (3in) tip cuttings in seed and cutting compost at 18–20°C (65–68°F); treat leaf with section of stem in same way from mid spring to early autumn
Potting	Houseplant potting compost
Problems	Red spider mite, tortrix moth caterpillar, aphid, stem and root rot from over-watering
Availability	Commonly available throughout year
Uses indoors	Good windowsill plant

The plant can be grown in association with succulents

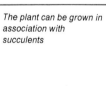

Persea americana

Although it is rarely available to buy as a plant, the Persea can be grown from the stone found inside the Avocado fruit. The stone can either be planted in seed and cutting compost or suspended over a tumbler of water with the broadest part just in contact with the surface of the water. Various methods can be employed to support the stone, such as matchsticks pushed into the skin, or looped wire, and many kitchen windowsills are often occupied by the experiment. Germination is perhaps more interesting than subsequent growth, as the Persea has a rather spindly habit and takes up a fair amount of space, as might be expected of a plant which in its natural environment grows to tree size.

COMMON NAME
Avocado Pear

Plant type	Foliage plant with erect habit
Season of interest	All year round
Size	100–300cm (39–117in)
Flower	Usually none as houseplant
Leaf	Oval, 7.5–12.5cm (3–5in) long, 5–7.5cm (2–3in) wide, green
Temperature	18–21°C (64–70°F)
Aspect/Light	Well-lit situation with sunlight
Humidity	Moderate
Watering	Evenly moisten compost in spring and summer; keep on drier side when dormant in autumn and winter
Feeding	Once every two to three weeks with houseplant fertilizer in spring and summer
Propagation	From Avocado Pear stone suspended over water or planted, with one third of stone exposed, in seed and cutting compost at 21°C (70°F)
Potting	Houseplant potting compost
Problems	Mealy bug, scale insect, premature lower leaf loss from over-watering
Availability	Rarely commercially available as plant; usually grown from Avocado Pear stone
Uses indoors	Floor standing specimen in well-lit position in lounge or heated conservatory

An Avocado Pear stone can be germinated by suspending it over water

Petroselinum crispum

Parsley is one of the most useful of all the culinary herbs, and though it is really happier outside it can also be grown in pots in the cool conservatory, where the growing season may be extended. The main problem with Parsley is the length of time taken for the seed to germinate. It can be sown at any time from early spring to mid summer, and germination may be speeded up if boiling water is poured on the soil before the seed is sown. Parsley will flourish in either full sun or partial shade, but requires a plentiful supply of moisture to do well. It is a biennial plant, flowering in the summer of its second year of growth, though it is most satisfactory to propagate new plants from seed each year.

COMMON NAME
Parsley

Plant type	Foliage plant with bushy habit
Season of interest	Late spring to autumn
Size	15–22.5cm (6–9in)
Flower	Small, white, in clusters
Leaf	Curled and deeply divided, mid-green, edible
Temperature	Minimum −2°C (28°F)
Aspect/Light	Full sun to light shade
Humidity	Moderate
Watering	Keep compost evenly moist throughout growing season
Feeding	Not normally needed
Propagation	Sow seed in seed and cutting compost at 19–24°C (66–75°F) from early spring to mid summer
Potting	Houseplant potting compost
Problems	Slow to germinate
Availability	Commonly available as seed from early winter onwards; or as pre-grown plants from early spring to late summer
Uses indoors	Pot plant for conservatory or greenhouse

Sow several groups of seeds in threes to achieve bushy growth

Philodendron 'Red Emerald'

In the right conditions this Philodendron will grow quite rapidly into a luxuriant plant. Its glossy leaves and upright habit make it a useful specimen plant for display, initially on a table then, as it grows larger, on the floor. To grow and display the plant to best effect it is a good idea to train it up a moss pole. Initially, the stem can be attached to the moss pole with wire rings. With time though, the plant should produce aerial roots, which will root into the moss around the pole, provided that the moss is kept evenly moist. This can be achieved easily by regularly misting the moss with tepid water using a hand mister. With its fleshy leaves and stem this Philodendron can become rather heavy, so the support provided by the moss pole is essential.

Plant type	Foliage plant with climbing habit
Season of interest	All year round
Size	100–200cm (39–78in)
Flower	None
Leaf	Elongated, heart-shaped, 15–20cm (6–8in) long, 7.5–17.5cm (3–5in) wide, green with reddish tinge
Temperature	16–21°C (61–70°F)
Aspect/Light	Moderate light
Humidity	Moderate to high
Watering	Evenly moisten compost in spring and summer; keep drier in autumn and winter
Feeding	Once every two to four weeks with houseplant fertilizer in spring and summer
Propagation	Plant 10cm (4in) tip or stem cutting in seed and cutting compost at 21°C (70°F) in late spring to early summer
Potting	Houseplant potting compost
Problems	Mealy bug, root rot from over-watering
Availability	Occasionally available throughout year
Uses indoors	Feature plant for lounge or dining room; useful in office as specimen plant or in associated planting
Other varieties	P. 'Green Emerald' – green leaves

Keep the moss pole moist with a mister

Philodendron scandens

This Philodendron can be a vigorous climber. Although the plant has relatively feeble stems, it can produce quite strong growth once adequately supported. Like *P.* 'Red Emerald', it grows well against a moss pole. However, provided care is taken not to allow the roots growing in the compost to suffer in any way, this plant can also be supported by no more than a bamboo cane, with wire rings looped around the stem. Although the leaves may initially look untidy as they are bent out of place, many will grow to face tidily outwards as they adapt to the direction of the light.

COMMON NAME
Sweetheart Plant

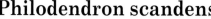
Use wire rings to support the plant

Plant type	Foliage plant with climbing habit
Season of interest	All year round
Size	60–250cm (24–98in)
Flower	None
Leaf	Heart-shaped, 5–7.5cm (2–3in), green
Temperature	16–21°C (61–70°F)
Aspect/Light	Moderate light, but will tolerate a little shade
Humidity	Moderate to high
Watering	Evenly moisten compost in spring and summer but do not over-water; keep drier in autumn and winter
Feeding	Once every two to four weeks with houseplant fertilizer in spring and summer
Propagation	Plant tip cuttings, 7.5–10cm (3–4in), in seed and cutting compost at 21°C (70°F) in mid spring to early autumn
Potting	Houseplant potting compost
Problems	Mealy bug, root rot from over-watering
Availability	Commonly available throughout year
Uses indoors	Very adaptable; can be used as table-top or floor-standing subject in home, conservatory or office
Other varieties	*P. hastatum* – larger and more angular; longer green leaves

Philodendron tuxla

A highly distinctive Philodendron with very large leaves, which have earned it the common name of Elephant's Ears. When young it has a semi-prostrate habit, but can be encouraged to climb up a moss pole. Anchor the stem to the pole with wire clips or rings to support the plant as it climbs. Eventually aerial roots will be produced and these can be encouraged to root into the moss by keeping the pole moist. The moss pole should be substantial as the plant can grow quite large and heavy. This Philodendron is quite easy to grow but care should be taken with watering as too much moisture can cause root rot. It is most susceptible to over-watering during the winter rest period, so allow the compost to dry out a little between waterings.

COMMON NAME
Elephant's Ears

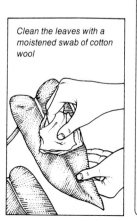
Clean the leaves with a moistened swab of cotton wool

Plant type	Foliage plant with climbing habit
Season of interest	All year round
Size	90–180cm (36–72in)
Flower	None indoors
Leaf	Elongated heart-shaped, 15–20cm (6–8in) long, 7.5–10cm (3–4in) wide, glossy, green
Temperature	16–21°C (61–70°F)
Aspect/Light	Moderate light
Humidity	Moderate to high
Watering	Evenly moisten compost in spring and summer; keep on drier side in autumn and winter
Feeding	Once every two to four weeks with houseplant fertilizer in spring and summer
Propagation	Plant 10cm (4in) tip cuttings in seed and cutting compost at 21°C (70°F) in late spring to early summer
Potting	Houseplant potting compost
Problems	Mealy bug, root rot from over-watering
Availability	Occasionally available throughout year
Uses indoors	Feature plant for lounge or dining room; useful in office as specimen plant or in associated planting

Phormium tenax

The sword-shaped leaves of the Phormium make a bold display in a group of conservatory shrubs. There are a number of striking cultivars available with brightly coloured and variegated leaves, many of which are smaller in size. They include *P. t.* 'Purpureum', which has bronze-purple foliage, and *P. t.* 'Variegatum', with green and yellow striped leaves. Although the Phormium is grown mainly for its foliage, it also has large panicles of dark red flowers in summer, borne on tall stems, which are followed by orange seed heads.

COMMON NAME
New Zealand Flax

Plant type	Foliage plant with tufted habit
Season of interest	All year
Size	30–180cm (12–72in)
Flower	Dark red, 10cm (2in) long, borne in panicles on long flower stems, followed by orange seed heads
Leaf	Sword-shaped, erect and slightly arched, to 180cm (72in) long, dark-green, bronze, purple, variegated
Temperature	−3–16°C (26–61°F)
Aspect/Light	Full sun
Humidity	Moderate
Watering	As required; do not over water
Propagation	Divide established plants in spring
Potting	Houseplant potting compost
Problems	Large plants may burst plastic, earthenware or wooden containers
Availability	Commonly available from mid spring to midsummer
Uses indoors	Feature plant in conservatory or greenhouse plant

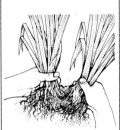

Divide and re-pot the plant every 5 years to avoid damage to pots from the strong roots

Pilea cadierei

An attractive plant with a silver or aluminium sheen to the leaves, hence the common name. It is useful in moderately lit positions, such as within the body of a room. Although it will probably grow for a number of years, the foliage can tend to become rather straggly and dull in colour. It is therefore advisable to renew the plant every year or two, either from tip cuttings taken from the original plant or by buying a new plant. In the spring and summer months take particular care to watch out for aphids, which can quickly cause great damage to the new shoots. If damage does occur, the damaged growth should be pinched off to a pair of leaves. This will encourage fresh growth, which should appear unmarked.

COMMON NAME
Aluminium Plant

Plant type	Foliage plant with compact, bushy habit
Season of interest	All year round
Size	10–30cm (4–12in)
Flower	Insignificant, produced in spring/summer
Leaf	Oval, slightly puckered, 5cm (2in), green and silver
Temperature	18–21°C (64–70°F)
Aspect/Light	Moderate light
Humidity	Moderate
Watering	Evenly moisten compost throughout year, taking care never to over-water and allowing to dry out a little before re-watering
Feeding	Once every two to three weeks with houseplant fertilizer in spring and summer
Propagation	Plant 6–7.5cm (2½–3in) tip cuttings in seed and cutting compost at 18–21°C (64–70°F) from mid to late spring
Potting	Houseplant potting compost
Problems	Aphid, mealy bug, leggy growth with lower leaf loss caused by over-watering and also age
Availability	Commonly available throughout the year
Uses indoors	Can be used in body of most rooms, away from direct sunlight
Other varieties	*P. spruceana* 'Norfolk' – bronze and silver leaves

Pinch out terminal shoots to help maintain a compact habit

Pilea mollis

This compact and low-growing Pilea is a useful subject for a bowl garden or similar planter. It is very effective when grouped with other plants and grows well with many foliage and flowering plants. As with other Pileas, bushy growth can be encouraged by regularly pinching out the growing shoots. These can be used to propagate new plants. The plant produces small, pinkish brown flowers in the summer, but these are of no particular interest and are best removed. This is a fairly easy plant to grow, provided it is given a certain amount of warmth, good light, and the compost is kept evenly moist. The textured leaf surfaces of the Pilea easily collect dust, which should be removed with tepid water applied through a mister.

COMMON NAME
Moon Valley Plant

To remove dust, lightly mist the foliage with tepid water

Plant type	Compact, low growing and bushy foliage plant
Season of interest	All year round
Size	10–15cm (4–6in)
Flower	Insignificant, pinkish brown, produced in summer
Leaf	Pointed oval, crinkled, 2.5–5cm (1–2in), green with brownish tinge
Temperature	18–21°C (64–70°F)
Aspect/Light	Moderate light
Humidity	Moderate
Watering	Evenly moisten compost throughout year, taking care never to over-water and allowing to dry out a little before re-watering
Feeding	Once every two to three weeks with houseplant fertilizer in spring and summer
Propagation	Plant 6–7.5cm (2½–3in) tip cuttings in seed and cutting compost at 18–21°C (64–70°F) from mid to late spring
Potting	Houseplant potting compost
Problems	Aphid, mealy bug, root rot from over-watering
Availability	Occasionally available throughout year
Uses indoors	Useful for most rooms, especially lounge or dining room; effective in bowl garden or similar group planting

Pleomele reflexa variegata

The Pleomele is very rarely seen nowadays, although it really is quite a choice plant. The green and yellow-green variegated foliage is attractive and becomes more interesting as the erect habit turns a little more wayward and starts to grow horizontally or in a semi-erect fashion. As this happens, it is advisable to provide the plant with some support using bamboo cane and wire rings. The plant requires a fairly high level of humidity, which can be provided by regular misting or by standing the pot in a tray of moist pebbles. The Pleomele is quite slow-growing, which means that it takes a considerable time to produce a plant of worthy proportions to display effectively.

COMMON NAME
Song of India

Wayward growth may need some support to prevent damage

Plant type	Foliage plant with erect, then semi-erect, habit
Season of interest	All year round
Size	100–300cm (39–117in)
Flower	None
Leaf	Lance-like, 10–20cm (4–8in) long, 2–2.5cm (¾–1in) wide, green and yellow-green striped
Temperature	18–21°C (64–70°F)
Aspect/Light	Well-lit situation, but out of direct sunlight
Humidity	Moderate to high
Watering	Evenly moisten compost throughout year, taking care not to over-water and allowing to dry out a little before re-watering
Feeding	Once every three to four weeks with houseplant fertilizer in spring and summer
Propagation	Plant 10cm (4in) tip cuttings in seed and cutting compost at 21°C (70°F) in early spring
Potting	Houseplant potting compost
Problems	Mealy bug, leaf loss from over-watering
Availability	Rarely available
Uses indoors	Prominent position in lounge, dining room or conservatory; good for office reception

Pseudopanax laetus

This large-leaved evergreen from New Zealand makes a useful shrub for use indoors or in the conservatory, either as a free-standing plant or fan-trained against a wall. The hand-shaped, sometimes toothed leaves may vary in shape but this is not normally to the plant's detriment. Green-leaved, silver and gold variegated forms exist and all are commonly available as houseplants from garden centres. Careful attention must be paid to watering and feeding and a quite large container is necessary to show off the plant to best advantage. As well as being a good subject to display on its own, the Pseudopanax is also useful as a background and foil to flowering plants and more colourful foliage plants.

COMMON NAME
Pseudopanax

Plant type	Foliage shrub with upright habit
Season of interest	All year round
Size	100–200cm (39–78in)
Flower	None of interest
Leaf	Hand-shaped, edges sometimes toothed, up to 15cm (6in) long
Temperature	7–20°C (45–68°F)
Aspect/Light	Moderately bright situation but will tolerate light shade; avoid strong, direct sunlight
Humidity	Moderate
Watering	Evenly moisten compost in spring and summer; keep on dry side in autumn and winter
Feeding	Once every three to four weeks with liquid houseplant fertilizer from spring to summer
Propagation	Root softwood cuttings in seed and cutting compost at 18–20°C (65–68°F) from spring to early summer
Potting	Houseplant or general potting compost
Problems	Red spider mite, vine weevil
Availability	Commonly available in spring
Uses indoors	Indoor or conservatory plant

Use the Pseudopanax as a background to flowering plants

Sansevieria trifasciata 'Laurentii'

This Sansevieria has been a popular indoor plant for some time and must be one of the easiest to look after, provided that it is grown in full light and not over-watered. It can tolerate slightly less well-lit conditions, although its leaf colour and habit may change. Whilst the plant can be propagated from sections of leaf, the golden-yellow edged variegation may be lost by this technique. It is therefore better to propagate by cutting off offshoots at the base, and separating a piece of the rhizome with the new shoot, as this preserves the true colour. The plant prefers to be grown in a container that is just large enough for it, but it is advisable to check the rate of growth from time to time, as the roots are capable of breaking a pot.

COMMON NAME
Mother-in-law's Tongue

Plant type	Semi-succulent foliage plant with erect habit
Season of interest	All year round
Size	45–90cm (18–36in)
Flower	30cm (1ft) spike of small, greenish white, delicately scented flowers, produced in late spring/summer
Leaf	Erect, strap-like, pointed, 30–90cm (12–36in), cream-bordered with light and dark green patterned middle
Temperature	13–28°C (55–82°F)
Aspect/Light	Full sun
Humidity	Low
Watering	Evenly moisten compost in spring and summer, allowing to dry a little before re-watering; keep on dry side in autumn and winter
Feeding	Once every three to four weeks with half strength flowering plant fertilizer in spring and summer
Propagation	Cut out 20cm (8in) offshoots, with rhizome, in late spring to mid summer and pot in cactus and succulent compost at 20–22°C (68–72°F)
Potting	Cactus and succulent compost or houseplant potting compost
Problems	Mealy bug, aphid (on flower spike), root and stem rot when over-moist or cold
Availability	Commonly available throughout year
Uses indoors	Windowsill or table close to sunny window in lounge, dining room or office

Propagation is best achieved by separating the plant

Sansevieria trifasciata 'Silver Hahnii'

This diminutive Sansevieria is a very attractive foliage plant that is particularly suited to a position where it can be exposed to full sunlight. This will certainly help to produce the best foliage colour. It is possible to move the plant within the body of the room away from the light, provided that it is not grown in the shade. However, a plant that is grown in less light is likely to lose its bright silvery hue in favour of a greener tinge, and suffer some etiolation. The low habit and relatively slow rate of growth make this Sansevieria an ideal subject for long-term display in an ornamental pot or bowl. However, it is wise to keep a check on the rate of growth as the plant is capable of breaking a pot by the slow but sure development of the rhizomatous root system. This is all the more vigorous in the taller growing variety *S.t. 'Laurentii'*.

Propagate the plant by separating offsets

Plant type	Semi-succulent foliage plant with low, upright habit
Season of interest	All year round
Size	10–15cm (4–6in)
Flower	None indoors
Leaf	Pointed, 10–15cm (4–6in), silvery green, produced in rosette
Temperature	13–28°C (55–82°F)
Aspect/Light	Full sun
Humidity	Low
Watering	Evenly moisten compost in spring and summer, allowing to dry a little before re-watering; keep on dry side in autumn and winter
Feeding	Once every three to four weeks with half strength flowering plant fertilizer in spring and summer
Propagation	Plant offsets or 5cm (2in) cut sections of leaf in cactus and succulent compost at 20–22°C (68–72°F) in spring and summer
Potting	Cactus and succulent compost or houseplant potting compost
Problems	Mealy bug, root mealy bug
Availability	Occasionally available all year round
Uses indoors	Windowsill or table close to window in lounge, dining room or office; suitable for display on its own or in association with other plants
Other varieties	S. t. 'Golden Hahnii' – golden yellow and green

Saxifraga stolonifera 'Tricolor'

The Saxifraga is attractive to display as a hanging plant, although its habit is not the most tidy and compact. The non-variegated form, *S. stolonifera*, has green and silver foliage and is much more dense, growing with greater vigour. Both forms are highly attractive to aphid (greenfly) and mealy bug, which freely attack them and can be a problem indoors all year round. The plant has an added interest in the way it propagates itself by producing young plantlets on the fine red runners. It is a useful hanging basket plant for a position with limited exposure to sunlight.

COMMON NAME
Mother of Thousands

Regularly inspect the foliage for pests

Plant type	Foliage plant with trailing habit
Season of interest	All year round
Size	15cm (6in) with 45–60cm (18–24in) trails
Flower	Small white flowers in summer
Leaf	Rounded, 2.5–7.5cm (1–3in) wide, pinkish cream and green variegated on red stems and trails
Temperature	10–18°C (50–64°F)
Aspect/Light	Well-lit position, with limited sunlight
Humidity	Moderate
Watering	Evenly moisten compost in spring and summer; water only enough to prevent drying out in autumn and winter
Feeding	Once every four to six weeks with houseplant fertilizer in spring and summer
Propagation	Gently push plantlet into pot of houseplant potting compost while still attached to runner; cut off 5cm (2in) plantlet and push into pot of compost at 15–18°C (60–65°F) in mid spring to early autumn
Potting	Houseplant potting compost
Problems	Mealy bug, aphid
Availability	Commonly available throughout year, particularly spring and summer
Uses indoors	Good plant for hanging basket in situation with limited sun
Other varieties	S. stolonifera – green and silver; more vigorous and dense

Stromanthe amabilis

The Stromanthe is a plant for the enthusiast who is prepared to lavish great care and attention on it. Not only does it dislike temperature fluctuations but it also hates draughts and warm dry air. Its thin leaves lose water quickly, dehydrating to produce brown tips and edges. To provide the best conditions for the plant requires reproduction of the conditions it would normally expect in its natural habitat, the rainforest. A moderate-to-high temperature and moderate light away from direct sunlight are essential. The plant is best grown in a bottle garden or terrarium, and/ or closely grouped with other plants.

Plant type	Foliage plant with semi-upright habit
Season of interest	All year round
Size	20–25cm (8–10in)
Flower	Uninteresting spike, produced in spring/summer
Leaf	Oval, 10–20cm (4–8in) long, 4–5cm (1½–2in) wide, light green with darker green herringbone pattern
Temperature	18–21°C (65–70°F)
Aspect/Light	Moderate to light shade
Humidity	High
Watering	Evenly moisten compost in spring and summer; keep a little drier in autumn and winter
Feeding	Once every two to four weeks with half strength houseplant fertilizer in spring and summer
Propagation	Divide mature plants and plant in seed and cutting compost at 21°C (70°F) in mid to late spring
Potting	Houseplant potting compost
Problems	Red spider mite, mealy bug, dry atmosphere causes leaf browning
Availability	Reasonably commonly available throughout year
Uses indoors	Bowl garden or terrarium; prefers draught-free, humid position; can be grouped effectively with other plants

Plant the Stromanthe in a terrarium or similar container for best results

Stromanthe sanguinea

An elegant plant with very attractive leaves. The green uppersides, with their distinctive herringbone pattern, contrast well with the reddish purple undersides, and the plant's height and habit of growth permit both sides to be seen with ease. An uninteresting flower spike is produced in spring or summer and can be removed if it is not wanted. Similar in its care requirements to *S. amabilis*, this plant prefers a high humidity and is therefore best grown in association with other plants. It is rather too large for a terrarium or other enclosed space but suits a trough or planter very well. The bold foliage provides a useful foil for smaller, more delicate foliage and flowering plants. When positioning this plant, avoid locations that might be draughty, as this can cause leaf loss.

Plant type	Foliage plant with semi-upright habit
Season of interest	All year round
Size	40–50cm (16–20in)
Flower	Uninteresting spike, produced in spring/summer
Leaf	Pointed oval, 15–40cm (6–16in) long, 7.5–12.5cm (3–5in) wide, shiny, light green with darker green herringbone pattern above, reddish purple below
Temperature	18–21°C (65–70°F)
Aspect/Light	Moderate to light shade
Humidity	High
Watering	Evenly moisten compost in spring and summer; keep a little drier in autumn and winter
Feeding	Once every two to four weeks with houseplant fertilizer at half strength in spring and summer
Propagation	Divide mature plants and plant in seed and cutting compost at 21°C (70°F) in mid to late spring
Potting	Houseplant potting compost
Problems	Red spider mite, mealy bug, dry atmosphere causes leaf browning
Availability	Reasonably commonly available throughout year
Uses indoors	Trough or planter; prefers draught-free, humid position; can be grouped effectively with other plants

Regularly mist the leaves with tepid water

Syngonium podophyllum

A vigorous plant that undergoes quite dramatic changes in habit and leaf shape as it grows. When young it produces arrow-shaped leaves on erect stems. As it gets older, though, the plant produces leaves that are divided into sections on stems which climb and semi-trail. The Syngonium is often featured in bowl plantings, but will quickly get out of control, so is best displayed on its own with a moss pole for support. Because of the untidy habit of growth, this plant is not as popular as the variety *S. p.* 'Emerald Gem'. This has more attractively coloured and shaped foliage, is slower-growing and smaller and more compact in stature.

COMMON NAMES
Arrowhead Plant, African Evergreen

A moss pole provides effective support

Plant type	Foliage plant with climbing habit that can trail
Season of interest	All year round
Size	100–200cm (39–78in)
Flower	Unlikely indoors
Leaf	Arrow-shaped on young plants, divided into sections as plant matures, 10–30cm (4–12in) long, 5–12.5cm (2–5in) wide, green
Temperature	13–19°C (55–66°F)
Aspect/Light	Well-lit situation, but out of direct sun
Humidity	Moderate to high
Watering	Evenly moisten compost in spring and summer, allowing to dry a little before re-watering; keep drier in autumn and winter
Feeding	Once every two to four weeks with houseplant fertilizer in spring and summer
Propagation	Plant 7.5–10cm (3–4in) tip cuttings in seed and cutting compost at 20–21°C (68–70°F)
Potting	Houseplant potting compost
Problems	Aphid, mealy bug
Availability	Commonly available throughout year
Uses indoors	Trough or planter where it can climb and trail in hall or well-lit room that does not get too warm
Other varieties	*S.p.* 'Emerald Gem' – light and dark green leaves; smaller and more compact

Tolmiea menziesii

Although difficult to pronounce, this plant's Latin name serves a useful purpose in distinguishing it from *Saxifraga stolonifera*, with which it shares the common name of Mother of Thousands. Unlike the Saxifraga, which produces its young plants on the thread-like runners, the Tolmiea produces young plants at the junction of the leaf and leaf stalk. For this reason, the other common name of Piggy-back Plant is probably more appropriate. The plant does not truly 'trail'; the effect is created by the weight of the leaves on the long stems, causing them to be held prostrate. This enables the plant to position the leaf and its potential new plant on nearby soil or compost so that the new plant can root and develop whilst still gaining nourishment from the mother plant.

COMMON NAMES
Piggy-back Plant, Mother of Thousands

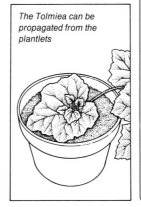

The Tolmiea can be propagated from the plantlets

Plant type	Foliage plant with loose, trailing habit
Season of interest	All year round
Size	10–30cm (4–12in)
Flower	Insignificant, greenish white flowers, but rare indoors
Leaf	Rounded heart-shaped, 4–7.5cm (1½–3in), green, with hairs on young growth, with young plantlets produced at top of leaf stalk and leaf
Temperature	13–20°C (55–68°F)
Aspect/Light	Well-lit position, but will tolerate medium light
Humidity	Moderate to high
Watering	Evenly moisten compost in spring and summer, taking care not to over-water; keep drier in autumn and winter
Feeding	Once every two to four weeks with houseplant fertilizer in spring and summer
Propagation	Place leaf with plantlet still attached on pot of compost and anchor with paper-clip; cut off leaf with plantlet and insert stem in seed and cutting compost at 18–20°C (65–68°F) in mid spring to late summer
Potting	Houseplant potting compost
Problems	Red spider mite
Availability	Commonly available throughout year, especially spring and summer
Uses indoors	Hanging basket plant for window in most rooms

Tradescantia fluminensis 'Quicksilver'

The Tradescantia was one of the pioneers that helped to establish the growing of plants indoors, and it remains popular. A very versatile plant, it is at home in a pot, bowl or hanging basket, and can be grown either singly or in a mixed arrangement. However, the foliage quickly becomes straggly as the stems grow and lose their lower leaves, so it is sensible to propagate fresh plants from the original. Take care to select good-quality propagation material, which has not reverted to green. It may even be wise to renew the stock plant from time to time to ensure that you have the best possible material. Like many variegated plants, the Tradescantia must have a well-lit position, otherwise the leaves will become dull and rather too green.

COMMON NAME
Wandering Jew

Plant type	Foliage plant with trailing habit
Season of interest	All year round
Size	7.5–10cm (3–4in) high
Flower	Small, white, produced spring/summer
Leaf	4–6.5cm (1½–2⅓in) long, 2–2.5cm (¾–1in) wide, silver-white and green striped
Temperature	15–22°C (59–72°F)
Aspect/Light	Well-lit situation with some exposure to sunlight
Humidity	Moderate to high
Watering	Evenly moisten compost in spring and summer, allowing to get on the dry side before re-watering; keep drier in autumn and winter and when plant slows down its rate of growth
Feeding	Once every two to four weeks with houseplant fertilizer in spring and summer
Propagation	Plant 7.5cm (3in) tip cuttings in seed and cutting compost at 18°C (65°F) in mid spring to late summer; or root cuttings in water
Potting	Houseplant potting compost
Problems	Leggy growth
Availability	Commonly available throughout year
Uses indoors	Hanging basket, bowl or pot in window, or on windowsill in most rooms
Other varieties	T. blossfeldiana 'Variegata' – green and cream variegated T. purpurea – reddish and purple leaves

Trim leggy growth; the tip cuttings can be used for propagation

Yucca elephantipes

For a plant that borders on the grotesque, the Yucca has gained considerable popularity. Apart from being sold as a small stump sprouting two or three tufts of foliage, it is also available several feet high, making an ideal feature or specimen plant in the home, if there is room, as well as being excellent for the office. Care with watering is critical, as it is relatively easy to over-water the Yucca, resulting in rapid wilting and possible death. When the plant grows too large it can be cut back to a more acceptable size using a pruning saw. Wear strong gloves for protection; it may be easier to lay the plant down to carry out the operation. Once pruned back, the plant should produce new shoots, and the piece of stem removed can be used for propagation.

COMMON NAME
Spineless Yucca

Plant type	Foliage plant with erect habit
Season of interest	All year round
Size	100–250cm (39–98in)
Flower	Spike of white flowers, produced in summer, but unlikely indoors
Leaf	Sword-like, 30–75cm (12–30in) long, 5–7.5cm (2–3in) wide
Temperature	13–21°C (55–70°F)
Aspect/Light	Well-lit situation with exposure to sunlight
Humidity	Prefers moderate to high humidity, but tolerates dry atmosphere
Watering	Evenly moisten compost in spring and summer, allowing to dry a little before re-watering; water just enough to prevent drying out in autumn and winter
Feeding	Once every three to four weeks with houseplant fertilizer in spring and summer
Propagation	Plant 10–20cm (4–8in) sections of stem or 20cm (8in) offsets in seed and cutting compost at 21°C (70°F) in spring or summer
Potting	Houseplant potting compost
Problems	Mealy bug, root rot from over-watering
Availability	Commonly available throughout year
Uses indoors	Floor-standing specimen plant for well-lit position in lounge, dining room or office

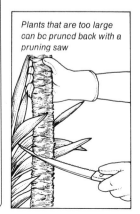

Plants that are too large can be pruned back with a pruning saw

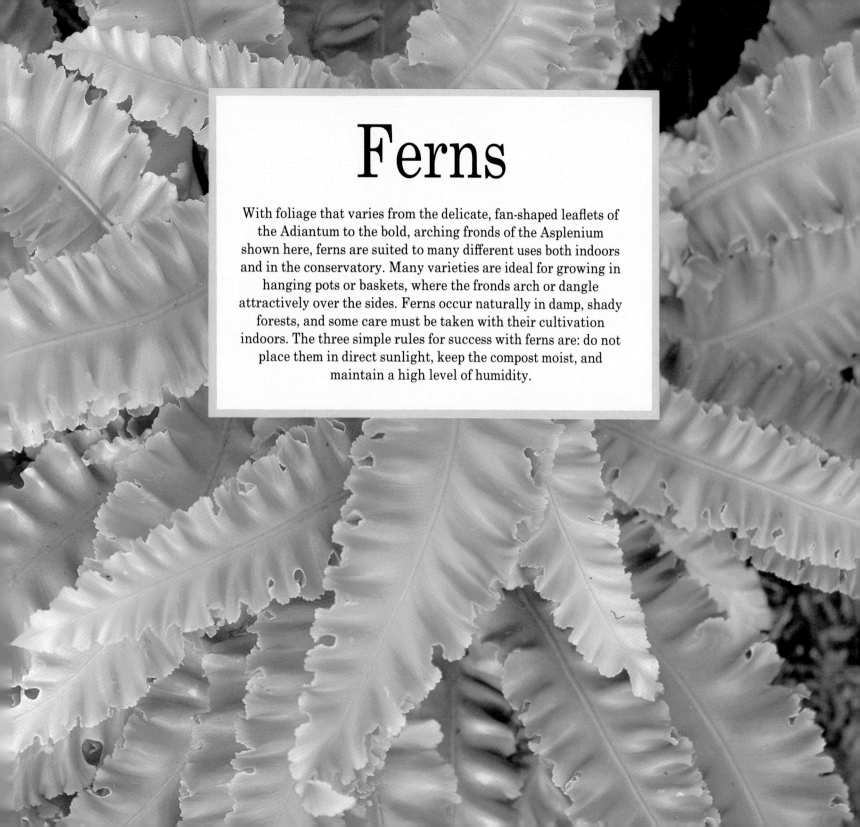

Ferns

With foliage that varies from the delicate, fan-shaped leaflets of
the Adiantum to the bold, arching fronds of the Asplenium
shown here, ferns are suited to many different uses both indoors
and in the conservatory. Many varieties are ideal for growing in
hanging pots or baskets, where the fronds arch or dangle
attractively over the sides. Ferns occur naturally in damp, shady
forests, and some care must be taken with their cultivation
indoors. The three simple rules for success with ferns are: do not
place them in direct sunlight, keep the compost moist, and
maintain a high level of humidity.

Adiantum capillus-veneris

An attractive little plant with delicate, pale green, fan-shaped fronds. The Adiantum is a versatile fern that can either be displayed on its own or used to add softness to a mixed planting. The main problem with the plant is that it is very susceptible to dehydration. If the compost becomes too dry or the humidity is not kept high enough, the thin fronds quickly wither and die. Plants that have suffered dehydration can sometimes be saved if remedial action is taken early enough. The shrivelled fronds may even become turgid again, but it is usually necessary to cut them off just above soil level, using sharp scissors. Associated planting will of course provide the plant with a more humid atmosphere.

COMMON NAME
Maidenhair Fern

Plant type	Fern with bushy, multi-stemmed, compact habit
Season of interest	All year round
Size	20–30cm (8–12in)
Flower	None
Leaf	Fan-shaped fronds, 20–30cm (8–12in), serrated, mid-green leaflets on brown to blackish stems
Temperature	16–20°C (60–68°F)
Aspect/Light	Moderate light, but out of direct sunlight
Humidity	Moderate to high; dislikes dry atmosphere
Watering	Keep compost evenly moist throughout year
Feeding	Once every three to four weeks with half strength houseplant fertilizer in spring and summer
Propagation	Divide plant into clumps in spring or summer and pot singly
Potting	Seed and cutting compost, or mixture of potting compost and medium to coarse sphagnum moss peat
Problems	Dehydration due to dry atmosphere or to compost drying out
Availability	Commonly available throughout the year
Uses indoors	Thrives in body of kitchen, bathroom or bedroom; may be tried in lounge or dining room if not too hot and dry
Other varieties	A. raddianum – more incised leaflets

Regularly check the compost to ensure that it is kept moist

Asplenium nidus

A beautiful fern with bright green, undulating fronds that are held in an upward-spreading rosette. The young fronds slowly unfurl from the centre, and have a soft, shiny texture. They are very delicate and should not be handled for the first few weeks. Mature fronds develop brown parallel lines on the underside, which later produce dust-like spores. The spores can be collected and used to propagate new plants. Although the Asplenium is often used in bowl gardens and mixed planters, it can quickly be overcome by more vigorous plants, so is best grown singly as a feature plant. A constant watch should be kept for scale insects, which can be difficult to control as the plant is sensitive to many spray chemicals. The safest way to deal with minor infestations is to simply remove the insects with a fingernail.

COMMON NAME
Birds-nest Fern

Plant type	Fern with upright habit
Season of interest	All year round
Size	30–75cm (12–18in)
Flower	None
Leaf	Tongue shaped fronds, 15–75cm (8–30in) long, 5–10cm (2–4in) across, bright green, arranged in rosette with brown central rib
Temperature	16–21°C (61–70°F)
Aspect/Light	Moderate light
Humidity	Moderate to high
Watering	Keep compost evenly moist in spring and summer; water a little less in autumn and winter, but do not allow compost to dry out
Feeding	Once every three to four weeks with half strength houseplant fertilizer in spring and summer
Propagation	Collect spores and scatter in pans or trays of seed and cutting compost at 21°C (70°F) in spring or summer; when large enough to handle, pot up singly
Potting	Houseplant potting compost
Problems	Scale insect, aphid, browning of fronds due to dry atmosphere
Availability	Quite commonly available throughout year
Uses indoors	Best grown singly in room that is not too hot or dry; prefers position within body of room, provided it is moderately well lit

To collect the spores, lightly tap the fronds over a sheet of paper

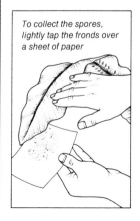

Nephrolepsis exaltata

The Nephrolepsis has long, sword-like fronds comprised of long leaflets on either side of a wiry midrib. Several varieties of the plant are available, with habits that range from erect to drooping, and leaflets that are either whole or divided by varying degrees, the finest being almost feathery. The different varieties are not always labelled correctly. Avoid growing the Nephrolepsis in an atmosphere that is either warm, dry or both. Such conditions will cause rapid dehydration, resulting in loss of the fronds or sometimes even the whole plant.

COMMON NAMES
Ladder Fern, Sword Fern, Boston Fern

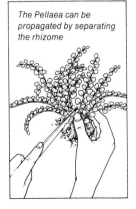

Trim back brown, dry fronds with sharp scissors

Plant type	Fern with upright, bushy habit
Season of interest	All year round
Size	45–75cm (18–30in)
Flower	None
Leaf	Fronds, 30–90cm (12–36in) long, 5–7.5cm (2–3in) across, consisting of long leaflets on either side of midrib; leaflets are either whole or divided
Temperature	15–21°C (59–70°F)
Aspect/Light	Moderate to reasonable light, but out of direct sunlight
Humidity	Moderate to high
Watering	Keep compost evenly moist in spring and summer; water less in autumn and winter; never allow to dry out
Feeding	Once every two to four weeks with half strength houseplant fertilizer in spring and summer
Propagation	Remove plantlets produced by runners and lay on surface of houseplant potting compost at 18–20°C (65–68°F); collect spores and scatter on seed and cutting compost at 21°C (70°F) in spring or summer
Potting	Houseplant potting compost
Problems	Scale insect, dehydration of fronds due to dry atmosphere
Availability	Commonly available throughout year
Uses indoors	Useful table-top plant for lounge or dining room, provided conditions are not too warm and dry

Pellaea rotundifolia

The Pellaea's button-shaped leaflets are unlike those of any other fern. Also unusual are the diminutive size and prostrate habit, which mean that the plant can be effectively used in bowl arrangements, bottle gardens and terrariums. Requiring a fairly high level of humidity, it grows well in close, associated plantings and can tolerate other plants growing around and through its foliage. When separating the rhizome for propagation, moisten the compost well first. The sections of rhizome, with fronds attached, can then be teased apart and cut away quite easily.

COMMON NAME
Button Fern

The Pellaea can be propagated by separating the rhizome

Plant type	Fern with loose, prostrate habit
Season of interest	All year round
Size	10–15cm (4–6in)
Flower	None
Leaf	Fronds, 10–30cm (4–12in) long, consisting of dark green, round leaflets on brown stems
Temperature	16–21°C (61–70°F)
Aspect/Light	Moderate light, away from direct sunlight
Humidity	Moderate to high
Watering	Keep compost evenly moist in spring and summer; water a little less in autumn and winter; never allow to dry out
Feeding	Once every three to four weeks with half strength houseplant fertilizer in spring and summer
Propagation	Separate rhizome in mid to late spring and pot in potting compost at 20°C (68°F); collect spores and scatter on seed and cutting compost at 21°C (70°F)
Potting	Houseplant potting compost
Problems	Aphid, scale insect, dehydration due to dry atmosphere
Availability	Occasionally available, usually in spring and summer
Uses indoors	Good plant for mixed bowl arrangements

Platycerium bifurcatum

An extraordinary plant with strange-looking fronds and a lop-sided habit of growth. The Platycerium produces two types of frond: sterile, shield-shaped fronds, which anchor the plant to its support; and fertile, antler-like fronds. The plant can either be grown in a hanging pot or basket or attached to a piece of cork bark and hung on a wall. Cover the root ball with a mixture of sphagnum moss and sphagnum moss peat, and attach the sterile fronds to the bark using plastic coated wire. Water the plant by either spraying the moss or immersing it in water for a few minutes.

COMMON NAME
Stag's Horn Fern

Plant type	Fern with unusual prostrate habit
Season of interest	All year round
Size	15–120cm (6–48in)
Flower	None
Leaf	Two distinct frond types: sterile frond at base of plant and wrapped around support; fertile frond prominent, antler-like, 30–90cm (1–3ft) long, green
Temperature	18–24°C (64–75°F)
Aspect/Light	Moderate to reasonable light, but away from direct sunlight
Humidity	Moderate to high
Watering	Evenly moisten compost throughout year, allowing to dry just a little before re-watering
Feeding	Once every four to six weeks with half strength houseplant fertilizer in spring and summer
Propagation	Collect spores from underside of fertile fronds and scatter on seed and cutting compost at 21°C (70°F) in spring and early summer
Potting	Mixture of sphagnum moss, peat and bark
Problems	Scale insect
Availability	Occasionally available throughout year
Uses indoors	Feature plant grown singly or in twos or threes, in hanging basket or attached to cork bark hung from wall; good conservatory plant

The Platycerium can be grown on a piece of cork bark

Pteris ensiformis 'Victoriae'

Unlike most ferns, which have plain green foliage, the Pteris produces leaflets with pretty silver bands running down the middle. Silver is a useful colour for mixed groupings, and the plant can be effectively combined with other ferns, foliage plants or even flowering plants. As well as bowls or troughs, it is also suited to bottle gardens and terrariums, although in these enclosed containers it will be necessary to remove any fronds that become too long. Associated planting will also help to maintain a fairly high level of humidity, which the Pteris needs in order to thrive. This plant requires quite a lot of water, so ensure that the compost is kept fairly moist.

COMMON NAME
Sword Brake

Plant type	Fern with loose, open habit
Season of interest	All year round
Size	20–25cm (8–10in)
Flower	None
Leaf	Fronds, roughly triangular, 15–25cm (8–10in) long, 7.5–10cm (3–4in) wide, consisting of broad green leaflets with silvery patterning, on thread-like stems
Temperature	16–21°C (61–70°F)
Aspect/Light	Moderately to reasonably well-lit situation, but away from direct sunlight
Humidity	Moderate to high
Watering	Keep compost evenly moist in spring and summer; water less in autumn and winter; never allow to dry out
Feeding	Once every three to four weeks with half strength houseplant fertilizer in spring and summer
Propagation	Divide rhizome in spring and pot in houseplant potting compost at 20–21°C (68–70°F); collect spores and scatter in seed and cutting compost at 21°C (70°F) in spring or summer
Potting	Houseplant potting compost
Problems	Aphid, dehydration in dry atmosphere
Availability	Occasionally available, usually in spring and summer
Uses indoors	Feature plant for table-top display; also useful for mixed planter or bowl
Other varieties	P. cretica 'Albolineata' – green fronds with white bands

Remove long fronds from bottle garden plants using a blade on a long stick

Palms

Palms are amongst the most evocative of plants, suggesting
exotic foreign lands and the grand interiors of the Edwardian
era. Their elegant, arching, finely divided leaflets, shown well in
the Chaemorops pictured here, can be used to grace many
situations. The large size of some varieties makes them
impressive floor-standing feature plants for spacious rooms and
conservatories. They can also be used to provide a shade canopy
over smaller flowering or foliage plants. Palms are relatively
easy to grow, as long as they have good drainage and are kept
well away from draughts.

Chamaedorea elegans

A compact, dwarf-sized palm that was formerly known by the Latin name *Neanthe bella*. Two or three plants are often sold together in the same pot and should not be separated as it is easy to tear the intertwined roots and kill the plants. The Chamaedorea thrives on a combination of moderately moist compost and fairly high humidity. Excessively dry air will turn the tips and edges of the fronds brown. If this should happen, they can be trimmed with sharp scissors, taking care to leave a thin edge of dead tissue. Apart from making an excellent specimen plant, the Chamaedorea is an ideal subject for a mixed grouping, especially when it is small, and this also helps to keep the humidity high. It can, however, cause a problem with pests, as the plant appeals to a number of pests that can be easily transferred.

COMMON NAME
Parlour Palm

Plant type	Palm with bushy fronds and compact, erect habit
Season of interest	All year round
Size	30–90cm (12–36in)
Flower	Uninteresting flower spike which can be cut off if not required
Leaf	Fronds, 15–60cm (6–24in), mid green
Temperature	20–24°C (68–75°F)
Aspect/Light	Moderately well-lit position, away from any direct sunlight
Humidity	Reasonably high
Watering	Keep compost evenly moist all year round, but allow to get on the dry side occasionally
Feeding	Once every three to four weeks with half strength houseplant fertilizer in spring and summer
Propagation	Sow seeds in seed and cutting compost at 21–24°C (70–75°F) in late spring to early summer; but note that seed germination is very difficult, irregular and slow
Potting	Houseplant potting compost
Problems	Rotting of stem base and roots, yellowing of fronds in direct sunlight, red spider mite, mealy bug, root mealy bug, scale insect
Availability	Commonly available
Uses indoors	Useful in most rooms, including offices, in position away from direct sunlight

The Chamaedorea is a useful subject for a bowl

Howea forsteriana

With its large, arching fronds borne on upright stems, the Howea is one of the most impressive and elegant palms. It is fast-growing and attains a height of 250cm (98in), so requires plenty of space. In most indoor locations it is best displayed in the corner of a room, either on the floor or on a low plant stand. The Howea is reputed to tolerate quite difficult conditions but it only really thrives when treated with great care. It is very susceptible to over-watering, which causes root failure and the collapse of the plant. Pests can also be a problem and a constant watch should be kept for red spider mites, mealy bugs and especially scale insects, which camouflage themselves well against the spots on the leaves and stems.

COMMON NAMES
Kentia Palm, Paradise Palm

Plant type	Palm with erect habit
Season of interest	All year round
Size	100–250cm (39–98in)
Flower	None indoors
Leaf	Erect fronds, 25–60cm (10–24in) long, on sturdy, green stems; each frond is comprised of leaflets, 15–30cm (6–12in) long, 2.5cm (1in) wide
Temperature	18–21°C (64–70°F)
Aspect/Light	Moderately to reasonably well-lit situation, but out of direct sunlight
Humidity	Moderate to high
Watering	Evenly moisten compost in spring and summer, taking care never to make too wet, and allowing to dry a little before re-watering; keep on dry side in autumn and winter
Feeding	Once every two to four weeks with houseplant fertilizer in spring and summer
Propagation	Sow seeds in seed and cutting compost at 27°C (80°F) in mid to late spring
Potting	Houseplant potting compost
Problems	Scale insect, mealy bug, root mealy bug, red spider mite, root rot due to over-watering
Availability	Commonly available throughout year
Uses indoors	Floor-standing feature plant in lounge, dining room, large hall or office
Other varieties	*H. belmoreana* – fronds more erect

Remove old fronds using a sharp knife

Phoenix canariensis

A distinctive and extremely attractive palm, with stiff leaflets and an upright but spreading habit. When small it makes an effective display plant for a table or other piece of furniture. As it grows taller and the habit spreads, the plant is best moved down to the floor. It is important to maintain a high level of humidity otherwise the leaflets will quickly turn brown at the ends and require trimming. If this becomes necessary, use sharp scissors and leave a thin edge of dead tissue. When the Phoenix produces new fronds, the leaflets tend to stick together as they emerge. These will normally free themselves as they grow, but if they begin to suffer tease them gently apart.

COMMON NAMES
Canary Date Palm, Canary Islands Date Palm, Feather Palm

Cut off brown leaf tips with sharp scissors

Plant type	Palm with erect but spreading habit
Season of interest	All year round
Size	100–300cm (39–117in)
Flower	None indoors
Leaf	Feather-like fronds 30–100cm (12–39in) long, comprised of many stiff leaflets, 10–20cm (4–8in) long, 0.5–1cm ($\frac{1}{4}$–$\frac{1}{2}$in) wide, green
Temperature	18–21°C (64–70°F)
Aspect/Light	Well-lit situation with some sunlight
Humidity	Moderate to high
Watering	Evenly moisten compost in spring and summer, allowing to dry just a little before re-watering; water less in autumn and winter
Feeding	Once every two to four weeks with houseplant fertilizer in spring and summer
Propagation	Sow seeds in seed and cutting compost at 27°C (80°F) in mid to late spring
Potting	Houseplant potting compost
Problems	Mealy bug, root mealy bug, scale insect, root rot due to over-watering, browning of leaves in dry atmosphere
Availability	Occasionally available throughout year
Uses indoors	Feature plant for table-top then floor indoors or in conservatory
Other varieties	*P. dactylifera* – more upright and vigorous

Phoenix roebelinii

This Phoenix is one of the best palms to grow indoors as it has a compact habit that can easily be accommodated in a number of home or office locations. It is also a very attractive plant with delicate, feathery fronds comprised of numerous fine leaflets. Like other Phoenix species, it cannot tolerate a warm, dry atmosphere, which will cause the foliage to dry out rapidly, with browning of the leaf tips. The white, waxy covering on newly emerging fronds can occasionally stick leaflets together. These should separate on their own in time, but sometimes need to be gently teased apart.

COMMON NAME
Miniature Date Palm

Gently separate leaflets that remain stuck together

Plant type	Palm with upright but spreading habit
Season of interest	All year round
Size	60–90cm (24–36in) with 60–120cm (24–48in) spread
Flower	None indoors
Leaf	Fronds, 30–90cm (12–36in) long, comprised of many fine leaflets 7.5–10cm (3–4in) long, 0.5cm ($\frac{1}{4}$in) wide, green with light waxy covering
Temperature	18–21°C (64–70°F)
Aspect/Light	Well-lit situation with some sunlight
Humidity	Moderate to high
Watering	Evenly moisten compost in spring and summer, allowing to dry just a little before re-watering; water less in autumn and winter
Feeding	Once every two to four weeks with houseplant fertilizer in spring and summer
Propagation	Sow seeds in seed and cutting compost at 27°C (80°F) in mid to late spring
Potting	Houseplant potting compost
Problems	Mealy bug, root mealy bug, scale insect, root rot due to over-watering, browning of leaves in dry atmosphere
Availability	Occasionally available throughout year
Uses indoors	Feature plant for table-top then floor display; good for lounge, dining room or office; needs space to accommodate spread

Trachycarpus fortunei

This evergreen palm with large fan-shaped leaves grows well in a large container and makes a good feature shrub for the conservatory. The pleated leaves, up to 90cm (36in) wide, are borne on strong, dark green leaf stalks clustered at the summit of a tall, rough, brown trunk. An individual leaf will remain on the plant for many years before it starts to discolour with age. The Trachycarpus also produces long panicles of small yellow flowers in early summer, which are followed by round blue-black fruits. No pruning is necessary apart from the occasional removal of old and damaged leaves.

COMMON NAME
Windmill Palm

Plant type	Palm with upright habit
Season of interest	All year round
Size	To 100–200cm (72–96in) when grown in a pot, if not double
Flower	Small, yellow, borne in panicles 60cm (24in) long
Leaf	Large, fan-shaped, to 90cm (36in) wide and 60cm (24in) long, mid-green, on long leaf-stalk.
Temperature	4–7°C (40–45°F)
Aspect/Light	Well-lit situation with exposure to direct sunlight
Humidity	Moderate
Watering	Keep compost evenly moist from spring to autumn; keep on drier side in winter
Feeding	Once every two weeks with houseplant fertilizer during summer growing period
Propagation	Sow seeds in seed and cutting compost at 24°C (75°F) in early spring
Potting	Soil-based potting compost
Problems	Overall size of leaves
Availability	Sometimes scarce
Uses indoors	Feature plant for conservatory or greenhouse

Remove old or dying lower leaves to improve the plant's appearance

Washingtonia filifera

An extraordinary palm with large, fan-like fronds and brown, fibrous threads hanging from the end of each leaflet. The Washingtonia is not often seen for sale, perhaps because the habit of growth is too wide for many locations indoors. As with most palms, the key to effective care is careful watering. The compost should be evenly moistened but should also be allowed to dry a little between waterings to prevent the roots from rotting. A high level of humidity is also important otherwise the leaf tips turn brown. Unlike most other palms it is not possible to trim the leaves without ruining the appearance of the plant, as the characteristic wispy threads will obviously be lost in the process.

COMMON NAMES
Washington Palm, Desert Fan Palm, Petticoat Palm

Plant type	Palm with erect but spreading habit
Season of interest	All year round
Size	100–250cm (39–98in)
Flower	None indoors
Leaf	Fan-shaped fronds, 45–60cm (18–24in) across, comprised of leaflets, 15–45cm (6–18in) long, 1–2.5cm (½–1in) wide, stiff, green, with wispy brown fibres hanging from the ends; leaflets radiate from 30–45cm (12–18in) stalk
Temperature	18–21°C (64–70°F)
Aspect/Light	Well-lit situation with some sunlight
Humidity	Moderate
Watering	Evenly moisten compost in spring and summer, taking care not to over-water, and allowing to dry a little before re-watering; water just enough to prevent drying out in autumn and winter
Feeding	Once every two to four weeks with houseplant fertilizer in spring and summer
Propagation	Sow seeds in seed and cutting compost at 27°C (80°F) in mid to late spring
Potting	Houseplant potting compost
Problems	Mealy bug, root mealy bug, scale insect, root rot due to over-watering, browning of leaf tips in dry atmosphere
Availability	Not often available
Uses indoors	Feature plant for floor display in lounge or dining room

Improve the humidity by standing the pot in a saucer of moist pebbles

Flowering Plants

Flowering plants provide a kaleidoscope of colours with which to enhance our interiors. The number of varieties is huge, with flowers ranging from the small, delicate blossoms of the Primulas shown here to the large, bold blooms of the Camellia and the unusual Strelitzia. Many species are scented and some produce colourful berries or fruits after the flowers.

Abutilon × hybridum

Saucer-shaped flowers, which closely resemble those of the Hibiscus, are the main attraction of this showy shrub. It is also worth growing for its handsome three-or-five lobed leaves, which are sometimes variegated. Their shape gives the plant its common name of Flowering Maple. Colourful varieties include 'Ashford Red', 'Boule de Neige' (white), 'Canary Bird' (yellow), and 'Kentish Belle' (bronze or copper). *A. striatum thompsonii* has variegated green and yellow leaves. Abutilons can grow quite large, so are most suitable for the conservatory, where they may be planted in a border or pot-grown. Pot-grown specimens will appreciate being stood outside in summer. These shrubs are quite easy to grow, but can become leggy if not pruned. Cut them back hard in autumn to encourage shapely growth.

COMMON NAME
Flowering Maple

Plant type	Flowering shrub with upright habit
Season of interest	Early summer to autumn
Size	To 180cm (72in)
Flower	Saucer-shaped, 5cm (2in), red, yellow, white or pink
Leaf	7.5cm (3in), 3–5 lobed, maple- shaped, green or variegated
Temperature	10–20°C (50–60°F)
Aspect/Light	Well-lit situation with some exposure to sunlight
Humidity	Moderate
Watering	Evenly moisten compost from spring to autumn; keep drier in winter
Feeding	Liquid plant fertilizer once every two weeks in spring and early summer
Propagation	Plant 10–15cm (4–6in) stem cuttings in seed and cutting compost at 15–18°C (59–64°F) in summer; sow seeds in seed and cutting compost at 15–18°C (59–64°F) in late winter
Problems	Mealy bug, aphid, rate of growth and overall size
Availability	Commonly available throughout the year
Uses indoors	Conservatory or greenhouse plant
Other varieties	*A. × h. savitzii* – leaves variegated green and white

Water large plants through a hollow tube to ensure the roots get water

Abutilon megapotamicum 'Variegatum'

Although rather a leggy subject, the Abutilon can be made to look quite attractive if it is trimmed in early spring and provided with a light framework of canes or some other form of support. The loose habit of growth is enhanced by the hanging, bell-shaped flowers. However, the thin leaves are quite frail and the plant is susceptible to dehydration if the air is too dry, resulting in loss of foliage and occasionally the entire plant. The Abutilon requires a sunny position, such as a windowsill. Failure to provide sufficient light will result in lack of flower and more drab colour of foliage. This plant can give two to three useful years' display before it begins to look unkempt.

COMMON NAME
Trailing Abutilon

Plant type	Flowering plant with loose, leggy, trailing habit that can be trained with support
Season of interest	Spring to summer
Size	30–200cm (12–78in)
Flower	Pendulous, bell-shaped, yellow and red, growing from leaf axils
Leaf	Elongated heart shaped, serrated, thin, 5–10cm (2–4in), green with occasional yellow spots
Temperature	18–21°C (65–70°F)
Aspect/Light	Well-lit situation
Humidity	Average, but dislikes excessively dry air, which can cause the leaves to shrivel
Watering	Evenly moisten compost in spring and summer; keep on dry side in autumn and winter
Feeding	Once every two to three weeks with flowering plant fertilizer in spring and summer
Propagation	Plant 7.5–10cm (3–4in) tip cuttings at 20–21°C (68–70°F) in mid spring to early summer
Potting	Potting compost
Problems	Red spider mite, scale insect
Availability	Late spring to early summer; infrequently available
Uses indoors	Grows well on sunny windowsill or in conservatory
Other varieties	*A. megapotamicum* – plain green leaves; trailing habit

A light framework will help to support the plant

Acacia armata

This Australian flowering shrub is the Mimosa seen in florists' shops. The Acacia deserves a place in the conservatory for the yellow, fluffy flowers, often sweetly scented, which appear in late winter and early spring. Year round interest is maintained by the evergreen, fern-like, bright green foliage. There are a number of other varieties available: *A. dealbata* has silvery foliage, as does *A. podalyriifolia*, the Queensland Wattle. Acacias grow fast and need plenty of space for their spreading branches. They should be cut back after flowering if growth needs to be controlled. Though watering should be reduced in winter, it is important not to let the compost dry completely, as the flower buds may drop before opening.

COMMON NAMES
Kangaroo Thorn, Wattle

Provide drainage material and keep the base of the pot off ground level

Plant type	Flowering shrub with upright habit
Season of interest	Late winter to early summer
Size	3m (10ft) when grown in a pot, if not double
Flower	Rounded, fluffy, 1.25cm (½in), bright yellow
Leaf	Narrow, spiny or pinnate, fern-like, 2.5cm (1in), dark or silvery green
Temperature	7–18°C (45–64°F)
Aspect/Light	Well-lit situation with exposure to sunlight
Humidity	Medium to dry
Watering	Evenly moisten compost from spring to autumn; reduce water in winter but do not allow to dry out completely
Feeding	Once every two weeks with flowering plant fertilizer in spring and early summer
Propagation	Plant 10cm (4in) stem cuttings in seed and cutting compost at 16–18°C (61–64°F) in summer; sow seeds in seed and cutting compost at 21°C (70°F) in spring
Potting	Soil-based potting compost
Problems	Flower buds drop if plant is allowed to dry out in winter
Availability	Commonly available throughout the year
Uses indoors	Conservatory or greenhouse plant

Acalypha hispida

With its long, trailing flower spikes, the Acalypha is an unusual plant, which looks at its best when young. Plants that grow larger tend to become rather lank and straggly, and should be pruned back in the spring to maintain some level of compactness; dead flower-spikes should also be removed. Alternatively, the plant can be renewed each year from tip cuttings. Insufficient light not only increases the legginess and untidiness but will also reduce the likelihood of flowering. However, the Acalypha should not be exposed to direct sun. Care should be taken to maintain a high level of humidity, which can often be low where light intensities are high. To keep the humidity high, stand the pot on moist pebbles and mist the foliage regularly.

COMMON NAMES
Chenille Plant, Foxtails, Red-hot Cat's Tail

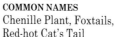
A tray of moist pebbles will improve the humidity

Plant type	Flowering plant with erect, bushy habit
Season of interest	Summer to early autumn
Size	30–60cm (12–24in)
Flower	Long, trailing, fluffy red spikes, 15–45cm (6–18in)
Leaf	Oval, 10–20cm (4–8in) long, 6–7.5cm (2½–3in) wide, green
Temperature	18–24°C (64–75°F)
Aspect/Light	Well-lit situation with light shade from direct sun
Humidity	High
Watering	Evenly moisten compost in spring and summer; keep on drier side in autumn and winter with just sufficient water to prevent compost drying out
Feeding	Once every two to three weeks with houseplant fertilizer in spring and summer
Propagation	Plant 7.5–10cm (3–4in) tip cuttings in seed and cutting compost at 20–24°C (68–75°F) in early to late spring
Potting	Houseplant potting compost
Problems	Red spider mite
Availability	Occasionally available in summer
Uses indoors	Table-top feature plant or windowsill plant where some protection from direct sun can be provided; useful plant for lounge or dining room

Achimenes grandiflora

An extremely colourful plant, the Achimenes flowers throughout the spring and summer. During this time the compost should be kept evenly moist, but in autumn and winter the plant should not be watered at all, as it becomes dormant and will 'rest' until the start of a new growing season. When this arrives, in the spring, the plant can be helped into new growth by watering the compost with warm water – hence the common name of Hot Water Plant. However, the water should not be too hot as this will damage or kill the rhizome.

COMMON NAMES
Cupid's Bower, Hot Water Plant

Plant type	Flowering plant with bushy habit
Season of interest	Late spring and summer
Size	10–40cm (4–16in)
Flower	2.5–4cm (1–1½in) wide, cerise-red flowers
Leaf	5–10cm (2–4in) long, 5cm (2in) wide, but can grow larger, green
Temperature	18–24°C (64–75°F)
Aspect/Light	Well-lit situation with exposure to sunlight but not excessively high levels for prolonged period
Humidity	Moderate to high
Watering	Evenly moisten compost in spring and summer; allow to dry in autumn and winter
Feeding	Once every two to four weeks with half strength flowering plant fertilizer in spring and summer
Propagation	Plant 7.5–9cm (3–3½in) tip cuttings in late spring to early summer in seed and cutting compost at 20–21°C (68–70°F); separate rhizomatous root in spring and plant as above
Potting	Houseplant potting compost
Problems	Red spider mite
Availability	Commonly available late spring and early summer
Uses indoors	Windowsill or hanging basket plant
Other varieties	*Achimenes* hybrids – generally smaller; pink, white, red or purple flowers

Use a light framework to support leggy plants

Aeschynanthus 'Mona Lisa'

This compact and low-growing Aeschynanthus is a relatively new variety. Like other trailing plants it may be used in a hanging pot or basket or displayed on a pedestal, but is perhaps better placed where the loose, somewhat straggly trails can lay almost semi-prostrate. It is particularly effective when grown in a bowl or trough where it associates well with many other plants. Position the Aeschynanthus at the front of the arrangement where the contrasting dark green leaves and reddish orange flowers can be seen to best effect.

Plant type	Flowering plant with loose, trailing habit
Season of interest	Summer
Size	10–15cm (4–6in) high, 20–100cm (8–39in) trails
Flower	Tube-like, 5–6cm (2–2½in) long, reddish orange
Leaf	Pointed oval, glossy, dark green, 5cm (2in) long
Temperature	15–21°C (59–70°F)
Aspect/Light	Well-lit situation, out of direct sunlight
Humidity	High
Watering	Keep compost evenly moist in summer when plant is in flower; allow to dry a little between waterings at other times
Feeding	Half strength flowering plant fertilizer every three to four weeks in spring and summer
Propagation	Plant 7.5–10cm (3–4in) tip or stem cuttings in seed and cutting compost at 21°C (70°F) in spring and summer
Potting	Houseplant potting compost
Problems	Mealy bug, aphid
Availability	Occasionally available late spring to early summer
Uses indoors	Low-growing feature plant for special display in lounge, dining room or conservatory; useful in bowl or trough or in mixed arrangement

This plant is a good subject for a mixed arrangement

Aeschynanthus speciosus

The Aeschynanthus is a superb plant for the enthusiast who favours vibrant colours, as it is a blaze of colour for many weeks whilst in flower. The life of the flowers is actually quite short, but as they are produced in succession, with each flower taking a while to mature fully before it finally fades and drops off, the interest is prolonged for some time. With its semi-trailing habit the plant is effective in a hanging basket, on a pedestal or when grown on a table or other piece of furniture. Whilst good light is essential, the Aeschynanthus should not be exposed to direct sunlight, as the leaves can turn yellow. Conversely, if the plant is not given enough light it will become weak and will be unlikely to flower.

COMMON NAMES
Lipstick Plant, Lipstick Vine, Basket Vine

Trim long, wayward shoots with a sharp knife or scissors

Plant type	Flowering plant with semi-trailing habit
Season of interest	Summer
Size	10–15cm (4–6in) high, with 30–45cm (12–18in) trails
Flower	Tube-like, 5–7.5cm (2–3in) long, bright orange with orange and yellow centre
Leaf	Pointed oval, 5–7.5cm (2–3in) long, green, fleshy
Temperature	15–21°C (59–70°F)
Aspect/Light	Well-lit situation, out of direct sunlight
Humidity	High
Watering	Keep compost evenly moist in summer when plant is in flower; allow to dry a little between waterings at other times
Feeding	Half strength flowering plant fertilizer every three to four weeks in spring and summer
Propagation	Plant 7.5–10cm (3–4in) tip or stem cuttings in seed and cutting compost at 21°C (70°F) in spring and summer
Potting	Houseplant potting compost
Problems	Mealy bug, aphid
Availability	Occasionally available late spring to early summer
Uses indoors	Excellent hanging basket plant, or pedestal or wall pot plant
Other varieties	*A. lobbianus* – bright red flowers

Allamanda cathartica

Surprisingly, perhaps, the Allamanda is not usually considered a climbing plant, but more a bushy shrub. However, the plant is really at its best if allowed to climb and provided with a means of support such as a light frame, a trellis or bamboo canes. Grown in such a way, it will look especially attractive if it is featured in a conservatory or next to a patio window, where it can be exposed to sufficient light. Without occasional trimming or pruning, the Allamanda can easily become rather straggly and untidy. When this happens it may be worth pruning back the growth by a half to two thirds in the latter part of winter before fresh growth starts. A less vigorous and more compact variety is *A.c.* 'Grandiflora'.

COMMON NAME
Golden Trumpet

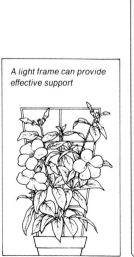

A light frame can provide effective support

Plant type	Flowering plant with bushy semi-trailing habit
Season of interest	Summer
Size	60–400cm (24–156in)
Flower	Trumpet-shaped, formed by five petals, 5–10cm (2–4in) wide, golden-yellow
Leaf	Oval, 7.5–12.5cm (3–5in) long, dark green
Temperature	18–21°C (64–70°F)
Aspect/Light	Well-lit situation, without too much direct sun
Humidity	High
Watering	Evenly moisten compost in spring and summer, allowing to dry just a little before re-watering; keep on drier side in autumn and winter
Feeding	Once every three to four weeks with flowering plant fertilizer in spring and summer
Propagation	Plant 7.5–10cm (3–4in) tip cuttings in seed and cutting compost at 21–22°C (70–72°F) in mid spring to early summer
Potting	Houseplant and potting compost
Problems	Aphid, red spider mite
Availability	Occasionally available in early summer
Uses indoors	Floor-standing plant next to patio window or in conservatory, climbing through trellis or similar support
Other varieties	*A.c.* 'Grandiflora' – more compact habit

Anisodontea halvastrum

Many members of the Mallow family adorn our gardens but this tender plant from the South Island of New Zealand requires the protection of a conservatory if it is to survive. Ideal for growing in a pot, the Anisodontea has an erect habit, evergreen foliage and rosy-magenta, mallow-shaped flowers, which are produced at each leaf-joint either singly or in threes. The flowering period lasts from spring until autumn. This is a versatile plant, which is suitable for growing singly or in a mixed planting with foliage plants. In summer, it can be moved outside and used as a patio plant if preferred.

COMMON NAME
Anisodontea

Plant type	Flowering shrub with erect habit
Season of interest	Spring to autumn
Size	Up to 100cm (39in) high, 100cm (39in) wide
Flower	Mallow-shaped, single, 2cm (¾in) wide, pale rosy-magenta
Leaf	Ovate with lobed edges, 2–3cm (¾in) long and wide, mid green
Temperature	0–20°C (32–68°F)
Aspect/Light	Full sun
Humidity	Average
Watering	Evenly moisten compost from late spring to early autumn; keep on dry side in winter
Feeding	Liquid houseplant fertilizer in mid spring and again in mid summer
Propagation	Root softwood cuttings in houseplant potting compost at 18–19°C (65–66°F)
Potting	General or houseplant potting compost
Problems	Vine weevil
Availability	Quite commonly available from late spring to summer
Uses indoors	Free-standing shrub; use as individual specimen or group with other foliage plants

The Anisodontea can be used as a patio plant in summer

Anthurium andreanum

The most apt of this plant's common names is Painter's Palette, as it can produce flower heads in several different colours. These are white, an almost gaudy pink (the Flamingo Flower or Lily), and bright red, which is the most common form. Rather demanding in its cultural requirements, the plant requires constantly high humidity, and the aerial roots should be mulched occasionally with sphagnum moss. However, if it can be grown satisfactorily, the Anthurium will produce its bright flowers for a long period. Left on the plant the flowers will last for several weeks before they fade and deteriorate, but will need support to display them at their best. Alternatively, they can be removed for use in cut flower arrangements.

COMMON NAMES
Flamingo Flower, Flamingo Lily, Painter's Palette, Oilcloth Flower

Plant type	Flowering plant with erect, open habit
Season of interest	Usually summer, but occasionally throughout year if conditions are favourable
Size	45–100cm (18–39in)
Flower	Spathe heart-shaped, 10–12.5cm (4–5in), white, pink or red; spadix poker-like, erect, 5–7.5cm (2–3in) long, white, yellow, on 30–45cm (12–18in) stem
Leaf	Heart-shaped, 15–25cm (6–10in) long, green, on 25–30cm (10–12in) stems
Temperature	18–24°C (64–75°F)
Aspect/Light	Moderate light with some shade
Humidity	High
Watering	Keep compost evenly moist in spring and summer; allow to dry very slightly before re-watering in autumn and winter
Feeding	Once every two to four weeks with houseplant fertilizer in spring and summer
Propagation	Separate plantlets in mid spring to mid summer and put into potting compost with sphagnum moss added at 24°C (75°F); sow seeds as above
Potting	Houseplant potting compost with sphagnum moss added
Problems	Aphid, red spider mite
Availability	Occasionally available throughout year
Uses indoors	Unusual feature plant for lounge, dining room or conservatory

Sphagnum moss may be used as a mulch around the aerial roots

Anthurium scherzerianum hybrids

Confusingly, this Anthurium shares with *A. andreanum* the common name of Flamingo Flower, although its other name of Pigtail Plant is more descriptive, because of the rather curly spadix. The flowers can be used in cut flower arrangements, but are more commonly left on the plant, where they provide a long display. For the best results, the flowers should be supported as their weight will cause the stems to bend and look untidy. Use wire rather than small sticks, as it is less obvious. Bend the wire into a loop to support the flower at the top and bend the sharp end back with a pair of pliers for safety. With its flowers suitably supported, this Anthurium makes an ideal feature plant for most rooms.

COMMON NAMES
Flamingo Flower, Pigtail Plant

Small wires can be bent to support the flowers

Plant type	Flowering plant with loose, erect habit
Season of interest	Usually summer, but occasionally throughout year if conditions are favourable
Size	30–45cm (12–18in)
Flower	Spathe heart-shaped, 7.5–10cm (3–4in), red, orange or white; spadix 5–7.5cm (2–3in) long, reddish orange, on 15–20cm (6–8in) stems
Leaf	Pointed oval, 15–20cm (6–8in), on 15–20cm (6–8in) stems
Temperature	18–24°C (64–75°F)
Aspect/Light	Moderate light, away from sunlight
Humidity	High
Watering	Evenly moisten compost in spring and summer; allow to dry very slightly before re-watering autumn and winter
Feeding	Once every two to four weeks with houseplant fertilizer in spring and summer
Propagation	Separate plantlets in mid spring to mid summer and plant in potting compost with sphagnum moss added at 24°C (75°F); sow seed as above
Potting	Houseplant potting compost with sphagnum moss added
Problems	Aphid
Availability	Usually available spring and summer
Uses indoors	Ideal feature plant for low table for lounge, dining room, kitchen, bathroom or office

Antirrhinum majus hybrids

Snapdragons make good container plants and are an excellent source of summer colour for the conservatory or greenhouse. Like most other annuals, they require plenty of light, water and food to provide a good display of flowers. They do not need high temperatures once the danger from frosts has passed. Pinch out the leading shoots to encourage a bushy habit of growth and remove dead flowers to encourage further flowering. There are many different varieties of Antirrhinum in a wide range of sizes and colours. *A. m.* 'Tom Thumb Mixed' is a large-flowered dwarf variety, 22.5cm (9in) high.

COMMON NAME
Snapdragon

Pinch back young plants to encourage a bushy habit of growth

Plant type	Flowering plant with erect habit
Season of interest	Early summer to late autumn
Size	15–30cm (6–12in)
Flower	Tubular, pinched together to form mouth surrounded by 5 broad lobes, in erect spikes; yellow, pink, red, orange, white
Leaf	Pointed oval, 2.5–7.5cm (1–3in) long, light to mid green
Temperature	4–7°C (40–45°F) for indoor flowering
Aspect/Light	Well-lit situation with some sunshine
Humidity	Moderate
Watering	Keep compost evenly moist throughout growing season
Feeding	Once every two weeks with flowering plant fertilizer during spring and summer growing season
Propagation	Sow seed in seed and cutting compost at 16–21°C (61–70°F) in late winter
Potting	Houseplant potting compost
Problems	Antirrhinum rust (rare)
Availability	Commonly available as seed from early winter to early spring and as potplants from early spring onwards
Uses indoors	Conservatory or greenhouse plant

Aphelandra squarrosa 'Louisae'

With its large, dark green, white veined leaves contrasting with a golden-yellow flower spike, the Aphelandra is as much a foliage as a flowering plant. Indeed, after the first flowering, it is perhaps best treated as a foliage plant, as it is difficult to create the cultural conditions that will encourage successful reflowering. Even as a foliage plant, however, the Aphelandra is not the easiest species to grow. The side shoots produced after the first season create a leggy growth and a palm tree shape as the lower leaves are lost. Pruning in the spring may help to maintain a more compact shape. When tending the plant, avoid handling the leaves, as they are weak and brittle and can be easily cracked or torn. The Aphelandra is also very susceptible to attack by scale insects and aphids.

COMMON NAMES
Saffron Spike, Zebra Plant

Plant type	Flowering plant with erect habit
Season of interest	Spring to early summer
Size	30–60cm (12–24in)
Flower	7.5–10cm (3–4in), golden-yellow spike with bracts from which tubular, 2.5–4cm (1–1½in) flowers appear
Leaf	Pointed oval, 15–25cm (6–10in), dark green with bold white veins
Temperature	18–24°C (64–75°F)
Aspect/Light	Well-lit situation, but out of direct sun
Humidity	High
Watering	Evenly moisten compost in spring and summer; allow to dry out a little before re-watering in autumn and winter
Feeding	Once every one or two weeks with houseplant fertilizer in spring and summer
Propagation	Plant 7.5cm (3in) tip cuttings or stem cuttings consisting of a pair of leaves and 5cm (2in) of stem below leaves in seed and cutting compost at 21–24°C (70–75°F) in mid spring to early summer
Potting	Houseplant potting compost
Problems	Aphid, mealy bug, scale insect, premature leaf loss
Availability	Commonly available spring and early summer
Uses indoors	Feature plant for lounge or dining room
Other varieties	A.s. 'Brockfeld' – more compact habit

Pruning in the spring after flowering may help to keep control of the plant

Begonia elatior hybrids

This Begonia is a popular and highly colourful plant that can provide a showy display for a very long time, often remaining in flower for several months. The plant can be used to brighten up a windowsill in virtually any room. One of its few weaknesses is that the growth is very floppy and rather brittle. Unsupported, the stems can easily sag and snap off. One other problem with this Begonia is its susceptibility to pests and diseases. A careful check should be kept for aphid, and any fading and dead flowers should be cleanly removed to prevent infection by diseases. Old leaves and other damaged tissue should be treated similarly.

Plant type	Flowering plant with erect, busy habit
Season of interest	Spring and summer
Size	15–30cm (6–12in)
Flower	4–5cm (1½–2in), red, pink or orange
Leaf	Rounded heart-shaped with slightly serrated edge, 5–10cm (2–4in), fleshy, green, crinkled
Temperature	15–19°C (59–66°F)
Aspect/Light	Well-lit situation with some exposure to sunlight
Humidity	Moderate to high
Watering	Evenly moisten compost in spring and summer, allowing to dry a little before re-watering; keep on dry side in autumn and winter
Feeding	Once every two to three weeks with flowering plant fertilizer in spring and summer
Propagation	Plant 7.5–10cm (3–4in) tip cuttings in seed and cutting compost at 20–21°C (68–70°F) in spring and summer
Potting	Houseplant potting compost
Problems	Aphid, botrytis, mildew
Availability	Commonly available in spring and summer
Uses indoors	Excellent windowsill plant for almost any room; good in kitchen

Use a light framework of sticks and twine to support the plant

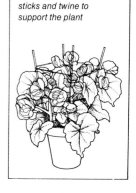

Beloperone guttata

An unusual plant with brownish pink, overlapping bracts. When first purchased the Beloperone is normally well formed and compact. However, within a few weeks the plant starts to produce lush, vegetative growth that can transform it into a leggy and untidy subject. Regular trimming will keep it in check to some degree, but maintaining the original habit is close to impossible, and within a few months the plant

Trimming the plant may help to keep it in check

may have to be discarded. The use of a flowering plant fertilizer rather than houseplant fertilizer may help to 'harden' the growth somewhat and reduce the production of lush vegetation.

COMMON NAME
Shrimp Plant

Plant type	Flowering plant with upright habit
Season of interest	Spring to early winter
Size	15–60cm (6–24in)
Flower	Curious spike of 5–10cm (2–4in), brownish pink 'shrimps', from which grow tubular, 2.5cm (1in), white flowers
Leaf	Soft, green, pointed, oval, 2.5–5cm (1–2in)
Temperature	16–20°C (61–68°F)
Aspect/Light	Well-lit situation with sunlight
Humidity	Moderate
Watering	Evenly moisten compost in spring and summer, allowing to dry just a little between waterings; keep on drier side in autumn and winter
Feeding	Once every two to three weeks with flowering plant fertilizer in spring and summer
Propagation	Plant 7.5cm (3in) tip cuttings or 5cm (2in) stem cuttings in seed and cutting compost at 20–21°C (68–70°F) in mid spring to early summer
Potting	Houseplant potting compost
Problems	Relatively trouble free
Availability	Common available from spring to autumn
Uses indoors	Good all year round windowsill plant for most rooms

Bougainvillea glabra

Despite the difficulty that may be encountered with its cultivation, the unusual and highly colourful Bougainvillea is worth all the effort. Avoid allowing the plant to dry to wilting point during the growing season, but keep it a little drier and slightly cooler for a short period in the winter. As the Bougainvillea starts to grow in the spring, the choice must be made as to whether it should be grown as a relatively loose bush, or encouraged to climb. As a climber the plant can be supported either by a bamboo cane or by a wire frame, possibly formed into a hoop. Care should be taken as the stems can produce sharp spines. It is essential to place the plant in direct sunlight, otherwise the growth becomes leggy and the flowering potential will be reduced. Aphids are strongly attracted to the Bougainvillea so make regular checks for them.

COMMON NAME
Paper Flower

Regularly train the growth to maintain a good shape

Plant type	Flowering plant with climbing habit
Season of interest	Spring and summer
Size	100–400cm (39–156in)
Flower	Small, white, amidst three 2.5–5cm (1–2in) pink or purple bracts
Leaf	Pointed oval, 5cm (2in), mid green
Temperature	16–20°C (61–68°F)
Aspect/Light	Well-lit situation with exposure to full sun
Humidity	Moderate
Watering	Evenly moisten compost in spring and summer, allowing to dry just a little before re-watering; keep on drier side in autumn and winter
Feeding	Flowering plant fertilizer once every two weeks in spring and summer
Propagation	Plant 10–15cm (4–6in) tip or stem cuttings in seed and cutting compost at 24°C (75°F) in mid spring to early summer
Potting	Houseplant potting compost
Problems	Aphid
Availability	Often available from mid spring to early summer
Uses indoors	Ideal for sunny windowsill or conservatory
Other varieties	B. buttiana – more compact; orange and rose-red bracts

Browallia speciosa

The pretty dark blue or violet flowers of the Browallia provide a very attractive display which can last for several weeks, possibly throughout the summer. To prolong the flowering period as much as possible, the plant should be kept at the cooler end of the temperature range; too high a temperature will reduce the flowering period considerably. The growth may need some support to promote a bushy habit, although the natural tendency of the Browallia is to semi-trail. If it becomes loose and untidy, the plant is perhaps best grown in a hanging pot or basket. The Browallia is best treated as an annual, to be discarded after flowering.

COMMON NAMES
Sapphire Flower, Bush Violet, Amethyst Flower

Plant type	Flowering plant with bushy, semi-trailing habit
Season of interest	Summer
Size	45–60cm (18–24in)
Flower	Five-petalled, 4–5cm (1½–2in) wide, dark blue
Leaf	Pointed oval, 5–6cm (2–2½in), green
Temperature	13–16°C (55–61°F)
Aspect/Light	Well-lit situation with exposure to sunlight
Humidity	Moderate
Watering	Evenly moisten compost throughout year, allowing to dry a little before re-watering
Feeding	Once every two weeks with flowering plant fertilizer from early summer until flowering finishes
Propagation	Sow seeds in seed and cutting compost at 18–20°C (65–68°F) in early to mid spring
Potting	Houseplant potting compost
Problems	Aphid
Availability	Occasionally available in the spring and early summer
Uses indoors	Good windowsill plant for virtually any bright window, including bedrooms; also suitable for hanging pot or basket
Other varieties	B.s. – 'Silver Bells' – white flowers; B. viscosa 'Alba' – compact; white flowers; B.v. 'Sapphire' – compact; blue flowers

Provide a light framework for support

Brunfelsia pauciflora calycina

The Brunfelsia's unusual common name of Yesterday, Today and Tomorrow Plant relates to the extraordinary development of the flowers. On the first day of opening they are purple in colour; by the second day they have faded to a paler blue; and by the third day they are an off-white colour. On the fourth day the flower deteriorates. The plant's erect, bushy habit can easily become rather leggy and get out of control. To maintain a more compact and balanced growth, the growing tips should be pinched out regularly and the plant should be trimmed back in the spring. The variety 'Floribunda' is a more compact and freely flowering plant, but it is less commonly available.

COMMON NAME
Yesterday, Today and Tomorrow Plant

Plant type	Flowering plant with erect, bushy habit
Season of interest	Spring and summer, occasionally all year round
Size	30–60cm (12–24in)
Flower	4–5cm (1½–2in), purple fading to pale blue then off-white, fragrant
Leaf	Oval, green, shiny 7.5–10cm (3–4in)
Temperature	16–20°C (61–68°F)
Aspect/Light	Well-lit situation, with some exposure to sun
Humidity	Moderate to high
Watering	Evenly moisten compost in spring and summer, allowing to dry out a little before re-watering; water just enough to prevent drying out in autumn and winter
Feeding	Once every three to four weeks with flowering plant fertilizer in spring and summer
Propagation	Plant 10cm (4in) tip cuttings or semi-hardwood cuttings in seed and cutting compost at 20–21°C (68–70°F) in spring
Potting	Houseplant potting compost
Problems	Red spider mite
Availability	Occasionally available
Uses indoors	Table-top plant, close to well-lit window
Other varieties	B.p.c. 'Floribunda' – more compact and freely flowering; B.p.c. 'Macrantha' – larger flowers, up to 5–7.5cm (2–3in) across

Regularly pinch out the growing tips to promote compact growth

Calceolaria herbeohybrida hybrids

With its colourful, balloon-shaped flowers, the Calceolaria provides an appealing display for a few weeks from late spring to early summer. The flower varieties are yellow, orange or red, with patterning produced by spots and freckles. Place the plant in a well-lit position, otherwise the growth will become leggy, and keep a constant watch for aphid and whitefly. Too much warmth can reduce the flowering period

considerably, so maintain a moderate temperature. Once flowering has finished, the Calceolaria is usually discarded.

Remove dead and fading flowers to maintain the plant's appearance

COMMON NAMES
Slipper Flower, Slipperwort, Pocketbook Plant, Pouch Flower

Plant type	Flowering plant with compact habit
Season of interest	Late spring to early summer
Size	15–30cm (6–12in)
Flower	Hollow, 2.5–4cm (1–1½in) yellow, orange or red, with spots
Leaf	Oval, 10–15cm (4–6in) long, variable width, slightly hairy, green
Temperature	12–18°C (54–64°F)
Aspect/Light	Well-lit situation out of direct sunlight
Humidity	Moderate to high
Watering	Keep compost evenly moist throughout year; do not allow to dry out
Feeding	Once every two to four weeks with half strength flowering plant fertilizer in spring and summer
Propagation	Sow seeds in seed and cutting compost at 18–20°C (65–68°F) from late spring to mid summer to flower the following year
Potting	Houseplant potting compost
Problems	Aphid, whitefly, dehydration if under-watered
Availability	Commonly available in late spring
Uses indoors	Limited life feature plant for table decoration

Calceolaria integrifolia 'Sunshine'

A spectacular, small tender perennial, normally grown as an annual, which is ideal for container planting and makes a showy pot plant in the cool conservatory. The Calceolaria is fairly easy to raise from seed and it should be massed in small or large groups for best effect. Its bright golden-yellow colour and long flowering period make it invaluable in a mixed display of flowering plants. For the best results, feed and

water well throughout the growing period and make sure the plant receives plenty of direct sunlight. The range of

colours in the varieties includes white, yellow, orange and red.

COMMON NAME
Slipperwort

Plant type	Flowering plant with bushy habit
Season of interest	Early summer to autumn
Size	25cm (12in) high
Flower	Bladder-like, 1.25cm (½in) across, borne in loose clusters, bright yellow
Leaf	Oval, 4–5cm (1½–2in) long, soft-textured and downy, grey-green
Temperature	0–5°C (32–41°)
Aspect/light	Sunny position
Humidity	Moderate
Watering	Water well throughout the summer growing period
Feeding	Flowering plant fertilizer every two weeks during the summer growing period
Propagation	sow seeds in seed and cutting compost at 18°C (64°F) in March/April
Potting	Houseplant potting compost
Problems	Whitefly
Availability	Commonly available in late spring to early summer
Uses indoors	Pot or container plant for summer colour in conservatory or greenhouse

Callistemon hybrids

Fluffy cylindrical flower spikes give this unusual Australian shrub its popular name of Bottle Brush. The variety most commonly seen is *C. citrinus* with deep red flower spikes, but yellow, white and even green flowers are also available.

The plant flowers in summer. Like most Australian shrubs, Callistemons need plenty of light, and pot-grown plants can be placed outside in summer. They can become straggly if left unpruned, and should be cut back in the autumn. However, before pruning too hard, bear in mind that the following year's flowers will appear on new growth made after flowering.

COMMON NAME
Bottle Brush

Plant type	Flowering shrub with upright habit
Season of interest	Summer to early autumn
Size	To 90cm (36in)
Flower	Cylindrical 'brush' made up of stamens, 7.5–10cm (3–4in) long, red, white, yellow, green, produced in summer to early autumn
Leaf	Narrow, evergreen, 7.5cm (3in) long
Temperature	−3–20°C (26–68°F)
Aspect/Light	Well-lit situation with exposure to sunlight
Humidity	Moderate to dry
Watering	Water well from spring to autumn; keep on drier side in winter
Feeding	Once every four weeks with flowering plant fertilizer in spring and early summer
Propagation	Plant 7.5–10cm (3–4in) stem cuttings in seed and cutting compost or low-lime compost at 15–18°C (59–6°F) in spring; sow seeds in seed and cutting compost at 13–18°C (55–65°F) in spring
Potting	Lime-free or ericaceous compost
Problems	May become open in habit
Availability	Quite commonly available throughout the year
Uses indoors	Conservatory or greenhouse plant

To cut down on water loss, plunge the roots into a peat substitute, gravel or soil

Camellia hybrids

Camellias are usually thought of as hardy plants but they are also ideal for growing in the conservatory. Their spectacular flowers make a welcome splash of colour in early spring. The glossy, dark, evergreen foliage makes a striking contrast to the beautiful single or double red, pink or white blooms. Camellias can be temperamental if they are not provided with the right conditions. They must be grown in lime-free or ericaceous compost, dislike sudden changes in temperature or moisture levels, and will not flourish in a hot, dry atmosphere. If possible, they should be watered with lime-free water or with rainwater. They require only light pruning in early spring to remove untidy shoots.

COMMON NAME
Camellia

Plant type	Flowering shrub with upright habit
Season of interest	Spring
Size	To 180 cm (72in)
Flower	Single or double, 7.5–12.5cm (3–5in), white, and shades of red and pink or bi-coloured
Leaf	Oval, 10cm (4in), dark green, glossy, evergreen
Temperature	−3–18°C (26–65°F)
Aspect/Light	Well-lit situation out of direct sun
Humidity	Moderate
Watering	Evenly moisten compost throughout the year; do not use water containing lime
Feeding	Once every two to three weeks with flowering plant fertilizer in late spring and early summer
Potting	Peat-based ericaceous potting compost
Propagation	Plant 10cm (3in) tip cuttings in low-lime compost at 13–16°C (55–61°F) in late summer
Problems	Dehydration in warm, dry atmosphere
Availability	Commonly available throughout the year
Uses indoors	Conservatory and greenhouse plant

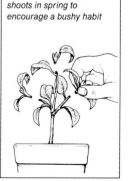

Pinch out the leading shoots in spring to encourage a bushy habit

Campanula isophylla

The Campanula produces masses of star-like flowers for many weeks. To prolong flowering, keep the plant at the cooler end of the temperature range. With its bushy, semi-trailing habit the Campanula is equally suited to a pot on a windowsill or to a hanging pot or basket. If displayed in a pot as a bushy subject, use a light framework of small canes linked with string for support. Although the plant benefits from moderate sunlight, excessive exposure to the brightest sun will bleach and scorch the leaves and flowers.

COMMON NAMES
Bellflower, Star of Bethlehem, Italian Bellflower, Falling Stars

When grown as a pot plant a light supporting framework will improve the appearance

Plant type	Flowering plant with semi-trailing habit
Season of interest	Summer
Size	10–15cm (4–6in) tall with 15–30cm (6–12in) trails
Flower	Profuse, five-petalled, star-shaped, 2.5–4cm (1–1½in), blue
Leaf	Heart-shaped, 2.5–3cm (1–1¼in), green
Temperature	10–16°C (50–61°F)
Aspect/Light	Well-lit situation with occasional exposure to some sunlight
Humidity	High
Watering	Evenly moisten compost in spring and summer; provide a little less water in autumn and winter
Feeding	Once every two to three weeks with flowering plant fertilizer in spring and summer
Propagation	Divide plant or insert 5–7.5cm (2–3in) tip cuttings in seed and cutting compost at 18–20°C (65–68°F) in spring
Potting	Houseplant potting compost
Problems	Aphid, botrytis (grey mould fungus)
Availability	Commonly available in spring and early summer
Uses indoors	Good feature plant for cool, well-lit position on table or windowsill; also useful in hanging pot or basket
Other varieties	*C.i.* 'Alba' – white flowers

Campsis tagliabuana 'Mme Gallen'

A spectacular flowering climber from China and Eastern Asia, suitable for a large conservatory or greenhouse. Its panicles of orange-red, trumpet-shaped flowers provide a brilliant splash of colour in late summer and early autumn. Orange and yellow-flowered varieties are also available. Although it is slow to establish itself, the Campsis will eventually cover an area of up to 10 × 10m (33 × 33ft) and should be trained on wires or a trellis. Unwanted shoots should be cut back after the leaves fall in autumn. Plenty of sunshine is needed if the plant is to flower well.

COMMON NAMES
Trumpet Climber or Creeper

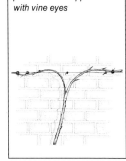

To train the growth horizontally, tie the plant to wires supported with vine eyes

Plant type	Flowering plant with climbing habit
Season of interest	Late summer to autumn
Size	To 10 × 10m (33 × 33ft)
Flower	In panicles of 6–12, Trumpet-shaped, to 7.5cm (3in) long, orange, orange-red or yellow
Leaf	Pinnate, 7–9 oval, toothed leaflets up to 7.5 cm (3in) long, light green, on twining stems
Temperature	Minimum −10°C (14°F) in winter
Aspect/Light	Well-lit situation with plenty of sunshine
Humidity	Moderate
Watering	As required
Feeding	In early summer with flowering plant liquid fertilizer
Propagation	Plant 7.5–10cm (3–4in) tip cuttings in seed and cutting compost at 16–21°C (61–70°F) in summer
Potting	For best results grow in open soil
Problems	May be slow to flower after planting
Availability	Commonly available throughout the year
Uses indoors	Climber for large conservatory or greenhouse
Other varieties	*C. tagliabuana* – orange flowers; *C. t.* 'Yellow Trumpet' – yellow flowers

Canna indica hybrids

This handsome perennial, from the tropics of South America, has large, oval, green or purple leaves, which show off to good effect the large columns of red, orange or yellow flowers. The combination of foliage and flower colour depends on the variety. The Canna is often used in the garden as a summer bedding plant. Given the protection of a conservatory, though, it can be grown for many years. Plants are normally propagated by removing short sections of the fleshy underground stems, which readily take root and send up strong leaves and flowering shoots in spring, to flower in summer.

COMMON NAME
Indian Shot

Plant type	Flowering and foliage plant with erect habit
Season of interest	All year round, especially summer and autumn
Size	100–120cm (39–48in) in height, 30–60cm (12–24in) in spread
Flower	In spikes, orange, red or yellow
Leaf	Oval to lance-shaped, 40cm (15in) or more long, 12cm (5in) wide, blue or purple
Temperature	5–77°C (41–77°F)
Aspect/Light	Full sun to light shade
Humidity	Average
Watering	Evenly moisten compost in spring and summer; reduce in autumn; water rarely in winter
Feeding	Liquid houseplant fertilizer after flowering
Propagation	Root 8cm (3in) sections of underground stem in houseplant potting compost in mid spring
Potting	Houseplant potting compost
Problems	Root-rot from over-watering
Availability	Quite commonly available as sections of underground stem in mid spring; occasionally available as plants
Uses indoors	Free-standing plant for conservatory or greenhouse

Propagate the plant from root cuttings in mid spring

Capsicum annuum

Colourful, edible fruits are the main feature of the Capsicum or Red Sweet Pepper. These are usually produced in shades of yellow, orange and red, though there are also purple varieties. The fleshy, cone-shaped or pointed fruits remain decorative for up to twelve weeks before becoming wrinkled and falling from the plant. The fruits are preceded by small white flowers in summer or autumn. The plant needs plenty of light for best results, and the compost must not be allowed to dry out otherwise both the leaves and the fruit may fall prematurely. Regular mist spraying of the leaves will also be appreciated by the plant. The Capiscum is usually grown from seed, but is not easy to propagate.

COMMON NAME
Red Sweet Pepper

Plant type	Fruiting plant with shrubby habit
Season of interest	Autumn to winter
Size	30–45cm (12–18in)
Flower	White, insignificant
Leaf	Oval, 5–10cm (2–4in), green
Temperature	13–21°C (55–65°F)
Aspect/Light	Well-lit situation with some direct sun
Humidity	Moderate
Watering	Keep compost evenly moist and do not allow to dry out
Feeding	Once every two weeks with houseplant fertilizer in spring and summer
Propagation	Sow seeds in seed and cutting compost at 21–24°C (70–75°F) in early spring; difficult
Potting	Houseplant potting compost
Problems	Leaves and fruit may drop if compost is allowed to dry out
Availability	Commonly available from autumn to early winter
Uses indoors	Indoor or as a conservatory or greenhouse plant

Spray the plant with water in summer and autumn to help pollinate the flowers

Cattleya hybrids

Orchids can make good indoor plants and the Cattleya is no exception. It is easy to care for and produces large, colourful and beautifully shaped flowers, which are often used for corsages. The plant usually flowers in the summer but can bloom at other times and may even produce flowers throughout the year, with short rests between each flowering. During these rests, which may last four to eight weeks, keep the compost a little drier and the plant cooler, at no less than 13°C (55°F). When propagating the Cattleya by division, gently tease the plant apart and cut the rhizome with a sharp knife.

COMMON NAME
Corsage Flower

Gently separate rhizomatous root when propagating

Plant type	Flowering orchid with erect habit
Season of interest	Summer, sometimes other seasons
Size	20–30cm (8–12in)
Flower	Magnificent, up to 15cm (6in) across, white, pink or purple
Leaf	Strap-like, 20–30cm (8–12in), green
Temperature	18–22°C (64–72°F)
Aspect/Light	Well-lit situation, shaded from direct sunlight
Humidity	Moderate to high
Watering	Evenly moisten compost in spring and summer, allowing to dry a little before re-watering; keep on dry side after flowering and in autumn and winter, watering just enough to prevent dehydration
Feeding	Once every four weeks with half strength flowering plant fertilizer in spring and summer
Propagation	Divide plant and plant in orchid compost at 21°C (70°F) in spring
Potting	Orchid compost
Problems	Mealy bug
Availability	Infrequently available
Uses indoors	Close to window in warm, well-lit position out of direct sunlight, possibly in kitchen

Celosia argentea

A striking plant with broad, deeply veined leaves and strange crested flower heads in shades of red and yellow. Celosias are sometimes grown outdoors as summer bedding plants, but they are also ideal as decorative pot plants for use in the house or conservatory, where they may remain in flower for several weeks. The flowering period is from mid to late summer. For best results, Celosias need a coolish, well-ventilated position with some direct sunlight, and they should be fed regularly to prolong the flowering period. When flowering has finished, the plants are usually discarded.

COMMON NAME
Cockscomb

Group odd numbers of pots together to produce a bold display

Plant type	Flowering plant with upright habit
Season of interest	Summer
Size	30–60cm (12–24in)
Flower	Crested plume, 7.5–15cm (3–6in), red and yellow
Leaf	Broad, lance-like, 10cm (4in), deeply veined
Temperature	10–16°C (50–61°F)
Aspect/light	Well-lit situation with some sunlight
Humidity	Moderate
Feeding	Every two weeks with flowering plant; fertilizer in spring and summer
Propagation	Sow seed in seed and cutting compost at 18°C (64°F) in early spring
Problems	Can look untidy towards end of flowering period
Availability	Quite commonly available throughout the year
Uses indoors	Good as part of mixed display in conservatory or greenhouse
Other varieties	C. plumosa – plume-like flower heads, coloured yellow, red, pink and orange

Cestrum hybrids

Cestrums are evergreen or semi-evergreen shrubs with attractive clusters of tubular flowers similar to those of the Jasmine.

They can grow quite tall and may be vigorous, so are best suited to the conservatory. The ideal growing position is near a wall or pillar. There are several types of Cestrum, most of which are sweetly scented. *C. nocturnum* and *C. parqui* are both night-flowering with strongly scented white flowers. *C. elegans* has red flowers and purple berries. *C. e.* 'Smith' has pinkish flowers. *C. auranticum* has orange flowers. All of these are day-flowering. Cestrums should be pruned back hard in late winter.

COMMON NAME
Hammer bush

Plant type	Flowering plant with spreading habit
Season of interest	Early summer to early autumn
Size	150cm (60in) when grown in a pot, if not double
Flower	tubular, 2.5cm (1in) long, borne in clusters, red, deep pink, orange or white
Leaf	Oval, 5–7.5 cm (2–3in), green or greyish green
Temperature	−3–16°C (26–61°F)
Aspect/Light	Well-lit situation, shaded from bright sunlight
Humidity	Moderate
Watering	Evenly moisten compost in spring and autumn; keep on the drier side in autumn and winter with just enough moisture to prevent drying
Feeding	Every two to three weeks with flowering plant fertilizer in spring and early summer
Propagation	Plant 7.5–10cm (3–4in) stem cuttings in seed and cutting compost at 18–20°C (65–68°F) in spring
Potting	Peat-based ericaceous potting compost
Problems	Whitefly
Availability	Quite commonly available all year
Uses indoors	Grow near wall or pillar in the conservatory or greenhouse

Plant the Cestrum at least 38–46cm (15–18in) away from the wall

Chrysanthemum morifolium

The 'AYR' in this plant's common name means All Year Round. However, this does not refer to any ability to remain in flower throughout the year, merely to the fact that it is always available in flower from plant stockists. The plant is tricked into flowering out of season by using blackout material to give it an artificially short day and long night. It is also treated with chemicals to retard the growth at dwarf size. The plant is therefore not an ideal subject for a permanent indoor plant, but worth using for a few weeks to provide a quick burst of colour. After this time the Chrysanthemum can be planted in the garden, where it will revert to its natural form. The habit will change dramatically, as the plant grows much taller, and the flowers will be produced in the autumn. Plants grown from cuttings will also reach normal size.

COMMON NAME
AYR Pot Chrysanthemum

Plant type	Flowering plant with erect, bushy habit
Season of interest	Available in flower throughout year
Size	20–30cm (8–12in)
Flower	Multi-petalled in ray formation 5–6.5cm (2–2½in) across, yellow, orange, pink, bronze, purple, red and white
Leaf	Multi-lobed, 7.5cm (3in) long, mid green
Temperature	15–19°C (59–66°F)
Aspect/Light	Well-lit position with exposure to sunlight, but some protection from excessive levels
Humidity	Moderate to high
Watering	Evenly moisten compost in growing period
Feeding	Once every two weeks with flowering plant fertilizer in growing period
Propagation	Plant 7.5–10cm (3–4in) tip cuttings in seed and cutting compost at 20–22°C (68–72°F)
Potting	Houseplant potting compost
Problems	Aphid, red spider mite, thrips
Availability	Commonly available throughout year
Uses indoors	Ideal for providing splash of colour in lounge, dining room, office, and most other rooms that are well lit and not too warm

Pinch out dead or fading flowers

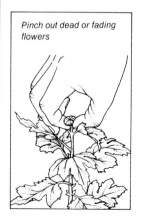

Citrofortunella mitis

Although the correct botanical name for this plant is *Citrofortunella mitis*, it is usually sold as *Citrus mitis*. An attractive, ornamental tree, it produces miniature oranges after the fragrant white flowers. The ripe oranges are edible but bitter-tasting. Although the plant prefers a moist condition, do not allow the compost to become too wet, otherwise root rot will set in, followed by rapid wilting and probably total leaf loss. Pests can also be a problem, especially the scale insect. As well as damaging the plant, it deposits sticky honeydew over the leaves and fruit, which quickly turns into an unsightly sooty mould. In the autumn and winter the plant prefers a rest. Keep the compost on the dry side and the temperature a little cooler, to a minimum of 10°C (50°F).

COMMON NAME
Calamondin Orange

Keep a close watch for scale insects

Plant type	Flowering and fruiting plant with erect, shrubby habit
Season of interest	Spring and summer, sometimes at other times
Size	60–90cm (24–36in)
Flower	1.5cm (½in) small, white, fragrant, followed by neat, round oranges, 3–4cm (1¼–1½in)
Leaf	Pointed oval, 5–7.5cm (2–3in), mid green
Temperature	15–20°C (59–68°F)
Aspect/Light	Well-lit situation with exposure to direct sunlight
Humidity	Moderate to high
Watering	Evenly moisten compost in spring and summer, allowing to dry a little between waterings; keep on drier side in autumn and winter
Feeding	Flowering plant fertilizer once every two to three weeks in spring and summer
Propagation	Plant 10–15cm (4–6in) stem cuttings in seed and cutting compost at 21°C (70°F) in mid spring to early summer
Potting	Houseplant potting compost
Problems	Mealy bug, red spider mite, scale insect, root rot if over watered
Availability	Occasionally available throughout year
Uses indoors	Feature plant for lounge, dining room or office

Clematis, large-flowered hybrids

These beautiful climbers come in a wide range of forms and colours. Clematis need a soil containing plenty of organic material, and though their heads like to be in sun, their roots should be shaded. As well as climbing up walls, trellises, and pillars, they can be used as ground cover over a low wire frame. There are several different ways of pruning Clematis, depending on variety and time of flowering. For varieties intended to flower early, the best method is to tidy and thin end shoots back to the main framework after flowering. There are many large-flowered hybrids suitable for the cool conservatory.

COMMON NAME
Clematis

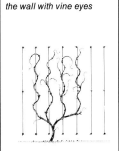

Train the plant up wires, 30cm (12in) apart, and held 5cm (2in) away from the wall with vine eyes

Plant type	Flowering plant with climbing habit
Season of interest	Mid spring to autumn
Size	To 210 × 210m (84 × 84in)
Flower	Flat, plate-shaped, 7.5–20cm (3–8in) wide, made up of 4–8 oval sepals; white, pink, red, mauve, purple, blue, single and double varieties; some varieties have coloured bar down centre of sepal
Leaf	Made up of 3–5 lance-like or oval leaflets, each up to 10cm (4in), mid-green, on twining leaf-stalks
Temperature	Minimum −5°C (23°F)
Aspect/Light	Full sun to light shade; roots must be shaded
Humidity	Moderate
Watering	Evenly moisten compost from spring to autumn, allowing to dry out a little before re-watering; keep on drier side in winter
Feeding	Every three weeks with flowering plant liquid fertilizer from mid spring to mid summer
Propagation	Plant 5cm (2in) internodal stem cuttings (2in) in sand and peat mix at 15–18°C (59–64°F) in summer
Potting	Soil-based potting compost
Problems	Clematis wilt and mildew, blackfly
Availability	Commonly available all year round
Uses indoors	Climber for cool conservatory or greenhouse

Clematis, small-flowered hybrids

All of the small-flowered Clematis grow well in the conservatory, where their flowers can be shown to good effect. Their foliage is delicate and can form a valuable shade canopy. Most varieties require pruning. Those that flower in spring should be pruned after flowering; those that flower in the autumn should be cut back hard in spring. An attractive way to display these plants is to fan-train them up the conservatory wall. Varieties include *C. flammula*, with white flowers, *C. texensis*, with red flowers, *C. viticella*, with purple-red flowers, *C. macropetala*, with blue flowers and *C. alpina*, with violet flowers.

COMMON NAME
Small-flowered Clematis

Plant type	Flowering plant with climbing habit
Season of interest	Spring, summer or autumn, depending on variety
Size	4–5m (13–16ft) in height and spread
Flower	Either monk's-capped or star-like in shape, wide range of colours
Leaf	Up to 8cm (3in) long and wide, often heavily lobed
Temperature	−10–20°C (14–68°F)
Aspect/Light	Prefers full sun but will tolerate light shade
Humidity	Average
Watering	Evenly moisten compost in spring and summer; keep on dry side in autumn and winter
Feeding	Liquid houseplant fertilizer in spring and early summer
Propagation	Root semi-ripe cuttings in grit sand at 21°C (70°F)
Potting	Soil-based potting compost
Problems	Aphid
Availability	Commonly available from spring to summer
Uses indoors	Conservatory or greenhouse plant

Train the plant in a fan-shape up a trellis

Clerodendrum thomsoniae

An extraordinarily attractive plant that provides a long period of display, almost all through the growing season. To grow at its best, the plant needs not only a relatively high level of light, but also humidity, which may make its cultivation difficult indoors. Nevertheless, with the right conditions it will grow quite vigorously and will need to be trained and kept in check. As a climbing plant the Clerodendrum will climb well up a cane frame, with additional support from wire ties. After flowering, the plant can be trimmed or pruned to improve the overall shape and appearance. An alternative method of display is to grow the plant in a large hanging basket, where it can both trail loosely over the sides and climb up the support chains.

COMMON NAMES
Bleeding Heart Vine,
Glory Bower

Plant type	Flowering plant with climbing habit that can also trail
Season of interest	Late spring to early autumn
Size	150–350cm (58–136in)
Flower	Star-shaped, red flowers appearing from 2.5cm (1in) white calyx, produced in clusters
Leaf	Oval, almost heart-shaped, 7.5–10cm (3–4in), dark green
Temperature	15–21°C (59–70°F)
Aspect/Light	Well-lit position with some shade to filter direct sunlight
Humidity	High
Watering	Evenly moisten compost in spring and summer; keep on drier side in autumn and winter
Feeding	Once every two to three weeks with flowering plant fertilizer in spring and summer
Propagation	10–15cm (4–6in) cuttings in seed and cutting compost at 21–22°C (70–72°F) from late spring to early summer
Potting	Houseplant potting compost
Problems	Red spider mite
Availability	Not commonly available, but may be seen late in spring and summer, normally as small, bushy plant
Uses indoors	Best as floor-standing feature plant near patio window or in conservatory
Other varieties	*C.t.* 'Delectum' – pink to violet flowers

The Clerodendrum can climb and trail effectively

Clianthus puniceus

This uncommon climber comes from Australia and New Zealand. Its curiously shaped curved red flowers have given it the common name of Parrot Beak or Parrot Bill. The Clianthus can be used as a houseplant, but is more suited to the conservatory. The large and colourful flowers appear in spring. There is also a white form, *C. p.* 'Albus'. The Clianthus is fairly easy to grow in spite of its exotic appearance but needs good drainage and plenty of light for the best results. It is prone to red spider mite, so leaves should be mist sprayed regularly in summer. It can be propagated either from seed or cuttings.

COMMON NAMES
Parrot's Beak, Parrot Bill

Water the Clianthus with rainwater if possible to avoid adding lime

Plant type	Flowering plant with climbing habit
Season of interest	Late spring to early summer
Size	180cm (72in) when grown in a pot, if not double
Flower	Unusual beak-like flowers, 7.5cm (2in) long, bright red or white
Leaf	Pinnate, green, 15cm (6in) long
Temperature	−2–20°C (28–68°F)
Aspect/Light	Very well-lit situation with shade only from brightest summer sun
Humidity	Moderate
Watering	Evenly moisten compost from spring to autumn; keep a little drier in winter
Feeding	Every two to three weeks with flowering plant fertilizer in spring and early summer
Propagation	Plant 7.5–10cm (3–4in) stem cuttings in seed and cutting compost at 16–18°C (61–64°F) in summer; sow seeds in seed and cutting compost at 13–16°C (55–61°F) in spring
Problems	Red spider mite
Availability	Quite commonly available throughout the year
Uses indoors	For conservatory or greenhouse on wall or trellis

Clivia miniata

A bold-looking plant with dark green, strap-like leaves produced symmetrically on either side of the flower spike. It looks particularly good when the pretty orange and yellow flowers open, creating a superb contrast. Flowering in the early part of the year, the plant provides colour at an often drab time. From autumn to early winter the Clivia prefers a rest. Keep the compost on the dry side and the plant a little cooler, to a minimum of 10°C (50°F). Avoid excessive sunlight, as this can scorch the foliage. Also, do not use too large a pot as the plant flowers better when the roots are a little restricted.

COMMON NAME
Kafir Lily

A clay pot that confines the roots helps to promote flowering

Plant type	Flowering plant with erect, open habit
Season of interest	Late winter to early spring
Size	40–45cm (16–18in)
Flower	Trumpet-like 5–7.5cm (2–3in) orange and yellow, on 40–45cm (16–18in) stalk
Leaf	Broad, strap-like, 45–60cm (18–24in) long, dark green
Temperature	15–21°C (59–70°F)
Aspect/Light	Well-lit situation with exposure to sunlight, but with some shade
Humidity	Moderate
Watering	Evenly moisten compost from late winter to summer; keep on dry side from autumn to early winter
Feeding	Once every two to three weeks with flowering plant fertilizer in spring and summer
Propagation	Tease apart offsets with at least three 25cm (10in) leaves and pot in houseplant potting compost at 18–20°C (65–68°F) in late summer
Potting	Houseplant potting compost
Problems	Mealy bug
Availability	Occasionally available from late winter to early spring
Uses indoors	Windowsill plant for most rooms, or table top plant provided very close to window

Convallaria majalis

This European native, with its strongly-scented bell-shaped white flowers, is one of the best-loved of garden plants. It is well-suited to growing in the conservatory, where it can be planted in hanging baskets or in pots and containers. For early flowering, plant 10–12 bare rooted pips (roots with a single crown bud) in a 15cm (6in) pot in autumn. Leave the pot in a cold frame in early winter, then bring it into a heated conservatory or room, where it should be kept at a temperature of 20°C (68°F). Water the plant well until flowering has finished, then reduce the frequency of watering as the leaves die back. Pot-grown Convallarias can be divided and planted out in the garden in autumn.

COMMON NAME
Lily of the Valley

Plant type	Flowering plant with erect habit
Season of interest	Late winter to spring
Size	To 20cm (8in)
Flower	5 small petals forming a bell-like flower, 15 or more to a stem, white, highly scented
Leaf	Pointed oval 15–20cm (6–8in) long and 5–7.5cm (2–3in) wide, light green with dark linear veining
Temperature	20°C (68°F) indoors for early flowering
Aspect/Light	Light shade
Humidity	Moderate
Watering	Keep compost evenly moist during growing season
Feeding	Every two weeks with flowering plant fertilizer during spring and early summer growing season
Propagation	Lift and divide clumps in autumn
Potting	Seed and cutting compost
Problems	Dislikes root disturbance
Availability	Bulbs available late winter to early spring; plants early spring to mid summer
Uses indoors	For early flowering in conservatory or indoors; plant in pots or hanging baskets

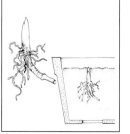

Plant root cuttings to produce early-flowering Convallaris

Convolvulus mauritanicus

This creeping relative of the Common Bindweed is one of the most attractive plants in its family, and fortunately it does not have the invasive nature of the garden weed. The long, silver-grey shoots, carrying the silver-grey foliage, provide an elegant background to the pale blue, trumpet-shaped flowers. The Convolvulus is ideal for the conservatory, where it can either be trailed from a hanging pot or basket or used to provide carpet cover in a large tub or conservatory bed. The creeping habit of growth makes this shrub a very useful subject for an associated planting with larger flowering or foliage plants.

COMMON NAME
Blue Convolvulus

Plant type	Flowering shrub with creeping habit
Season of interest	Mid spring to late summer
Size	Up to 100cm (39in) spread
Flower	Open-ended trumpet, pale blue
Leaf	Oval, 5cm (2in) long, grey to blue-grey
Temperature	−2–20°C (27–68°F)
Aspect/Light	Full sun; dislikes shade
Humidity	Moderate
Watering	Keep compost evenly moist from late spring to early autumn; keep on dry side in winter
Feeding	Liquid fertilizer in mid spring
Propagation	Sow seed at 18–20°C (64–68°F); root semi-ripe cuttings in grit sand in mid summer
Potting	Houseplant potting compost
Problems	Red spider mite, vine weevil
Availability	Quite commonly available as a bedding plant or houseplant, particularly in spring and summer
Uses indoors	Conservatory or indoor plant

Create an attractive feature by growing the Convolvulus in an old chimney pot

Crossandra infundibuliformis

A fairly compact, brightly coloured plant that can remain in flower from spring right through to the end of summer. The tubular, orange-red flowers are borne on erect flower spikes. Remove dead flowers to prolong the flowering period. The Crossandra requires a constant reasonably high temperature and will not tolerate any temperature fluctuation. For this reason, coupled with its preference for only a moderate light, it is best sited within the body of a room. As well as being suitable for use on its own, the plant grows and can be displayed well in association with many other plants.

COMMON NAME
Firecracker Plant

Remove dead and fading flowers to maintain the plant's appearance

Plant type	Flowering plant with compact, upright habit
Season of interest	Spring and summer
Size	30–60cm (12–24in)
Flower	Lobed, 2.5–3cm (1–1¼in), orange-red produced from erect spike
Leaf	Pointed oval, 5–7.5cm (2–3in), green, shiny
Temperature	18–22°C (64–72°F)
Aspect/Light	Moderate, away from high light intensities in summer
Humidity	High
Watering	Evenly moisten compost in spring and summer, allowing to dry a little before re-watering; keep on drier side in autumn and winter
Feeding	Once every two to three weeks with flowering plant fertilizer in spring and summer
Propagation	Plant 5–7.5cm (2–3in) tip cuttings in seed and cutting compost at 21–22°C (70–72°F)
Potting	Peat-based houseplant potting compost
Problems	Aphid, red spider mite, leaf loss with low temperature
Availability	Commonly available in spring and summer
Uses indoors	Useful flowering plant for table decoration in lounge or dining room; also good for kitchen or bathroom

Cyclamen persicum hybrids

Despite its popularity, the Cyclamen often presents considerable problems as far as its care is concerned. Usually the plant fails within a very short time, completely collapsing from the inside out, with all of the flowers and leaves flopping over the side of the pot. There are various reasons for this, all of which point to the fact that the plant does not like to be cosseted. It prefers a cool, light and airy position, and positively hates central heating. It also dislikes being watered from above, as the water can easily rest amongst the foliage and the top of the corm, causing a fungal rot which rapidly spreads and kills the plant. The Cyclamen should therefore be watered only from below, by adding water to the saucer the plant stands in and pouring the surplus away after a few minutes.

COMMON NAMES
Poor Man's Orchid, Alpine Violet

Water the plant from below

Plant type	Flowering plant with compact habit
Season of interest	Autumn, winter and spring
Size	15–20cm (6–8in)
Flower	Unusual, swept back, 5–7.5cm (2–3in) petals coloured white, pink, purple or red, on 15–20cm (6–8in) stalks
Leaf	Rounded heart shaped, 5–10cm (2–4in), fleshy, dark green with silvery patterning
Temperature	13–18°C (55–64°F)
Aspect/Light	Well-lit situation, lightly shaded from direct sunlight
Humidity	Moderate to high
Watering	In growing season add water to saucer pot is standing in, pouring away excess after a few minutes; never water from above; keep almost dry when foliage has died and the plant is resting
Feeding	Flowering plant fertilizer every two to three weeks in growing season
Propagation	Sow in seed and cutting compost at 18–20°C (65–68°F) in late autumn
Potting	Houseplant potting compost
Problems	Aphid, thrip, botrytis, collapse from warm dry atmosphere
Availability	Very commonly available
Uses indoors	Good windowsill plant or colourful feature plant for most rooms that are too warm

Cymbidium hybrids

The Cymbidium is a beautiful plant which, under the right environmental conditions, can provide a great deal of pleasure. Several flower colours are available, and the flowering period can last for many weeks, even a couple of months. After flowering, the flower stems should be cut back. The long, reed-like leaves give the plant interest even when it is not in flower. Also, unlike many orchids the growth does not become too untidy. To succeed with the Cymbidium it is important to be careful with watering. Excessive moisture can easily damage or kill the plant so it should be watered sparingly and allowed to get on the dry side before re-watering. The condition of the compost is best judged by probing beneath the surface with a finger.

Plant type	Flowering orchid with erect, slightly loose habit
Season of interest	Spring, summer
Size	30–45cm (12–18in)
Flower	5–6.5cm (2–2½in) white, yellow, pink or red flowers, sometimes fragrant, borne several to a stem
Leaf	Reed-like, spreading loosely outwards, 30–60cm (12–24in), green
Temperature	15–21°C (59–70°F)
Aspect/Light	Well-lit situation, slightly shaded from direct sunlight
Humidity	High
Watering	Evenly moisten compost in spring and summer, allowing to dry a little before re-watering; keep on dry side in autumn and winter, watering just enough to prevent drying out
Feeding	Once every two to three weeks with flowering plant fertilizer in spring and summer
Propagation	Divide plant after flowering and plant in orchid compost at 20–21°C (68–70°F) in spring or summer
Potting	Orchid compost
Problems	Scale insect, mealy bug, root loss when over wet
Availability	Occasionally available in spring and summer
Uses indoors	Spectacular feature plant for special postion in lounge or dining room

Provide the flower spike with a cane for support

Cytisus × racemosus

This hybrid cross between the Canary Islands and Madagascan Broom is an elegant, arching shrub, which often exceeds 120cm (48in) in height and spread. The three-fingered, grey, hairy leaves and grey-green stems provide a perfect foil for the racemes of bright yellow flowers, which are produced in late spring and also intermittently through the summer. With its Broom parentage, this plant is tolerant of hot, sunny, dry conditions, making it an ideal choice for the conservatory. It requires a fair amount of space to show off its graceful, arching habit to best effect.

COMMON NAME
Tender Broom

Plant type	Flowering shrub with arching habit
Season of interest	Spring to early summer
Size	100–200cm (36–72in) or more
Flower	Racemes, 5–10cm (2–4in) long, bright yellow
Leaf	Three-fingered, oval to round, up to 2cm (¾in) long, silky-hairy, grey-green, evergreen
Temperature	0–10°C (32–50°F)
Aspect/Light	Full sun; dislikes shade
Humidity	Average
Watering	Moisten compost sparingly in spring and summer; keep on dry side in autumn and winter
Feeding	Once every spring with liquid houseplant fertilizer
Propagation	Grown by grafting; best purchased as finished plant
Potting	Houseplant potting compost with 25 per cent grit sand added to aid drainage
Problems	Limited attacks of red spider mite, aphid
Availability	Quite commonly available from spring to summer
Uses indoors	Large conservatory or greenhouse plant

Add a surface layer of pebbles to the pot to keep the stem dry

Datura arborea

The spectacular white, trumpet-shaped flowers of the Datura make an exotic show in the conservatory, but should be handled with caution as all parts of the plant are poisonous. The flowers, which are very fragrant, appear from early summer to autumn. The Datura is a large shrub, up to 3m (10ft) tall. It should be pruned in early spring, cutting back the previous year's shoots to within 15cm (6in) of the base of the plant. A similar species, often confused with *D. arborea*, is *D. × candida*. This has even larger flowers, up to 30cm (12in) long, which are usually white, but may also be cream or pink.

COMMON NAME
Angel's Trumpet

Prune the Datura back in early spring to control the growth

Plant type	Flowering plant with erect habit
Season of Interest	Summer to autumn
Size	3m (10ft)
Flower	Trumpet-shaped, 18–20cm (7–8in) long, white, fragrant
Leaf	Oval, pointed, 22.5cm (9in), mid-green, hairy
Temperature	10–20°C (5–68°F)
Aspect/Light	Well-lit situation with shade from summer sun
Humidity	Moderate
Watering	Keep compost evenly moist from spring to autumn; keep on drier side in winter
Feeding	Every three weeks with houseplant liquid fertilizer from mid spring to mid summer
Propagation	Plant 10–15cm (4–6in) tip cuttings in seed and cutting compost at 15–18°C (59–64°F) in late spring
Potting	Soil-based potting compost with 25 per cent extra organic material such as rotted leaf mould
Problems	Red spider mite
Availability	Limited availability throughout the year
Uses indoors	Indoor, conservatory or greenhouse plant for container or border
Other varieties	*D. × candida* – white, cream or pink flowers

Eccremocarpus scaber

This evergreen climber from South America is suitable for the conservatory, where it will be protected from autumn frosts. It has a scrambling, twining habit and may be trained on wires or a trellis against a wall or pillar, or grown through another shrub. The racemes of narrow tubular flowers, usually bright orange in colour but also yellow or red, are set off well by the delicate, light-green, pinnate leaves. Flowering lasts from early summer until well into autumn. The Eccremocarpus requires little pruning, but it can be trimmed back in spring to encourage flowers and new growth in summer.

COMMON NAME
Chilean Glory Flower

Cover freshly sown seeds with a sheet of glass to aid germination

Plant type	Flowering plant with climbing habit
Season of interest	Early summer to autumn
Size	240cm (96in) when grown in a pot, if not double
Flower	Tubular, 2.5cm (1in) long, in racemes, orange, red, yellow
Leaf	Pinnate, 4cm (1½in) long, light green
Temperature	Minimum 4–10°C (40–50°F)
Aspect/Light	Well-lit situation with plenty of sunshine
Humidity	Moderate
Watering	Water well throughout growing season from late spring to mid summer
Feeding	Once very two weeks with flowering plant fertilizer during growing season
Propagation	Sow seeds in seed and cutting compost at 13–16°C (55–61°F) in late winter
Potting	Houseplant potting compost
Problems	Aphid, red spider mite
Availability	Commonly available from mid spring to early summer
Uses indoors	Climber for conservatory or greenhouse

Episcia dianthiflora

With its attractive, fringed white flowers that contrast well with the dark green foliage, the Episcia produces an effective display. The flowering period is rather short, although as the plant trails well it retains its appeal throughout the year. The Episcia prefers high humidity and a fairly well-lit situation, shielded from direct sunlight. For this reason it is a useful subject for an opaque bathroom window; a kitchen is also suitable if the conditions are right. Although it is usually grown in a hanging basket, the Episcia can also look highly effective on a pedestal if space permits. Care should be taken with watering as the plant is susceptible to root rot from excessive moisture.

COMMON NAME
Lace Flower

Plant type	Flowering plant with trailing habit
Season of interest	Summer
Size	7.5cm (3in) tall, with 30–90cm (12–36in) trails
Flower	2.5cm (1in) fringed, white
Leaf	Oval to almost round, 2–3cm ($\frac{3}{4}$–$1\frac{1}{4}$in), mid green, soft and hairy
Temperature	15–20°C (59–68°F)
Aspect/Light	Moderately to reasonably well-lit situation with some light shade
Humidity	High
Watering	Evenly moisten compost in spring and summer, allowing to dry a little before re-watering; keep on drier side in autumn and winter
Feeding	Once every two to three weeks with flowering plant fertilizer in spring and summer
Propagation	Divide roots and plant in houseplant potting compost at 21–22°C (70–72°F) in mid spring to early summer
Potting	Houseplant potting compost
Problems	Aphid, mealy bug, root rot if over-watered
Availability	Occasionally available in late spring and early summer
Uses indoors	Hanging basket plant for kitchen or bathroom; also good on a pedestal
Other varieties	*E. cupreata* – larger, more highly coloured leaves; red flowers

Remove dust by spraying the foliage with tepid water

Episcia reptans

This Episcia is not only a useful flowering plant, producing extremely pretty red flowers, but also a very attractive foliage plant, creating an effective display throughout the year. The Episcia prefers high humidity and a fairly well-lit situation, shielded from direct sunlight. For this reason it is a useful subject for an opaque bathroom window; a kitchen is also suitable if the conditions are right. A low-growing plant, it can be displayed to good effect in a bowl or pan, and is also suitable for associated planting. Care should be taken with watering as the plant is susceptible to root rot from excessive moisture. This is particularly important in the winter months when the plant is resting and at its most vulnerable.

COMMON NAME
Flame Violet

Plant type	Flowering plant with colourful foliage and low habit
Season of interest	Summer for flowers, otherwise all year round
Size	7.5–10cm (3–4in) tall
Flower	Five-petalled, 2.5cm (1in) across, red
Leaf	7.5–10cm (3–4in) long, 3–5cm ($1\frac{1}{2}$–2in) wide, brown or bronze green, with pale veining
Temperature	15–20°C (59–68°F)
Aspect/Light	Moderately to reasonably well-lit situation with some light shade
Humidity	High
Watering	Evenly moisten compost in spring and summer, allowing to dry a little before re-watering; keep on drier side in autumn and winter
Feeding	Once every two to three weeks with flowering plant fertilizer in spring and summer
Propagation	Divide roots and plant in houseplant potting compost at 21–22°C (70–72°F) in mid spring to early summer
Potting	Houseplant potting compost
Problems	Aphid, mealy bug, root rot if over-watered
Availability	Occasionally available in late spring and early summer
Uses indoors	Useful for group planting with taller plants in bowl where it can produce good cover

This Episcia is a useful subject for a low bowl or pan

Euphorbia pulcherrima

A boldly coloured plant that is a popular feature at Christmas. The large bracts, which may be red, pink, or creamy white, remain attractive for three or four months. After this time the plant should be pruned hard back, by a half to two-thirds. It can then be left to grow as a foliage plant or an attempt can be made to encourage the bracts to grow again the following winter. This involves keeping the plant in complete darkness after the hours of daylight at the end of summer. To avoid leaf loss keep the plant at a constant temperature and avoid over-watering.

COMMON NAMES
Poinsettia, Flower of the Holy Night, Christmas Plant

In mid spring cut the plant back by a half to two-thirds

Plant type	Flowering plant with upright, bushy habit
Season of interest	Winter and early spring
Size	20–100cm (8–39in)
Flower	Tiny, petal-less yellow flowers produced amidst red, pink or cream-white bracts, 10–15cm (4–6in)
Leaf	Lobed, 7.5–12.5cm (3–5in) long, mid to dark green with pinkish red stems
Temperature	16–21°C (61–70°F)
Aspect/Light	Well lit position with very slight shade from brightest sun
Humidity	Moderate
Watering	Evenly moisten compost from spring to autumn, allowing to dry out a little before re-watering; keep drier in winter
Feeding	Once every two to three weeks with flowering plant fertilizer in spring and summer
Propagation	Plant 7.5cm (3in) tip cuttings in 6cm (2½in) diam. pot of seed and cutting compost at 21–22°C (70–72°F) from mid spring to early summer
Potting	Houseplant potting compost
Problems	White fly, leaf loss if over-watered or subjected to draughts or cold
Availability	Commonly available, especially around Christmas
Uses indoors	Seasonal plant for table-centre display in lounge, dining room or office; good conservatory plant

Exacum affine

The Exacum is quite an easy plant to grow and makes an ideal subject for a windowsill; several plants massed together in a large bowl look especially effective. The pretty blue, fragrant flowers cover the plant for many weeks in the summer, as long as it is not exposed to too much sun and not over-heated. The plant requires a high level of humidity and this can be maintained by standing the pot in a tray of moist pebbles. To prolong the flowering period, pinch out or cut off faded or fading flowers. This helps prevent the plant from producing seeds, which will reduce its flowering potential. The Exacum is usually treated as an annual and discarded once flowering has finished.

COMMON NAMES
Persian Violet, Arabian Violet, German Violet

Remove faded or dead flowers to prolong flowering

Plant type	Flowering plant with compact, bushy habit
Season of interest	Summer
Size	15–30cm (6–12in)
Flower	Five-petalled, 1.5cm (½in), scented, pale blue with yellow stamens
Leaf	Pointed oval, 2.5cm (1in), glossy, green
Temperature	15–20°C (59–68°F)
Aspect/Light	Well-lit situation with some light shade
Humidity	High
Watering	Evenly moisten compost during growing period, but do not make too wet
Feeding	Once every two weeks with flowering plant fertilizer in growing period
Propagation	Sow seeds late winter to mid spring to flower early autumn of same year or sow early in autumn to flower following mid to late spring
Potting	Houseplant potting compost
Problems	Aphid
Availability	Quite often available late spring to early summer
Uses indoors	Good windowsill plant

Felicia amelloides

Pretty blue daisy-like flowers with yellow centres can be found on this dainty shrub for much of the year, though the summer is its main flowering season. These flowers will open fully only in sunshine, so this plant needs plenty of light and a sunny position. The leaves of the Felicia are green or variegated. For the best display, and to maintain a compact, bushy shape, growing tips should be pinched back regularly. When doing this be careful to avoid pinching out the stems which carry the flower buds. Keep the compost moist at all times. The Felicia needs plenty of water and sunshine to flower well.

COMMON NAME
Blue Marguerite

Plant type	Flowering plant with bushy habit
Season of interest	All year round, especially summer
Size	30–60cm (12–24in)
Flower	Daisy-like, 2.5cm (1in) across, blue with yellow centre
Leaf	Oval, 2.5cm (1in), dark green or variegated
Temperature	0–3°C (32–37°F)
Aspect/Light	Well-lit situation with exposure to sunlight
Humidity	Moderate
Watering	Keep compost moist at all times
Feeding	Every three weeks with flowering plant liquid fertilizer from late spring to late summer
Propagation	Plant 7.5–10cm (3–4in) stem cuttings in seed and cutting compost at 4–10°C (40–50°F) in spring; sow seed in seed and cutting compost at 16°C (61°F) in summer.
Potting	Houseplant potting compost
Problems	None
Availability	Commonly available as a bedding plant in spring; at other times as a houseplant
Uses indoors	Small shrub for indoors, conservatory or greenhouse

Remove the lower leaves of cuttings then root them in sharp sand

Fuchsia hybrids

The Fuchsia is an extremely popular indoor plant, available in an enormous range of varieties. There are many different colours, shapes and sizes of flowers and the habits vary from erect and bushy, through standard, to semi-trailing. Such variation means that the Fuchsia is useful in a number of different indoor locations, as well as being excellent for outer areas such as porches, conservatories, patios and glasshouses. Conditions should be kept moderate, so wherever the plant is grown inside should be freely ventilated. Flowering lasts from spring right through to autumn, after which the Fuchsia will rest until the following spring. Regular checks should be made for diseases and pests, such as whitefly and especially aphid, which can cause problems even in the winter if there is new growth to feed on.

COMMON NAME
Ladies Eardrops

Plant type	Flowering plant with standard, semi-trailing or erect, bushy habit
Season of interest	Spring to early autumn
Size	15–100cm (6–39in)
Flower	Hanging, with upward curving sepals and overlapping petals, forming corolla, 4–6.5cm (1½–2½in) across, white, pink, red or purple
Leaf	Oval, 4–6.5cm (1½–2½in), mid green
Temperature	13–20°C (55–68°F)
Aspect/Light	Well-lit situation with exposure to sun
Humidity	Moderate
Watering	Evenly moisten compost in spring and summer, allowing to dry just a little before re-watering; water only enough to prevent dehydration in autumn and winter
Feeding	Once every one to two weeks with flowering plant fertilizer in spring and summer
Propagation	Plant 7.5–10cm (3–4in) tip cuttings in seed and cutting compost at 15–20°C (60–68°F) from mid to late spring to early autumn
Potting	Houseplant potting compost
Problems	Aphid, whitefly, red spider mite, fungal rust
Availability	Commonly available from spring to summer
Uses indoors	Good for porch, or windowsill in cool room when smaller; also patio

Inspect flower buds and growing tips regularly for aphids

Gardenia jasminoides

The rich, almost heady fragrance of the Gardenia must be one of the most distinctive perfumes in the world. The plant prefers to grow in an acid compost and should ideally be watered with rain water to avoid the problems caused by the calcium in tap water. The Gardenia can also suffer from chlorosis, a yellowing of the leaves caused by an iron deficiency. This can usually be corrected by watering with a solution of sequestrated iron (iron sequestrene), which will turn the leaves back to a healthy, deep green colour. To prevent the plant becoming leggy and untidy, it should be pruned lightly in early spring. Alternatively, a more drastic prune, by up to a half or even two thirds, may encourage the plant to grow back more in balance.

COMMON NAMES
Gardenia, Cape Jasmine

Lightly trim in very early spring

Plant type	Flowering plant with bushy habit
Season of interest	Summer
Size	15–100cm (6–39in)
Flower	5–7.5cm (2–3in) double, white, with rich, heavy fragrance
Leaf	Oval, 5cm (2in) long, glossy, dark green
Temperature	18–21°C (64–70°F)
Aspect/Light	Well-lit situation with shade from direct sun
Humidity	High
Watering	Evenly moisten compost in spring and summer, allowing to dry a little before re-watering; keep on drier side in autumn and winter
Feeding	Once every two to three weeks with flowering plant fertilizer in spring and summer
Propagation	Plant 7.5–10cm (3–4in) tip cuttings in seed and cutting compost at 15–20°C (60–68°F) from mid to late spring or early autumn
Potting	Ericaceous compost
Problems	Aphid, mealy bug, scale insect, red spider mite, chlorosis
Availability	Often available in spring and summer
Uses indoors	Table-top plant close to window in lounge, dining room or other rooms that are warm and humid enough, including conservatory

Gerbera jamesonii

The Gerbera, a native of South Africa, is grown both as a cut flower and as a flowering plant for use indoor or in the conservatory. It has attractive single or double daisy-like flowers in a range of vivid colours, including pink, red, orange, yellow and white; all varieties have yellow centres to the flowers. The flower stalks can be up to 60cm (24in) long and the height of the plant makes it especially suitable for a mixed flowering display in the conservatory. The Gerbera likes a brightly-lit position with some sunshine. It should not be over-watered, and requires good drainage. This plant is a perennial, and can be propagated by division in spring as well as grown from seed.

COMMON NAME
Gerbera

Stand a few pots in an ornamental bowl to achieve a good display

Plant type	Flowering plant with upright habit
Season of interest	Spring; some imported plants at other times
Size	To 60cm (24in)
Flower	Daisy-like, 5cm (2in) across, single or double, red, pink, orange, yellow or white, with yellow centre
Leaf	Lobed, 15cm (6in), green
Temperature	10–21°C (50–70°F)
Aspect/Light	Well-lit situation with exposure to sunshine
Humidity	Moderate
Watering	Keep compost moist from spring to autumn, but do not over-water; keep on the dry side in winter
Feeding	Every two weeks with flowering plant fertilizer during the mid spring to early summer growing period
Propagation	Sow seed in seed and cutting compost at 18–21°C (65–70°F) in spring; divide established plants in spring
Potting	Houseplant potting compost
Problems	Greenfly, red spider mite
Availability	Moderate availability throughout the year
Uses indoors	Pot or tub plant for indoors, conservatory or greenhouse

Gloriosa rothschildiana

The flowers of the Gloriosa are amongst the most spectacular of all indoor plants, being bright red and yellow in colour and an unusual, lily-like shape. The long, glossy leaves bear tendrils at their tips, and the plant must be provided with a frame or trellis to climb up. All of the growth on the plant, which can be prodigious, is produced in one year's growing season. At the end of the season the plant dies back to its tuberous root, which should be kept fairly dry and cool, at 10–13°C (50–55°F). When spring arrives, the moisture and warmth can be increased to encourage the plant to break out of dormancy. The tuber does not always respond immediately so it is sometimes necessary to persevere for a while until the new growth begins.

COMMON NAME
Glory Lily

Plant type	Flowering plant with climbing habit
Season of interest	Summer
Size	100–200cm (39–78in)
Flower	Formed from six recurved petals, 7.5–10cm (3–4in) across, red and yellow
Leaf	Pointed, thin, 7.5cm (3in) long, shiny, dark green
Temperature	15–20°C (59–68°F)
Aspect/Light	Well-lit situation with exposure to sunlight
Humidity	High
Watering	Evenly moisten compost in spring and summer; keep on dry side in autumn and winter
Feeding	Once every two to three weeks with half-strength flowering plant fertilizer in spring and summer
Propagation	Separate tuber and pot in potting compost at 18–20°C (65–68°F) in very early spring; sow seeds as above in mid spring
Potting	Houseplant potting compost
Problems	Aphid, difficulty in breaking out of dormancy
Availability	Occasionally available
Uses indoors	Conservatory or close to patio window

A frame is useful for the plant to climb up

Hebe speciosa hybrids

Hebes are hardy shrubs that are usually thought of as garden plants. However, they respond well to the protected conditions provided by a conservatory. The range of flower colours, foliage sizes and plant sizes is very wide. Watering and feeding are important and neglect of either can result in failure. Larger-leaved varieties should be cut back hard every second or third year and allowed to regenerate new foliage. At the same time, the plants should be repotted to encourage the development of a larger root system. This will give the newly constituted plant the energy to produce new growth. Smaller-leaved varieties require less pruning and can often be left for years without being pruned.

COMMON NAMES
Hebe, Veronica

Plant type	Flowering shrub with upright habit
Season of interest	All year round, particularly summer and early autumn
Size	20–150cm (8–60in), depending on variety
Flower	Short or long racemes, white, blue, purple, mauve, pink or red
Leaf	Oval or lance-shaped, 0.5–4cm ($\frac{1}{4}$–1$\frac{1}{2}$in) long, grey, green, purple or variegated
Temperature	−5–10°C (23–50°F)
Aspect/Light	Moderately to reasonably bright situation but will tolerate some shade
Humidity	Moderate
Watering	Keep compost evenly moist all year round; do not allow plant to dry out
Feeding	Once every three to four weeks with liquid houseplant fertilizer from spring to early summer
Propagation	Root sem-ripe cuttings in houseplant potting compost at 18–19°C (65–66°F)
Potting	Houseplant or general potting compost
Problems	Red spider mite, vine weevil, dehydration
Availability	Commonly available from spring to summer
Uses indoors	Conservatory plant

Cut the plant back hard every second or third year

Hibiscus rosa-sinensis hybrids

The magnificent flowers of the Hibiscus may last for only a day or so individually, but if conditions are right they will be produced in steady succession throughout the spring and summer. Great care must be taken to ensure that the plant is not subjected to sudden environmental changes such as drying out, over-watering, or temperature fluctuation, as it will very rapidly shed the young flower buds. These quickly turn yellow and drop off, although if the shock is too great they may even be shed when still green. The plant may produce flowers out of season, but normally prefers a rest in winter, at a minimum temperature of 13°C (55°F), and with reduced watering.

COMMON NAMES
Rose of China, Chinese Rose, Rose Mallow, Chinese Hibiscus

In early spring a light trim can help to shape the plant

Plant type	Flowering plant with erect, bushy habit
Season of interest	Mostly spring and summer, but can flower at other times of year
Size	20–100cm (8–39in)
Flower	7.5–12.5cm (3–5in) across, red, pink, salmon, orange, yellow or white, with pronounced stamens
Leaf	Pointed oval with serrated edge, 5–7.5cm (2–3in) long, dark green
Temperature	15–21°C (59–70°F)
Aspect/Light	Well-lit situation with some sunlight
Humidity	Moderate to high
Watering	Evenly moisten compost in spring and summer, allowing to dry a little before re-watering; keep on drier side in autumn and winter
Feeding	Once every two to three weeks with flowering plant fertilizer in spring and summer
Propagation	Plant 7.5cm–10cm (3–4in) tip cuttings in seed and cutting compost at 21°C (70°F) from mid spring to late summer
Potting	Houseplant potting compost
Problems	Aphid, red spider mite, whitefly, bud drop with low temperature or dryness
Availability	Commonly available in spring and summer
Uses indoors	Windowsill – provided it is moved just away from window overnight in early spring – or table very close to window
Other varieties	*H. r-s.* 'Cooperi' – variegated foliage

Hoya bella

This Hoya is one of the best plants for a hanging pot. The flowers are attractive when viewed from above or from the side, but they are most beautiful when viewed from below, as the rose-purple centres can be seen. Apart from being a good trailing plant, it can also climb weakly, with support from a small frame or trellis. It is a delicate subject and particular care should be taken to avoid over-watering, temperature fluctuations or physical disturbance, any of which can cause the developing flowers to be shed. A clay pot is perhaps the best container as it provides more stability and allows the roots to be aerated. To keep stress to a minimum, the plant should be repotted only when it becomes absolutely necessary.

COMMON NAME
Miniature Wax Plant

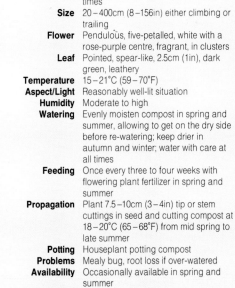

A clay pot will provide more stability

Plant type	Flowering plant with trailing, semi-climbing habit
Season of interest	Spring and summer, occasionally other times
Size	20–400cm (8–156in) either climbing or trailing
Flower	Pendulous, five-petalled, white with a rose-purple centre, fragrant, in clusters
Leaf	Pointed, spear-like, 2.5cm (1in), dark green, leathery
Temperature	15–21°C (59–70°F)
Aspect/Light	Reasonably well-lit situation
Humidity	Moderate to high
Watering	Evenly moisten compost in spring and summer, allowing to get on the dry side before re-watering; keep drier in autumn and winter; water with care at all times
Feeding	Once every three to four weeks with flowering plant fertilizer in spring and summer
Propagation	Plant 7.5–10cm (3–4in) tip or stem cuttings in seed and cutting compost at 18–20°C (65–68°F) from mid spring to late summer
Potting	Houseplant potting compost
Problems	Mealy bug, root loss if over-watered
Availability	Occasionally available in spring and summer
Uses indoors	Good hanging basket plant for most rooms, including conservatory

Hoya carnosa

An attractive, freely flowering plant that is quite easy to grow, provided it is not over-watered. It is a particularly useful climbing plant, having long stems that rapidly entwine the support. As it can climb to quite a height it is best displayed at floor level. The variety *H.c.* 'Variegata' is a little less hardy and freely flowering, but it does have quite attractive foliage. Both types are particularly prone to infestation by the mealy bug, which can be difficult to control. The pest is very good at hiding amongst the entwined stems and foliage, and as the plant is quite 'stiff', it is not easy to treat by general spraying. It is therefore best to make regular checks and spray each bug as it is found.

COMMON NAMES
Wax Plant, Wax Flower

Plant type	Flowering plant with climbing habit
Season of interest	Summer
Size	100–250cm (39–98in)
Flower	Fragrant, white to pale pink with red centre, in clusters of ten to thirty
Leaf	Pointed oval, fleshy, 7.5cm (3in) long, green, leathery
Temperature	18–21°C (64–70°F)
Aspect/Light	Well-lit situation with exposure to sunlight
Humidity	Moderate
Watering	Evenly moisten compost in spring and summer, allowing to dry a little before re-watering; keep on drier side in autumn and winter, watering just enough to prevent drying out
Feeding	Once every three to four weeks with flowering plant fertilizer in spring and summer
Propagation	Plant 10–12.5cm (4–5in) tip or stem cuttings in seed and cutting compost at 20°C (68°F) in spring
Potting	Houseplant potting compost
Problems	Mealy bug, root loss if over-watered
Availability	Occasionally available in spring and summer
Uses indoors	Floor-standing, climbing plant for lounge near patio window, conservatory or bright office
Other varieties	*H.c.* 'Variegata' – variegated foliage; more shy to flower

The plant may be displayed on a frame

Hydrangea macrophylla 'Hortensia'

An excellent feature plant that produces a magnificent flower head. The flowering period can last for about six weeks provided the plant is kept at the cooler end of the temperature range and the compost is not allowed to dry out. The Hydrangea is available in a number of varieties, with white, pink, red, blue or purple flowers. The blue-flowered form requires a high acid content in its soil, otherwise it will change to pink. Acidity can be maintained by feeding the plant with alum (aluminium sulphate), often sold as 'Hydrangea colourant'. The vigour and care requirements of the Hydrangea make it difficult to grow for successive years when confined to a pot, so after the first flowering it should be planted outside in the garden, taking care to water it well until it becomes established.

Plant type	Flowering plant with erect, shrubby habit
Season of interest	Spring to early summer
Size	30–100cm (12–39in)
Flower	Round flower head, 10–15cm (4–6in) across, of four-petalled flowers, 1.25–2.5cm (½–1in), white, pink, red or blue
Leaf	Oval, 7.5–15cm (3–6in), serrated, green
Temperature	13–18°C (55–64°F)
Aspect/Light	Well-lit position with some shade
Humidity	Moderate to high
Watering	Keep compost evenly moist from early spring as soon as growth starts; keep on dry side in autumn and winter when dormant
Feeding	Once every two weeks with flowering plant fertilizer in spring and summer
Propagation	Plant 7.5–10cm (3–4in) tip or stem cuttings in seed and cutting compost at 18–20°C (64–68°F) from late spring to mid summer
Potting	Ericaceous, low-lime compost
Problems	Aphid, red spider mite, mildew
Availability	Occasionally available in spring
Uses indoors	Good porch plant or feature plant for windowsill or near window in cool room, including conservatory

A light frame may help to support the heavy blooms

Impatiens hybrids

The Impatiens is one of the most popular indoor plants, with a flowering period that lasts several months. Many different varieties and hybrids are available, with flower colours that range from white, through pink and orange, to red; some forms are striped. Leaf colours include pale green, bronze and variegated. Once the plant has finished flowering it tends to become rather straggly and untidy so is best discarded and replaced the following year. The Impatiens attracts a number of pests, so regular checks must be made as they can quickly disfigure the plant. Trimming of the foliage or stems should be done with a sharp knife to reduce the risk of damaging the growth.

COMMON NAMES
Busy Lizzie, Patience Plant, Patient Lucy

Trim leggy growth with a sharp knife

Plant type	Flowering plant with loose, bushy habit
Season of interest	Late spring to late summer
Size	20 – 45cm (8 –18in)
Flower	Irregularly circular, 2.5 – 4cm (1 –1½in) across, white, pink, orange or red
Leaf	Pointed oval, 2.5 – 5cm (1 – 2in) pale green to bronze or variegated
Temperature	13 – 20°C (55 – 68°F)
Aspect/Light	Well-lit situation with some shade
Humidity	Moderate to high
Watering	Evenly moisten compost in spring and summer, allowing to dry just a little before re-watering; keep on drier side in autumn and winter
Feeding	Once every two to three weeks with flowering plant fertilizer in spring and summer
Propagation	Plant 7.5cm (3in) tip cuttings in seed and cutting compost, or place in water, at 18 – 20°C (65 – 68°F) from late spring to early autumn; sow seeds in this compost at 21°C (70°F)
Potting	Houseplant potting compost
Problems	Aphid, whitefly, red spider mite
Availability	Quite commonly available spring and summer
Uses indoors	Good windowsill plant for most rooms, especially kitchen or bathroom; also feature plant for fairly cool dining room

Ipomoea hederacea

Ipomoea hederacea, the Morning Glory, is one of the most striking of all the Convolvulus family. Normally grown as an annual climber outdoors, it is also suitable for displaying in the conservatory. Its twining habit of growth will enable it to scramble over wires or trellis, or through the branches of a shrub. This is an extremely fast-growing plant – grown in a conservatory bed it should reach a height and spread of 3.7 x 3.7m (12 x 12ft) within the first year. The Ipomoea needs a sunny position to do well, where its bright blue trumpet-shaped flowers will be produced freely from mid summer to autumn, opening each day with the morning sun and fading at night.

COMMON NAME
Morning Glory

Plant several Ipomoeas together to achieve a bold display

Plant type	Flowering plant with climbing habit
Season of interest	Mid summer to early autumn
Size	180 x 180cm (72 x 72in) when grown in a pot, if not double
Flower	Five-petalled, trumpet-shaped, 6cm (2½in) wide, bright blue with white eye
Leaf	Broad, heart-shaped, up to 12.5cm (5in) long
Temperature	10 – 20°C (50 – 68°F)
Aspect/Light	Full sun
Humidity	Moderate
Watering	Water well during growing period
Feeding	Every two weeks with flowering plant fertilizer during late spring to early summer
Propagation	Sow seed in seed and cutting compost at 18°C (64°F) in early spring
Potting	Houseplant or soil-based potting compost
Problems	Slugs and snails may damage leaves; young plants very susceptible to over-watering
Availability	Commonly available as a bedding plant from late spring to early summer or seed from early winter
Uses indoors	Fast-growing climber for summer colour in conservatory or greenhouse

Jasminum polyanthum

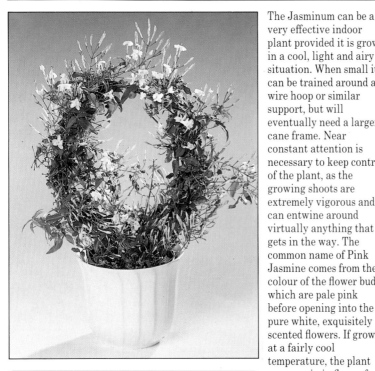

The Jasminum can be a very effective indoor plant provided it is grown in a cool, light and airy situation. When small it can be trained around a wire hoop or similar support, but will eventually need a larger cane frame. Near constant attention is necessary to keep control of the plant, as the growing shoots are extremely vigorous and can entwine around virtually anything that gets in the way. The common name of Pink Jasmine comes from the colour of the flower buds, which are pale pink before opening into the pure white, exquisitely scented flowers. If grown at a fairly cool temperature, the plant can remain in flower for many weeks, from the middle of winter to the middle of spring.

COMMON NAMES
Pink Jasmine, Indoor Jasmine, Jessamine

Plant type	Flowering plant with climbing habit
Season of interest	Mid winter to mid spring
Size	100–300cm (39–117in)
Flower	Five-petalled, 1.25cm (½in) across, white, scented, in clusters
Leaf	Five to seven leaflets produced in opposite pairs
Temperature	10–15°C (50–59°F)
Aspect/Light	Well-lit situation with some exposure to sunlight
Humidity	Moderate
Watering	Evenly moisten compost in spring and summer, allowing to dry very slightly between waterings; keep on drier side in autumn and winter
Feeding	Once every two to four weeks with flowering plant fertilizer in spring and summer
Propagation	Plant 10cm (4in) tip or stem cuttings in seed and cutting compost at 18–20°C (65–68°F) from late spring to early autumn
Potting	Houseplant potting compost
Problems	Aphid
Availability	Commonly available from mid winter to mid spring
Uses indoors	Cool bedroom windowsill when small, then as floor-standing plant for cool porch, conservatory or other cool, well-lit room

Regularly train the growing shoots to prevent them becoming tangled

Lagerstroemia indica

This attractive shrub, a native of China, may also be grown outdoors in some areas, but is not reliably hardy when exposed to temperatures below freezing. It makes an ideal subject for featuring in the conservatory, where its clusters of deep-pink or purple flowers should appear in profusion in late summer. There is also a white form, *L. i.* 'Alba'. The Crepe Myrtle grows up to 10m (30ft) when used outdoors, so plants grown in the conservatory need to be pruned back hard each winter to keep their size in check. This is a deciduous shrub and it may lose its leaves in autumn.

COMMON NAME
Crepe Myrtle

Plant type	Flowering shrub with upright habit
Season of interest	Mid to late summer
Size	To 180cm (72in) when grown in a pot, if not double
Flower	White, pink or purple, 2–3in (5–7cm) wide, in panicles
Leaf	Oval, 4–7.5cm (1½–3in) long, on short stalks
Temperature	0–3°C (32–37°F)
Aspect/Light	Well-lit situation
Humidity	Moderate
Watering	Keep compost evenly moist, allowing to dry a little before re-watering
Feeding	Every three weeks with flowering plant liquid fertilizer from late spring to mid summer
Propagation	Root 7cm (3in) stem cuttings in sand and grit at 10–12°C (50–55°F) in early summer
Potting	Soil-based potting compost
Problems	Red spider mite, overall size
Availability	Limited throughout the year
Uses indoors	Conservatory or greenhouse plant

Remove old flower heads after flowering to encourage new flowers

Lantana alba

The individual florets which make up the Lantana's round, tightly-packed flower heads change colour as they age, so that each head contains several different shades of colour. Colours include yellows, oranges, pinks, reds, bicolours and white. The flowering season lasts from spring to late autumn, so this is a very desirable shrub for any conservatory. If left unpruned it will reach a height of about 120cm (48in), but it can be restricted to 30–60cm (12–24in) by cutting back in late winter. This shrub can also be grown as a standard. Lantanas need plenty of sunlight and good drainage in order to flower well.

COMMON NAME
Lantana

The Lantana can be grown as a standard plant

Plant type	Flowering shrub with upright habit
Season of interest	Mid-spring to late autumn
Size	30–120cm (12–48in)
Flower	Circular heads of tightly-packed florets, 5cm (2in) across, varying shades of yellow, orange, pink, red or white
Leaf	Oval, pointed, 5cm (2in) long, grey-green
Temperature	10–21°C (50–70°F)
Aspect/Light	Well-lit situation with plenty of sunshine
Humidity	Moderate
Watering	Evenly moisten compost from spring to autumn, allowing to dry a little before re-watering; keep on the drier side in winter
Feeding	Once every two weeks with flowering plant fertilizer from spring to autumn
Propagation	Plant 7.5cm (3in) tip cuttings in seed and cutting compost at 16–18°C (61–64°F) in late summer
Potting	Houseplant potting compost
Problems	Red spider mite
Availability	Quite commonly available throughout the year
Uses indoors	Indoor, conservatory or greenhouse plant

Lapageria rosea

Lapageria rosea, the Chilean Bellflower, is one of the most attractive climbing plants suitable for the conservatory. The distinctive, bell-shaped flowers are produced almost all year round and last extremely well. The best-known varieties of the plant are pink or white but there are now a number of hybrids available, including doubles and bicolours, in all shades from cream and pale pink to near-red. The Lapageria is a lime-hater, so must be grown in a lime-free or ericaceous compost. It requires plenty of shade in summer and the roots should never be allowed to dry out. Propagation is possible by layering as well as from seed and stem cuttings.

COMMON NAME
Chilean Bellflower

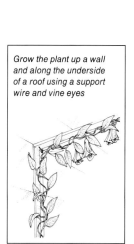

Grow the plant up a wall and along the underside of a roof using a support wire and vine eyes

Plant type	Flowering plant with climbing habit
Season of interest	All year round
Size	To 180cm (72in) if grown in a pot, if not, double
Flower	Bell-shaped, to 7.5cm (3in) long, white to deep pink, single or double
Leaf	Oval, 7.5–15cm (3–6in) long, dark green, shiny
Temperature	Minimum 0–5°C (32–41°F)
Aspect/Light	Well-lit situation, shaded from direct summer sun
Humidity	Moderate
Watering	Keep compost evenly moist, allowing to dry out a little before re-watering
Feeding	Every three weeks with houseplant liquid fertilizer from late spring to mid summer
Propagation	Plant 7.5cm (3in) stem cuttings in seed and potting compost at 15–18°C (60–65°F) in early summer; sow seed at the same temperature all year round; peg down new shoots in seed and cutting compost in early summer
Problems	Aphids, mealy bug
Availability	Quite commonly available throughout the year
Uses indoors	Climber for year-round colour in conservatory or greenhouse

Lippia citrodora

The leaves and stems of this small deciduous shrub have a lovely lemon scent when crushed, and are the source of an aromatic oil. The Lippia can be displayed in the house in a sunny spot, such as on a windowsill, but it is best suited to the conservatory, where it can be planted in a tub or container. It is a neat and attractive-looking plant, with grey-green leaves and panicles of pale-mauve flowers appearing in summer. A warm spot with plenty of sunshine will suit the Lippia best, and it should be pruned in spring, when the growth produced in the previous season can be cut back by a half.

COMMON NAME
Lemon Verbena

Plant type	Flowering plant with bushy habit
Season of interest	Spring to autumn
Size	To 90cm (36in)
Flower	Small, pale mauve, borne in terminal panicles in summer
Leaf	Lanceolate, 8–10cm (3–4in) long, grey-green, with strong lemon scent
Temperature	Minimum −2°C (28°F) in winter
Aspect/Light	Full sun
Humidity	Moderate
Watering	Evenly moisten compost in spring and summer, allowing to dry a little before re-watering; keep on dry side in autumn and winter
Feeding	Every three weeks with flowering plant liquid fertilizer from mid spring to mid summer
Propagation	Plant 7.5cm (3in) stem cuttings in seed and cutting compost at 16–18°C (51–64°F) in mid summer
Potting	Houseplant or soil-based potting compost
Problems	None
Availability	Quite commonly available throughout the year
Uses indoors	Shrub for sunny position indoors, or in conservatory or greenhouse

Cut and dry surplus branches in mid summer for potpourri

Mandevilla sanderi

A very prettily flowered plant that at first looks more like a compact shrub than a climbing plant. It can in fact grow quite vigorously and will require a framework for support, or just a bamboo cane to climb up. To get the most from the Mandevilla it must be provided with a high level of humidity. The pink, trumpet-shaped flowers are first produced when the plant is still quite small, sometimes when it is only a few centimetres (an inch or so) above the rim of the pot. The flowers are produced on the previous year's growth. As well as training the plant on to a frame, it may be worth lightly trimming or pruning the foliage at the top in spring to promote more compact side growth, which will produce flowers the following year. This plant is also known by the latin name *Dipladenia sanderi*.

Plant type	Flowering plant with climbing habit
Season of interest	Summer
Size	100–250cm (39–98in)
Flower	Five petals forming trumpet, 5–7.5cm (2–3in) across, pink
Leaf	Pointed oval, 5cm (2in), green, glossy
Temperature	16–21°C (61–70°F)
Aspect/Light	Well-lit situation with some light shade from direct sunlight
Humidity	High
Watering	Just moisten compost in spring and summer, allowing to dry a little before re-watering; water just enough to prevent drying out in autumn and winter
Feeding	Once every two to three weeks with flowering plant fertilizer in spring and summer
Propagation	Plant 7.5cm (3in) tip cuttings in seed and cutting compost at 27°C (80°F) in spring
Potting	Houseplant potting compost
Problems	Aphid, red spider mite
Availability	Occasionally available, usually as small, erect, bushy specimen
Uses indoors	Next to patio window with some shade; as floor-standing specimen in lounge; as table-top feature plant when small

A light frame will help to support the plant as it grows

Medinilla magnifica

A spectacular flowering plant that truly lives up to its name. The hanging flowerheads, which are up to 30cm (12in) long, consist of panicles of large bracts, rosy-pink in colour, with central purple and yellow anthers and forward-arching filaments. The colourful flowerheads contrast well with the broad, dark green, shiny leaves, making the Medinilla a handsome addition to the conservatory. Flowering mainly in spring, the plant may also bloom at other times of the year, depending on its cultivation. Being a tropical species, it requires a fair amount of warmth and should be sprayed with water once or twice a day throughout the year to increase the humidity level. *M. m* 'Rubra' is a variety with deeper pink flowers.

Use a wire coat hanger bent into a 'Y' shape to support the flower heads

Plant type	Flowering plant with upright habit
Season of interest	Spring
Size	80–100cm (18–39in)
Flower	In panicles, 30cm (12in) long, pink flowers with purple and yellow anthers
Leaf	Oval, up to 30cm (12in) long, dark green, evergreen
Temperature	20–24°C (68–75°F)
Aspect/Light	Moderately to reasonably bright situation; avoid strong sunlight, which will cause scorching
Humidity	High
Watering	Keep compost evenly moist in spring and summer; water less in autumn and winter
Feeding	Once every three to four weeks with liquid houseplant fertilizer from spring to summer
Propagation	Root softwood cuttings in sand in closed case at not less than 21°C (70°F)
Potting	Houseplant potting compost
Problems	Mealy bug, root mealy bug, vine weevil; lack of humidity will lead to poor health
Availability	Quite commonly availble in spring
Uses indoors	Conservatory plant

Myrtus communis

This highly attractive Mediterranean shrub makes an ideal plant for the conservatory. It is valuable for its scented leaves as well as for the flowers which appear throughout the summer, to be followed by purple berries in autumn. The variety most commonly grown indoors is *M. c. microphylla*, the Dwarf Myrtle. Myrtles can be pruned to the required shape by trimming the young shoots in spring. However, too-vigorous pruning will reduce the flowering potential. These plants require a lime-free soil and plenty of light. Pot-grown specimens can be put outside in summer if desired.

COMMON NAME
Myrtle

Myrtles can be clipped into a ball shape

Plant type	Flowering plant with shrubby habit
Season of interest	Early summer to autumn
Size	60–180cm (24–72in)
Flower	White with prominent gold stamens, scented, 2cm (¾in) across
Leaf	Oval, 5cm (2in) long, dark green or variegated, aromatic
Temperature	0–3°C (32–37°F)
Aspect/Light	Well-lit situation with protection from bright summer sun
Humidity	Low to moderate
Watering	Water regularly from spring to autumn, allowing top layer of compost to dry out between waterings; keep on the dry side in winter
Feeding	Once very two weeks with flowering plant fertilizer in spring and early summer
Propagation	Plant 7.5–10cm (3–4in) stem cuttings in seed and cutting compost at 16°C (61°F) in summer
Potting	Lime-free or ericaceous compost
Problems	None
Availability	Quite commonly available throughout the year
Uses indoors	Conservatory or greenhouse plant

Nerium oleander hybrids

An attractive, colourful plant that flowers freely throughout the summer. The large, occasionally fragrant blooms are borne in clusters above the lance-like leaves. Several varieties are available, producing pink, white or rose-red flowers. The disadvantage of the Nerium is that all parts of the plant are extremely poisonous, so it should be positioned well out of the reach of children. Provided this safety requirement can be met, it makes an ideal subject for a conservatory, porch or windowsill. In the summer, the plant will benefit from a spell outdoors. The Nerium is easy to propagate, from tip cuttings, although it is advisable to wear protective gloves when doing so or otherwise tending to the plant.

COMMON NAMES
Common Oleander, Rose Bay

Plant type	Flowering plant with erect habit
Season of interest	Summer
Size	30–150cm (12–59in)
Flower	2.5cm (1in) across, pink, occasionally white or rose-red, in clusters of six to eight
Leaf	Lance-like, 10–15cm (4–6in) long, dark green
Temperature	15–21°C (59–70°F)
Aspect/Light	Full sun
Humidity	Moderate
Watering	Evenly moisten compost in spring and summer, allowing to dry a little before re-watering; keep on drier side in autumn and winter
Feeding	Once every two to three weeks with flowering plant fertilizer in spring and summer
Propagation	Plant 7.5–15cm (3–6in) tip cuttings in seed and cutting compost, or place in water, at 20–21°C (68–70°F) in early summer
Potting	Houseplant potting compost
Problems	Scale insect, mealy bug, aphid
Availability	Occasionally available from late spring to early summer
Uses indoors	Windowsill, conservatory or porch, but well away from children

Treat the plant with great care as all parts of it are poisonous

Passiflora caerulea

Provided cultural conditions are suitable, the Passiflora will produce its unusual and beautiful flowers in near continuous succession from summer to early autumn. With luck, these may be followed by the yellow to orange fruits. This plant is tidy and compact when young, but soon produces long, straggly growth with tendrils that latch on to almost anything nearby. It must therefore be carefully and regularly trained around an adequate supporting frame. If space is limited, the growth can be cut back hard each spring to keep the plant to a more manageable size. The Passiflora is a hardy subject, requiring cool conditions. In summer it can be stood outdoors if desired.

COMMON NAME
Passion Flower

Plant type	Flowering plant with climbing habit
Season of interest	Summer to early autumn
Size	60–400cm (24–156in)
Flower	7.5cm (3in) across, formed of five white sepals and five white petals with purple blue filaments radiating from centre, and with five yellow anthers and three brown stigmas, occasionally followed by 5cm (2in) yellow to orange fruit
Leaf	Lance-like, lobed, 7.5–10cm (3–4in), dark green, in clusters of five to nine
Temperature	16–21°C (61–70°F)
Aspect/Light	Well-lit position with sunlight
Humidity	Moderate to high
Watering	Evenly moisten compost in spring and summer, allowing to dry a little before re-watering; keep on dry side in autumn and winter
Feeding	Once every two to three weeks with flowering plant fertilizer in spring and summer
Propagation	Plant 10cm (4in) tip or stem cuttings in seed and cutting compost at 18–20°C (65–68°F) in early to mid summer
Potting	Houseplant potting compost
Problems	Aphid
Availability	Occasionally available in spring and early summer
Uses indoors	Windowsill plant when small, then as floor-standing plant close to patio window or in conservatory

Provide the plant with an adequate frame for support

Pelargonium domesticum

Pelargoniums are amongst the most popular flowering indoor plants. Not only are they easy to grow, tolerating a certain amount of neglect, but they offer a long and rewarding flowering period. Preferring cool, well-lit positions, they are ideal plants for windowsills, porches and conservatories. There are a number of varieties and cultivars available. *P. domesticum* has attractively patterned flowers, produced from late spring to early autumn, and pretty, scalloped leaves. It is, however, prone to attack by whitefly. *P. hortorum*, the Zonal Pelargonium, often called the Geranium, is the most common variety. It produces vibrantly coloured flowers nearly all year round, and is relatively free from problems. *P. peltatum* is a trailing variety with ivy-shaped leaves. It is a good plant for hanging pots and planters.

COMMON NAME
Regal Pelargonium

Remove faded flowers regularly

Plant type	Flowering plant with bushy habit
Season of interest	Late spring to early autumn
Size	15–60cm (6–24in)
Flower	Five-petalled, 5cm (2in), white, pink, lilac or red, clustered on 15–20cm (6–8in) stems
Leaf	Rounded heart-shaped with slightly serrated edge, 5–7.5cm (2–3in)
Temperature	16–20°C (61–68°F)
Aspect/Light	Well-lit position with sunlight
Humidity	Moderate
Watering	Evenly moisten compost in spring and summer, allowing to dry a little before re-watering; keep on drier side in autumn and winter, with just enough to prevent drying out
Feeding	Once every two to three weeks with flowering plant fertilizer in spring and summer
Propagation	Plant 10cm (4in) tip cuttings in seed and cutting compost at 18–20°C (65–68°F) from early to late summer
Potting	Houseplant potting compost
Problems	Whitefly, botrytis on fading flowers and leaves in cool, damp conditions
Availability	Commonly available spring and summer
Uses indoors	Windowsill, porch or conservatory plant; patio plant in summer
Other varieties	*P. hortorum* – 'zoned' leaf *P. peltatum* – ivy-shaped leaf

Petunia hybrids

The Petunia is an excellent plant for the conservatory, where it is especially suitable for containers or hanging baskets. There are many different hybrids available in a wide range of forms and colours. The two main types of Petunia are Multiflora and Grandiflora. The first have many smaller flowers, the second have fewer but larger flowers. Good varieties include *P.* 'Apple Blossom', with apple-blossom pink flowers; *P.* 'Resisto', in a wide range of colours; *P.* 'Starfire', with red and white striped petals, and *P.* 'Pendula', a low-growing form with trailing stems, suitable for hanging baskets.

COMMON NAME
Petunia

For a colourful display, sink the Petunia into a larger pot and surround it with ivy

Plant type	Flowering plant with bushy habit
Season of interest	Early summer to autumn
Size	23–38cm (9–15in)
Flower	Trumpet-shaped, up to 4in (10cm) long and wide, single or double; mono- or multi-coloured, white, yellow, pink, red, purple
Leaf	Oval, 5–10cm (2–4in) long, soft and hairy, light green
Temperature	Minimum 5–10°C (40–50°F)
Aspect/Light	Full sun
Humidity	Moderate
Watering	Evenly moisten compost throughout growing period, allowing to dry out a little before re-watering
Feeding	Once every 2 weeks with flowering plant fertilizer from mid summer to autumn
Propagation	Sow seed in seed and cutting compost at 15°C (59°F) in early spring
Potting	Houseplant potting compost
Problems	Will deteriorate if not watered regularly
Availability	Commonly available as seed from early winter onwards or as tray or pot plants for mid spring
Uses indoors	In container or hanging basket indoors or in conservatory or greenhouse

Phalaenopsis hybrids

A choice flowering plant that will produce a spectacular display provided that it is well cared for. In its natural environment, the rainforest, the Phalaenopsis is an epiphytic or tree-living plant, so it prefers a very open compost. Quite often it is grown in rock wool, the material that is used in roof insulation, but this can easily become too wet, causing the roots to rot off. Ideally, the plant should be grown in either specialist orchid compost or a mixture of coarse peat and bark. The Phalaenopsis produces flowers at various times throughout the year. The flowers often grow from the same spike, so it should only be cut back to just under the previous dead flowers. Alternatively, a fresh spike may be produced.

COMMON NAME
Moth Orchid

Plant type	Flowering orchid with low but upright habit
Season of interest	Flowers at various times throughout year
Size	20–60cm (8–24in)
Flower	5–7.5cm (2–3in) across, white to pink flowers on 30–60cm (1–2ft) flower stems
Leaf	Broad, strap-like, fleshy, 15–30cm (6–12in) long, 5–7.5cm (2–3in) wide, mid green
Temperature	18–22°C (64–72°F)
Aspect/Light	Reasonably well-lit situation out of direct sunlight
Humidity	High
Watering	Evenly moisten compost throughout year, allowing to dry a little before re-watering; water with great care
Feeding	Once every three to four weeks with half strength flowering plant fertilizer in spring and summer
Propagation	Separate side shoots and plant in specialist orchid compost at 20–22°C (68–72°F) in spring or summer
Potting	Orchid compost or coarse peat/bark mixture
Problems	Fungal rotting of roots if over-watered
Availability	Occasionally available at various times of the year
Uses indoors	Feature plant for lounge, dining room or kitchen

Provide the flower spike with support if necessary

Pittosporum tobira

Pittosporums are Australian or New Zealand shrubs grown for their rosettes of shiny, dark green or variegated oval leaves; for their scented flowers in summer; and for the fruits which follow the flowers. *P. tobira* is not frost-hardy, so it is ideal for the conservatory. The tubular flowers are white or cream, borne in clusters. Their orange-blossom scent gives the plant its common-name of Mock Orange. The Pittosporum needs plenty of light to flower well, but it should be moved to a cool position for a rest in winter months. The variegated fir *P. t. variegatum* has added foliage attraction.

COMMON NAME
Mock Orange

Plant type	Flowering plant with shrubby habit
Season of interest	Flowers in summer; foliage all year round
Size	120–150cm (48–60in)
Flower	Tubular, scented, 1.25cm (½in) across, white or cream, followed by fruits
Leaf	Oval, shiny, dark green or variegated, 10cm (4in) long, borne in rosettes
Temperature	4.5–18°C (40–65°F); rest at 10°C (50°F) in winter
Aspect/Light	Well-lit situation with protection from direct summer sun
Humidity	Moderate
Watering	Water regularly in spring and summer, allowing top layer of compost to dry out between waterings; keep on dry side in autumn and winter
Feeding	Once every two weeks with flowering plant fertilizer in spring and early summer
Propagation	Plant 7.5cm (3in) tip cuttings in seed and cutting compost at 16–18°C (61–64°F) in spring
Problems	None
Availability	Limited availability throughout the year; often found in florists
Uses indoors	Ideal for a cool conservatory or greenhouse

Use the Pittosporum as a background to pot-grown bedding plants

Plumbago capensis

The sky-blue flowers of this lovely South African shrub make it a must for every conservatory. Produced in quantity in late summer and autumn, the tubular blossoms make a wonderful show at a time of year when flowering plants are becoming scarce. The flowers are produced on growth made the same year, so the old growths should be cut back by about two-thirds in early spring to encourage the plant to shoot vigorously during the growing season. The Plumbago makes a particularly attractive feature if the stems are trained up the conservatory wall in a fan-shape. As well as the blue Plumbago, there is a white form, *P. c.* 'Alba', but this is less spectacular.

COMMON NAME
Leadwort

Cut back old flowering shoots 2in (5cm) from the stem in early spring

Plant type	Flowering plant with leggy, upright habit
Season of interest	Late summer to autumn
Size	90–120cm (36–48in) when grown in a pot, if not double
Flower	Tubular with star-shaped face, 2.5cm (1in) across, clear blue or white
Leaf	Oval, mid-green, 5cm (2in) long
Temperature	7–20°C (45–68°F)
Aspect/Light	Well-lit situation with some sun
Humidity	Moderate
Watering	Keep compost evenly moist throughout growing period; keep on dry side in winter
Feeding	Once every two weeks with flowering plant fertilizer in spring and early summer
Propagation	Plant 7.5–10cm (3–4in) stem cuttings in seed and cutting compost at 21°C (70°F) in late summer; sow seed in seed and cutting compost at 21–24°C (70–75°F) in spring
Potting	Soil-based potting compost
Problems	Weak leggy habit of growth; overall size once established
Availability	Commonly available from late spring to early winter; limited availability at other times
Uses indoors	Conservatory or greenhouse plant

Primula malacoides

Although the flowering period of this Primula may last only a few short weeks, the plant provides an attractive display during the normally drab months of late winter and early spring. Unlike *P. vulgaris*, which produces its flowers on short stalks close to the plant, this species bears its flowers in clusters on long erect stems giving the plant a dainty and delicate appearance, hence its common names of Baby or Fairy Primrose. Remove dying leaves and fading flowers to maintain the plant's appearance. The Primula does not like warm dry conditions and tends to etiolate and become unsightly after a few weeks indoors. It is therefore usually treated as an annual and renewed each year.

COMMON NAMES
Baby Primrose,
Fairy Primrose

Remove yellowing leaves or fading flowers with a sharp knife

Plant type	Flowering plant with relatively compact, loose rosette
Season of interest	Late winter to early spring
Size	20–30cm (8–12in)
Flower	1.25cm (½in), white, pink or red, on 20–30cm (8–12in) stems
Leaf	Serrated, 5–7.5cm (2–3in) long, 5cm (2in) wide, light green, hairy, on slender stems
Temperature	10–15°C (50–59°F)
Aspect/Light	Well-lit situation, with some sunlight
Humidity	Moderate
Watering	Evenly moisten compost throughout year, but do not make over-wet
Feeding	Once every two to three weeks with flowering plant fertilizer in late winter to early spring
Propagation	Sow seeds at 16–20°C (61–68°F) in seed and cutting compost in mid summer
Potting	Houseplant potting compost
Problems	Whitefly, leaf browning due to dry atmosphere
Availability	Commonly available from late winter to early spring
Uses indoors	Useful for display on its own or in a mixed arrangement in cool, well-lit position in bedroom, kitchen or porch

Primula vulgaris hybrids

The cultivated Primula has the same foliage, habit and flower shape as the Primrose, but is available in a range of bright colours. The white, yellow, blue or red blooms, produced in clusters in a rosette of leaves, are a welcome harbinger of spring. Sadly though, the flowering period is quite limited. Kept in optimum conditions, in a cool but well-lit place, the plant will flower for only a few weeks. It is best to buy the plant early, before many flower buds have opened. After flowering, the Primula is best planted in the garden, where it should flower in successive years.

COMMON NAME
Primrose

Plant type	Flowering plant with low growing habit
Season of interest	Late winter to early spring
Size	7.5–10cm (3–4in) high, 10–15cm (4–6in) wide
Flower	Five-petalled, 2.5cm (1in), single, white, yellow, blue, red, pink or mauve, on 2.5–5cm (1–2in) stalks
Leaf	Broadly strap-like with slightly wavy edge and uneven surface, 7.5–15cm (3–6in), pale green
Temperature	10–15°C (50–59°F)
Aspect/Light	Well-lit situation, with some sunlight
Humidity	Moderate
Watering	Evenly moisten compost throughout year, but do not make over-wet
Feeding	Once every two to three weeks with flowering plant fertilizer in late winter and early spring
Propagation	Sow seeds at 16–20°C (61–68°F) in seed and cutting compost in mid summer
Potting	Houseplant potting compost
Problems	Aphid, red spider mite, botrytis
Availability	Commonly available from late winter to early spring
Uses indoors	Seasonal splash of colour for indoor bowl or trough; good windowsill plant for cool, light position such as bedroom, kitchen or porch
Other varieties	P. obconica – white, pink, red or mauve flowers in sprays, with irritant foliage

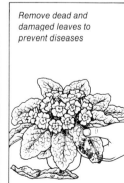

Remove dead and damaged leaves to prevent diseases

Prunus persica

Peaches and Nectarines may be grown in the conservatory with much success. They are best trained as fans against a wall, and should be planted in a border rather than pot-grown. They must be pruned hard after planting, taking the vertical central shoot down to the level of the first horizontal branches. The side branches are then tied in on wires. Regular pruning is needed in late winter, when shoots which have borne fruit must be cut back to new shoots. Flowering is in early spring when few insects are about, so flowers must be hand-pollinated to ensure a good crop of fruit in the autumn.

COMMON NAMES
Peach, Nectarine

Plant type	Flowering and fruiting tree with upright habit
Season of interest	Early spring to autumn
Size	To 4.6m (15ft)
Flower	Single, 2.5–4cm (1–1½in) across, pink; followed by round, fleshy, fuzzy or smooth skinned fruit, yellow flushed with red
Leaf	Lance-shaped, 5–10cm (2–4in), mid-green
Temperature	−5–16°C (23–61°F)
Aspect/Light	Well-lit situation with some direct sunlight
Humidity	Moderate
Watering	As required in spring and summer; drier in winter
Feeding	Every three weeks with liquid houseplant fertilizer from mid spring to midsummer
Propagation	Difficult to propagate young trees; best purchased from garden centre or nursery
Potting	Soil-based potting compost
Problems	Peach-leaf curl, red spider mite
Availability	Quite commonly available throughout the year
Uses indoors	Fruiting plant for cool conservatory or greenhouse; best fan-trained against a wall

Brush the flowers with a rabbit's tail to pollinate the plant

Punica granatum

The Punica, better known as the Pomegranate, is grown indoors or in the conservatory mainly for its beautiful bright scarlet flowers, which appear from late spring until well into the summer. The orange-yellow fruit which most people associate with the plant will sometimes be formed on a conservatory-grown specimen, but may well not ripen enough to be edible. Pomegranates require plenty of light during the growing period and pot-grown specimens can be put outside in summer. Pruning is not normally needed for this plant, but straggling or crowded branches can be cut back in early winter if desired.

COMMON NAME
Pomegranate

Stand the pot on a layer of stones to aid drainage

Plant type	Flowering and fruiting shrub
Season of interest	Late spring to autumn
Size	To 180cm (72in); dwarf form to 90cm (36in)
Flower	Single or double, bright orange-red, bell-shaped, 4cm (1½in) across; followed by hard, round, yellow to orange-red fruits
Leaf	Oval, glossy, 2.5cm (1in) long, mid-green
Temperature	13–20°C (55–65°F); rest in winter at minimum 7°C (45F)
Aspect/Light	Brightly-lit situation with plenty of sun during summer
Humidity	Moderate
Watering	Keep compost evenly moist from spring to autumn; keep on the dry side in winter
Feeding	Once every two weeks with liquid fertilizer during spring and summer growing period
Propagation	Plant 7.5 cm (3in) stem cuttings in seed and cutting compost at 16–18°C (61–64°F) in summer
Potting	Potting compost
Problems	Red spider mite, whitefly
Availability	Limited throughout the year
Uses indoors	Shrub for conservatory or greenhouse; dwarf form may be grown indoors

Rhododendron simsii

Although the correct botanical name of this plant is *Rhododendron simsii*, it is still usually sold as *Azalea indica*. If properly cared for, the plant can give many years of great pleasure. Having flowered, it may be placed outside in the garden from late spring to late summer or early autumn, provided the chance of frosts has passed. During this time it should continue to be watered and fed and at no time neglected, especially during the height of the summer, when it could easily dry out. If the plant needs repotting, then this should also be carried out during this time, preferably early on to enable the plant to establish its roots in the fresh compost before flowering. Bring the Rhododendron back indoors at the beginning of autumn. With sufficient light, moisture and warmth, it will flower again during the winter to spring period.

COMMON NAME
Indian Azalea

Watering may be carried out by immersing the pot

Plant type	Flowering plant with compact habit
Season of interest	Winter to spring
Size	15–60cm (6–24in)
Flower	Single or double, 4–5cm (1½–2in), white, pink, red or bi-coloured
Leaf	Oval, 2.5cm (1in), dark green
Temperature	10–18°C (50–64°F)
Aspect/Light	Well lit situation out of direct sunlight
Humidity	High
Watering	Evenly moisten compost throughout year
Feeding	Once every two to three weeks with flowering plant fertilizer in spring and summer
Propagation	Plant 5–7cm (2–3in) tip cuttings in seed and cutting compost or low-lime compost at 20–21°C (68–70°F) in late spring to early summer
Potting	Low-lime or ericaceous compost
Problems	Aphid, dehydration if under-watered or over-heated in dry atmosphere
Availability	Widely available mid winter to early spring
Uses indoors	Good plant for cool, well-lit room such as bedroom or cool conservatory

Rosa banksia lutea

This flowering climber is both very beautiful and a rather tender specimen which will benefit from the winter protection of a conservatory. Its double, canary-yellow flowers appear in profusion in late spring and early summer, and occasional blooms are produced right through until autumn. This rose also has attractive light-green foliage and bright green stems which give interest in winter. It is a strong-growing plant so should only be attempted in a large conservatory. Pruning is carried out after flowering, when one third of the oldest flowering growth should be cut back to just above ground level.

COMMON NAME
Yellow Banksian Rose

Plant type	Flowering plant with climbing habit
Season of interest	Late spring to autumn
Size	To 6 × 6m (20 × 20ft)
Flower	Double, 2.5cm (1in) across, canary yellow
Leaf	Five light-green leaflets, 12cm (5in) long, borne on bright green stem
Temperature	Minimum winter temperature −10°C (14°F)
Aspect/Light	Well-lit situation
Humidity	Moderate
Watering	Keep compost evenly moist from spring to autumn; keep on dry side in winter
Feeding	Pure fertilizer in mid spring
Propagation	Purchase container-grown plants
Potting	Best grown as a border plant
Problems	Black spot, mildew, greenfly, blackfly
Availability	Not widely available except from specialist nurseries
Uses indoors	Conservatory or greenhouse plant

After flowering, cut back one-third of the oldest shoots to near ground level

Rosmarinus hybrids

Rosmarinus or Rosemary is valuable both as a foliage shrub and as a culinary herb. Although it is normally grown in the garden, it is slightly tender, especially in some of its choicer varieties, and younger specimens in particular may not survive a hard winter. Grown in the cool conservatory, Rosemary will do well, and the aromatic evergreen foliage provides interest all year round. The small but attractive flowers are available in varying shades of blue as well as white and pink. They are produced mainly in late spring and early summer. Rosemary can also be trained in a fan shape against a wall or pillar.

COMMON NAME
Rosemary

Plant type	Flowering evergreen plant with shrubby habit
Season of interest	All year round
Size	To 120 × 150cm (48 × 60in)
Flower	Small, produced in clusters on leaf axils, mauve to bright blue, white, pink
Leaf	Narrow, lance-shaped, 0.5–3.5cm (¼–1¼in) long, grey to grey-green with white underside, some variegated
Temperature	Minimum −3°C (27°F)
Aspect/Light	Well-lit situation with some sunlight
Humidity	Moderate
Watering	Evenly moisten compost in spring and summer, allowing to dry out a little before re-watering; keep on dry side in autumn and winter
Feeding	In mid spring with liquid houseplant fertilizer
Propagation	Plant 7cm (3in) stem cuttings at 4–7°C (40–45°F) in trays of sharp sand from late spring to early summer
Potting	Soil-based potting compost
Problems	Becomes woody if not pruned regularly
Availability	Commonly available throughout the year
Uses indoors	Border or fan-trained shrub for conservatory or greenhouse

Root 7cm (3in) semi-ripe cuttings in sharp sand

Saintpaulia ionantha hybrids

The Saintpaulia is available in a wide range of flower colours from white through to purple. If conditions are right the plant can flower for many months, sometimes all year round, with just a short break between each flowering. Plants that refuse to flower successively should be kept a little drier for a while. Although the Saintpaulia requires high humidity, its foliage should not be misted as water droplets will mark the leaves and can also cause scorching. It is therefore best to create a humid environment for the plant, by growing it in a bowl or trough arrangement.

COMMON NAME
African Violet

Always water the plant from below

Plant type	Flowering plant with prostrate habit
Season of interest	Various times throughout year
Size	7.5–12.5cm (3–5in) high, 10–15cm (4–6in) wide
Flower	White, pink, rose, blue or purple, occasionally two-toned, single or double, 2.5cm (1in)
Leaf	Rounded heart-shaped, 4–5cm (1½–2in), mid to dark green, hairy, on 5–7.5cm (2–3in) fleshy stalks
Temperature	18–22°C (64–72°F)
Aspect/Light	Moderate light away from direct sun
Humidity	High
Watering	Evenly moisten compost throughout year, allowing to dry a little before re-watering; always water into saucer
Feeding	Once every two to four weeks with half strength flowering plant fertilizer in spring and summer
Propagation	Plant leaf cuttings in seed and cutting compost at 21–24°C (70–75°F) at any time of the year, although mid spring to early summer is best period; sow seeds as above; divide and plant as above
Potting	Houseplant potting compost
Problems	Aphid, tarsonemid mite, mealy bug, mildew, botrytis
Availability	Commonly available throughout year
Uses indoors	Good feature plant for lounge or trough, planter or bowl garden; can also do well in kitchen or bathroom

Sinningia speciosa hybrids

The summer-flowering Sinningia makes an attractive feature plant for a table-top. After flowering, the plant may become a little more leafy, although it usually fades and eventually withers and dies back to the corm. The corm should be stored dry over the winter, then started back into growth again in the spring by watering the compost and ensuring the temperature is kept within the recommended range. Take care when handling the Sinningia as the large leaves are very brittle and can easily be broken. Remove broken or bruised leaves with a sharp knife before any fungal infection develops.

COMMON NAME
Gloxinia

Damaged leaves should be cut off cleanly to prevent rotting

Plant type	Flowering plant with low habit
Season of interest	Summer
Size	10–20cm (4–8in) high, 20–30cm (8–12in) wide
Flower	Bold, bell-shaped, 4–6cm (1½–2½in) across, white, pink, red or purple
Leaf	Broadly heart-shaped, 10–20cm (4–8in) long, 7.5–15cm (3–6in) wide, mid green, hairy
Temperature	18–22°C (64–72°F)
Aspect/Light	Reasonably well-lit situation out of direct sunlight
Humidity	Moderate to high
Watering	Evenly moisten compost in spring and summer, allowing to dry a little before re-watering; always water into saucer; keep dormant tubers dry in autumn and winter
Feeding	Once every two to three weeks with flowering plant fertilizer in spring and summer
Propagation	Plant leaf cuttings in seed and cutting compost at 21°C (70°F) in mid spring to early summer; sow seeds as above
Potting	Houseplant potting compost
Problems	Aphid, thrip
Availability	Commonly available in early summer
Uses indoors	Feature plant for table-top display in lounge or dining room

Solanum capsicastrum

The Solanum has a long and varied season of interest. Tiny, star-shaped flowers are formed in the summer and last until autumn, when they are followed by green, shiny berries. These ripen to a bright orange in winter, remaining on the plant for several weeks. The berries are poisonous so the plant should be positioned well away from children. To enable the Solanum to produce berries in successive years, it must be placed outside in the summer, where the flowers can be pollinated by insects. Once the berries appear, it can be brought indoors.

COMMON NAMES
Winter Cherry, Fake Jerusalem Cherry

Plant type	Flowering and berry-forming plant with bushy habit
Season of interest	Summer, autumn and winter
Size	15–45cm (6–18in)
Flower	Five-petalled, star-like, 1cm ($\frac{1}{2}$in), white, followed by berries, green turning to bright orange, shiny, poisonous 1–2cm ($\frac{1}{2}$–$\frac{3}{4}$in)
Leaf	Pointed oval, 2.5–5cm (1–2in), mid green
Temperature	10–15°C (50–59°F)
Aspect/Light	Well-lit situation with exposure to sunlight
Humidity	Moderate to high
Watering	Evenly moisten compost throughout year; keep on drier side for about six weeks in spring when semi-dormant
Feeding	Once every two to three weeks with flowering plant fertilizer in spring and summer
Propagation	Sow seeds in seed and cutting compost at 21°C (70°F) in spring
Potting	Houseplant potting compost
Problems	Aphid, whitefly, leaf loss due to over-watering
Availability	Commonly available from late summer to early winter
Uses indoors	Good windowsill plant for most rooms, including offices; also suitable for seasonal planting in bowls, troughs and planters

Place the plant outside in summer so that insects pollinate the flowers

Solanum melongena

The Aubergine is easy to grow in the conservatory, and with its purple, edible fruit and large handsome leaves it is both useful and ornamental. The plant is a perennial but it is usually cultivated as an annual. It is suitable for growing in a tub or pot, and will reach up to 90cm (36in) in height. As the fruits form, the plant will need a stake or a wire to support their weight. The variety most often grown is *S. m. esculentum*. This has varying forms, ranging from dark purple fruit, through pale violet to striped purple and white, and pure white. The shape of the fruit may be short and round as well as long and thin.

COMMON NAMES
Aubergine, Egg Plant

Plant type	Flowering and fruiting plant with erect habit
Season of interest	Spring to autumn
Size	To 90cm (36in) when grown in a pot, if not double
Flower	Single, 4cm (1$\frac{1}{2}$in) across, purple
Leaf	Irregular oval, 10–20cm (4–8in) long, light green
Temperature	Minimum 5–10°C (40–50°F)
Aspect/Light	Well-lit situation with some direct sunlight
Humidity	Moderate
Watering	Evenly moisten compost throughout growing period, allowing to dry out a little before re-watering
Propagation	Seed grown in early to mid spring in peat-based seed and cutting compost at 18–20°C (65–68°F)
Potting	Peat-based houseplant potting compost
Problems	Whitefly
Availability	Commonly available as seed from early winter; plants from mid to late spring
Uses indoors	Container plant for conservatory or greenhouse

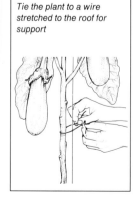

Tie the plant to a wire stretched to the roof for support

Sparmannia africana

This evergreen flowering shrub from South Africa is a very handsome plant for the conservatory. It has large, heart-shaped, pale green leaves, which are slightly hairy in texture, and clusters of white flowers on long stalks. The flowers are four-petalled, with a prominent tuft of yellow stamens in the centre. Sparmannias can be grown either in the conservatory border or in a large container such as a tub. They need plenty of light but should be protected from direct sun, which can scorch the leaves. These plants grow fast given the right conditions, and if they become too large they can be pruned back hard after the main flush of flowering is over. *S. a.* 'Nana' is a dwarf form, which is suitable as a houseplant.

COMMON NAME
African Hemp

Stand tall, bushy plants in a corner, where they will take up less space

Plant type	Flowering shrub with upright habit
Season of interest	All year round
Size	120–180cm (48–72in)
Flower	Four-petalled, 2.5–5cm (1–2in), white with prominent yellow stamens
Leaf	Heart-shaped, 22.5cm (9in) long, pale green, slightly hairy
Temperature	7–18°C (45–65°F)
Aspect/Light	Well-lit situation with protection from direct sunlight
Humidity	Moderate
Watering	Keep compost evenly moist from spring to autumn; keep on dry side in winter
Feeding	Once every two weeks with liquid fertilizer from early spring to mid summer
Propagation	Plant 10–12.5cm (4–5in) stem cuttings in seed and cutting compost at 18–21°C (65–70°F) in spring
Potting	Houseplant potting compost
Problems	Whitefly, red spider mite
Availability	Limited availability throughout the year
Uses indoors	Shrub for conservatory or greenhouse

Spathiphyllum wallisii

An elegant flowering and foliage plant that is still not enjoying the popularity it deserves. With its lance-shaped leaves on long stems that form a well-balanced habit of growth, the plant is attractive throughout the year. The unusual creamy white, sometimes fragrant flowers provide added beauty for several days in spring, summer and sometimes also in autumn. The Spathiphyllum is long-lived and the growth is easily kept under control. A very dry atmosphere may cause the leaf tips to turn brown, but these can be cut off, taking care to leave a small edge of dead tissue to help prevent further browning. For most homes, *S. wallisii* is the easiest variety to grow. The larger *S.* 'Mauna Loa' is probably best grown by specialists. It is sometimes used in interior landscaping.

COMMON NAMES
White Sails, Peace Lily

Remove dead flower spikes with sharp scissors

Plant type	Flowering plant with erect habit
Season of interest	Spring, summer and occasionally other times of the year
Size	30–40cm (12–16in)
Flower	Pointed oval, 7.5–10cm (3–4in), white spathe around knobbly, 5–7.5cm (2–3in), creamy white spadix, sometimes fragrant, on 25–30cm (10–12in) stalk
Leaf	Lance-like, 15–30cm (6–12in), dark green, on 15–30cm (6–12in) stalks
Temperature	16–21°C (61–70°F)
Aspect/Light	Moderate light away from direct sun
Humidity	Moderate to high
Watering	Evenly moisten compost throughout year, allowing to dry a little before re-watering
Feeding	Once every two to three weeks with flowering plant fertilizer in spring and summer
Propagation	Divide plant and pot in houseplant potting compost at 20–21°C (68–70°F) in mid to late spring
Potting	Houseplant potting compost
Problems	Red spider mite
Availability	Occasionally available throughout year
Uses indoors	Superb plant for feature display on furniture or floor within body of most rooms, including offices
Other varieties	*S.* 'Mauna Loa' – larger; can be more difficult to grow

Stephanotis floribunda

A pretty climbing plant with glossy leaves and star-shaped, tubular flowers, which are often used in bridal bouquets. The Stephanotis is very sensitive and if not properly cared for, will quickly shed its foliage. It is essential to maintain an even temperature for the plant and to neither under- nor over-moisten the compost. Particular care should be taken when the plant has just been purchased and is struggling to adapt to its new environment. If it gets over the initial trauma, though, the Stephanotis should thrive, and grow with increasing vigour, requiring additional support and a larger pot. When the plant is in flower, the pot should not be moved, otherwise the blooms will be shed. The Stephanotis can grow quite tall and older specimens are best displayed on the floor.

COMMON NAMES
Madagascar Jasmine, Wax Flower

Plant type	Flowering plant with climbing habit
Season of interest	Spring to summer
Size	100–250cm (39–98in)
Flower	Five-lobed, tubular, 4cm (1½in), white, wax-like, fragrant, in clusters
Leaf	Oval, 7.5–10cm (3–4in), dark green, glossy, leathery
Temperature	18–22°C (64–72°F)
Aspect/Light	Well-lit situation away from direct sunlight
Humidity	Moderate
Watering	Evenly moisten compost in spring and summer, allowing to dry a little before re-watering; keep on drier side in autumn and winter
Feeding	Once every two to three weeks with flowering plant fertilizer in spring and summer
Propagation	Plant 10cm (4in) tip cuttings in seed and cutting compost at 20–22°C (68–72°F) from mid spring to early summer
Potting	Houseplant potting compost
Problems	Mealy bug, scale insect, low temperature causing leaf loss, over-watering
Availability	Quite commonly available in spring and early summer
Uses indoors	On furniture or floor in lounge or dining room close to window with some shade from direct sun

Regularly train the plant around a support frame

Strelitzia reginae

A spectacular plant with long, paddle-shaped leaves, and orange and blue flowers that arise in a crest from a beak-shaped bud. Some patience is required, as the flowers do not appear until the plant is six or seven years old. The blooms are produced in succession for several weeks from spring to early summer. The Strelitzia needs plenty of space. The leaves can grow up to 125cm (48in) high, and if brushed against they can very easily become ragged. Badly damaged leaves should be removed at the base of the leaf stalk with a sharp knife. When the leaves become dusty or dirty, simply wipe them gently with a damp sponge. The Strelitzia is quite an easy subject to grow, and makes a superb feature plant.

COMMON NAME
Bird of Paradise Flower

Plant type	Flowering plant with erect habit
Season of interest	Spring to early summer
Size	60–125cm (24–49in)
Flower	Unusual, 10–15cm (4–6in), orange and blue, growing from 12.5–20cm (5–8in) horizontal bract
Leaf	Oval, lance-shaped, leathery mid green leaves 20–40cm (8–16in), on 30–60cm (12–24in) stems
Temperature	12–22°C (55–72°F)
Aspect/Light	Well-lit situation with some exposure to sunlight
Humidity	Moderate
Watering	Evenly moisten compost in spring and summer, allowing to dry a little before re-watering; keep on drier side in autumn and winter
Feeding	Once every two to three weeks with flowering plant fertilizer in spring and summer
Propagation	Sow seeds in seed and cutting compost at 24°C (75°F) in spring; divide plant and pot in houseplant potting compost at same temperature in mid to late spring
Potting	Houseplant potting compost
Problems	Scale insect
Availability	Rarely available
Uses indoors	Feature plant for conservatory or next to patio window

After flowering cut off the flower spike with a sharp knife

Streptocarpus hybrids

The Streptocarpus produces its attractive, trumpet-shaped flowers from spring right through until autumn. A variety of bold colours are available, and a beautiful display can be created by massing several different hybrids in a shallow bowl. Faded flowers should be removed with a sharp knife. An interesting propagation technique is to cut a leaf in half down the central vein and gently dib each half into the compost with the cut side down. When the plantlets appear they can be cut apart and potted individually.

COMMON NAMES
Cape Primrose, Cape Cowslip

The plant can be propagated from half a leaf

Plant type	Flowering plant with low-growing habit
Season of interest	Late spring to early autumn
Size	15–30cm (6–12in)
Flower	Five-lobed, tubular, 2.5–5cm (1–2in) across, white, pink, red, blue or mauve, with veined throat, on 10–30cm (4–12in) stalks
Leaf	Strap-shaped, 15–30cm (6–12in), mid to dark green
Temperature	15–22°C (59–72°F)
Aspect/Light	Reasonably well-lit situation, lightly shaded from direct sunlight
Humidity	Moderate to high
Watering	Evenly moisten compost in spring and summer, allowing to dry a little before re-watering; keep on drier side in autumn and winter
Feeding	Half strength flowering plant fertilizer every two to three weeks in spring and summer
Propagation	Sow seeds in seed and cutting compost at 21°C (70°F) in early to mid spring; dib sections of leaf into, or lay entire leaves on, same compost at 20–21°C (68–70°F) in spring
Potting	Houseplant potting compost
Problems	Mealy bug, mildew
Availability	Usually available in spring and summer
Uses indoors	Table-top plant close to window in lounge, dining room or kitchen

Styrax japonica

The common name of this small tree, Japanese Snowbell, describes well the white, hanging, scented flowers, which are produced from late spring to early summer. When grown outdoors it reaches in excess of 5m (19ft). A container-grown plant will attain about a third of this size, yet it will still flower in profusion, making it a useful shrubby specimen for use in the larger conservatory or the greenhouse. The Styrax's deciduous foliage is also attractive, particularly in autumn when it turns a bright yellow colour. Interest is further provided by the plant's unusual tiered habit of growth.

COMMON NAME
Japanese Snowbell

Tie the plant to a cane for support

Plant type	Flowering tree with upright habit
Season of interest	Late spring to early summer
Size	100–200cm (39–78in)
Flower	Small, bell-shaped, hanging in clusters along the undersides of the branches, snow-white, scented
Leaf	Oval, pale green turning yellow in autumn
Temperature	−5–20°C (23–68°F)
Aspect/Light	Moderately well-lit situation
Humidity	Average
Watering	Evenly moisten compost in spring and summer; keep on dry side in autumn and winter
Feeding	Liquid houseplant fertilizer every two to three weeks in spring and summer
Propagation	Root semi-ripe cuttings in seed and cutting compost at 18–20°C (65–68°F) in mid summer
Potting	Lime-free ericaceous potting compost
Problems	Aphid, but to no real detriment
Availability	Occasionally available all year round
Uses indoors	Feature plant for larger conservatory or greenhouse

Thunbergia alata hybrids

A climbing plant that produces orange to yellow flowers with a dark centre or 'eye', hence the common name of Black-eyed Susan. Given the correct care, the Thunbergia will remain in flower from the end of spring to the beginning of autumn. Dead or dying flowers should be removed before rotting occurs or seeds are set, as either will reduce the flowering period. The plant's twining stems grow vigorously and can completely cover a screen or trellis in the first season. It can look particularly attractive when trained to grow up strings in front of a window. Although the Thunbergia is a perennial, the growth can become very leggy and straggly, and the plant is often discarded after the first flowering.

COMMON NAME
Black-eyed Susan

Plant type	Flowering plant with climbing habit
Season of interest	Late spring to early autumn
Size	30–200cm (12–78in)
Flower	Five-lobed, 2.5–5cm (1–2in) across, yellow to orange with dark brown to black centre, growing from tubular base
Leaf	Angular, roughly heart-shaped, crinkly, 5–7.5cm (2–3in), mid green
Temperature	13–19°C (55–66°F)
Aspect/Light	Well-lit situation with exposure to sunlight
Humidity	Moderate
Watering	Evenly moisten compost at beginning of season in spring, adding more water as plant requires
Feeding	Once every two to three weeks with flowering plant fertilizer in spring and summer
Propagation	Sow seeds in seed and cutting compost at 18–19°C (64–66°F) in early spring
Potting	Houseplant potting compost
Problems	Aphid
Availability	Occasionally available from late spring to early summer
Uses indoors	Trellis, screen or strings near window in most rooms, including conservatory, provided they are not too warm

Remove dead flowers to prolong flowering

Trachelospermum jasminoides

An attractive evergreen climber from China, the Trachelospermum has clusters of fragrant white flowers in mid-summer, and grey-green oval leaves. There is also a variegated form, *T. j.* 'Variegatum', whose white-edged leaves take on pink autumn tints which last until the following spring. This plant is suitable for training against a wall or trellis, where it will need to be tied to wires or anchor points. It dislikes very dry conditions and needs plenty of light. Though sometimes slow to become established, the Trachelospermum will reach about 4.6 x 4.6m (15 x 15ft) at maturity.

COMMON NAME
Trachelospermum

Plant type	Flowering plant with climbing habit
Season of interest	Flowers in summer; foliage all year, especially variegated form
Size	To 240cm x 240cm (96 x 96in) if grown in a pot, if not double
Flower	Five-petalled, fragrant, 2.5cm (1in) across, white, in clusters
Leaf	Oval, pointed, up to 11cm (4½in) long, grey-green or variegated green and white with pink tint in winter
Temperature	Minimum −8°C (17°F) in winter
Aspect/Light	Well-lit situation with some sunlight
Humidity	Moderate
Watering	Keep compost evenly moist from spring to autumn; keep on drier side in winter but do not allow to dry out completely
Feeding	Liquid houseplant fertilizer every month in summer
Propagation	Plant 7.5–10cm (3–4in) stem cuttings in seed and cutting compost at 18–20°C (65–68°F) in summer
Potting	Soil-based potting compost
Problems	Can be slow to establish but worth the wait
Availability	Quite commonly available throughout the year
Uses indoors	Climber for conservatory or greenhouse wall or trellis

Grow the plant up a pillar or pole to show off the flowers to best effect

Verbena × hybrida

This colourful perennial may be overwintered in the conservatory, where it makes an ideal container plant. The jewel-like flowers, in shades of bright red, pink, purple and white, form dense, rounded clusters against the attractive grey-green foliage. With adequate water and food, the flowers will be freely produced from early summer to mid-autumn. Regular dead-heading will also encourage

Stand plants with a semi-weeping habit on bricks to enhance the display

repeat flowering. The prostrate varieties are good for displaying in hanging pots or baskets. Established plants can be used for the propagation of new stock for the following season.

COMMON NAME
Verbena

Plant type	Flowering plant with erect or prostrate habit
Season of interest	Early summer to autumn
Size	20–35cm (8–14in)
Flower	Saucer-shaped, in upward-facing clusters, 4–5cm (1½–2cm) across, pink, red, purple, white
Leaf	Oval, 5–8cm (2–3in) long, indented edges, hairy, light grey-green
Temperature	Minimum 5–10°C (40–50°F)
Aspect/Light	Full sun to light shade
Humidity	Moderate
Watering	Evenly moisten compost from spring to autumn, allowing to dry out a little before re-watering; keep on drier side in winter
Feeding	Once every two weeks with flowering plant fertilizer from late spring to early summer
Propagation	Plant stem cuttings in seed and cutting compost at 18–20°C (65–68°F) from late summer to early autumn; sow seed in seed and cutting compost at 13–18°C (55–65°F) in spring
Potting	Houseplant potting compost
Problems	Whitefly
Availability	Commonly available from mid spring to mid summer
Uses indoors	Conservatory or greenhouse plant for container or hanging basket

Viola cornuta

The Viola is one of the gems of the many alpines that can be grown in the conservatory. It is available in a wide range of flower colours, each with its own 'face', and has attractive pansy-like foliage. With its carpeting habit it is ideal for a small pot and can also be used as ground cover in a conservatory bed or grown in a mixed group. Varieties to look out for are *V. c.* 'Broughton Blue', with light blue flowers, *V. c.* 'Jack

The Viola is a good plant to grow in a hanging basket

Snapes', with bright yellow flowers marked red and brown, *V. c.* 'Prince John', with golden-yellow flowers, and *V. c. foliis aureiis* 'Tony Venison', with blue flowers striped white.

COMMON NAME
Viola

Plant type	Flowering plant with low-growing habit
Season of interest	Spring to early summer
Size	60–80cm (24–30in) in spread
Flower	Violet-like, in wide range of colours
Leaf	Pansy-like, 2cm (¾in) long and wide, dark green, glossy, evergreen
Temperature	−5–10°C (23–50°F)
Aspect/Light	Prefers well-lit situation but will tolerate light shade; avoid strong, direct summer sun
Humidity	Average
Watering	Evenly moisten compost in spring and summer; keep on dry side in autumn and winter
Feeding	Every three to four weeks with liquid houseplant fertilizer in spring and summer
Propagation	Sow seed in pans at 18–20°C (65–68°F) from late spring to early summer
Potting	Houseplant or general potting compost
Problems	Limited attacks of wine weevil
Availability	Commonly available in spring
Uses indoors	Conservatory plant for use individually or in associated planting

Vitis vinifera

Grape Vines have large, lobed leaves, which turn gold or red in autumn, and attractively gnarled stems, but the main attraction is the purple or green, edible fruit. Conservatory-grown vines should be planted in an outside border and trained through into the conservatory to give the roots the space they need. Young plants should be cut back to within (30cm) 12in of soil in early spring and the shoots that follow trained on wires. In the second year after planting, reduce vertical shoots to within 30cm (12in) of origin and reduce side shoots to one bud. Tie in the growths and repeat every year until the required height.

COMMON NAME
Grape Vine

Plant type	Fruiting plant with climbing habit
Season of interest	Late summer to autumn
Size	To 7m (20ft)
Flower	Greenish-yellow, insignificant, followed by round, purple or green, edible fruit in hanging bunches
Leaf	Palmate, 3 or 5 lobed, up to 15cm (6in) long, mid-green, edible when young
Temperature	Minimum 13°C (55°F) in summer and autumn when fruit is ripening
Aspect/Light	Well-lit situation with some direct sunlight
Humidity	Moderate
Watering	As required
Feeding	Houseplant fertilizer in mid spring
Propagation	Plant vine eyes (buds) with a small area of stem, or 10–15cm (4–6in) stem cuttings in winter
Potting	Well-prepared garden soil
Problems	Mildew
Availability	Commonly available throughout the year
Uses indoors	For large conservatory or greenhouse; can be trained on walls or under roof

Prune the stems back in early spring

Wisteria sinensis

The Wisteria is one of the most beautiful of all climbing shrubs, with its long racemes of mauve-blue flowers produced in profusion in spring. Added interest is provided by the finely divided leaflets, which turn yellow in autumn. The plant needs an extensive root run and is ideal for training up a wall or trellis. Though it is hardy and normally grown outdoors it will also thrive in a cool conservatory where the flower buds are protected from spring frosts. Once the desired shape has been established, cut back the growth in late summer and again in winter every year. There are a number of varieties, including *W. s.* 'Alba', with white flowers, *W. s.* 'Plena, with blue flowers, and *W. s.* 'Black Dragon', with dark purple flowers.

COMMON NAME
Chinese Wisteria

Plant type	Flowering plant with climbing habit
Season of interest	Spring
Size	To 15 × 15m (50 × 50ft)
Flower	Pea-like, in hanging racemes, 15–25cm (6–9in) long, blue, mauve or white, fragrant
Leaf	Pinnate, with 7–9 leaflets, 30–45cm (12–18in) long, light green, yellow autumn colour
Temperature	Minimum −10°C (14°F) in winter
Aspect/Light	Well-lit situation with some direct sunlight
Humidity	Moderate
Watering	As required
Feeding	In mid spring with a general liquid fertilizer
Propagation	Must be grafted for reliable result; buy bare-rooted or container-grown from nursery or garden centre
Potting	Soil-based potting compost
Availability	Commonly available throughout the year
Uses indoors	Climber for large conservatory or greenhouse

Cut back the new growth by a third in late summer, then to two buds in winter

Zantedeschia aethiopiaca

This is not a true lily, in spite of its common names. Its spectacular flowers consist of a golden spadix surrounded by a white spathe, up to 25cm (10in) long. The plant should be allowed to dry out in summer, when it is dormant. During the growing season, which commences in autumn, gradually increase watering until the plant is in full leaf, when the compost should be kept moist at all times. The flowers appear from late winter into the spring and once flowering is over watering is gradually reduced until the leaves die down. The plant can then be left in its pot in a dry place until the following autumn.

COMMON NAMES
Arum Lily, Calla Lily

When the plant is in full leaf, stand the pot in water for up to 4 hours per day

Plant type	Flowering plant with upright habit
Season of interest	Late winter to spring
Size	45–90cm (18–36in)
Flower	Yellow spadix surrounded by white spathe, 12.5–25cm (5–10in) long
Leaf	Arrow-shaped, 45cm (18in) long, deep green, glossy, on long leafstalk
Temperature	10–16°C (50–61°F) during growing season
Aspect/light	Well-lit situation with some direct sun
Humidity	High during growing season
Watering	Increase watering as leaves appear and keep moist at all times when in full growth; dry out after flowering
Feeding	Once every two weeks with flowering plant fertilizer from spring to early summer
Propagation	Divide rhizomes in autumn
Potting	Houseplant potting compost
Problems	Lack of water
Availability	Quite commonly available throughout the year
Uses indoors	Conservatory or greenhouse plant; good when grown beside an indoor ornamental pool

Zinnia elegans

A number of bedding plants are suitable for the conservatory but few are finer than the Zinnia. Its large, bold, dome-shaped flowers, which are available in many vibrant colours, make it a perfect container plant for use from mid summer to late autumn. It can be displayed individually or combined with foliage or other flowering plants in an associated planting. Many garden centres now offer Zinnias as growing plants, from mid summer onwards. They require a sunny position, and the growing tips should be pinched out to encourage branching. These plants die in winter so are discarded when flowering has finished.

COMMON NAME
Youth-and-Old-Age

Use a cane to support the flowerheads

Plant type	Flowering plant with erect habit
Season of interest	Mid summer to late autumn
Size	40–60cm (15–24in)
Flower	Bold, dome-shaped, consisting of many petals, often up to 8cm (3in) across, wide range of colours
Leaf	Oval, 8–10cm (3–4in) long, carried on tall, upright shoots, mid green
Temperature	10–20°C (50–68°F)
Aspect/light	Well-lit situation with sunlight
Humidity	Average
Watering	Keep compost evenly moist from late spring to late autumn
Feeding	Once a with liquid houseplant fertilizer in spring and summer
Propagation	Sow seed in seed and cutting compost at 15–21°C (60–70°F) in spring
Potting	Houseplant or general potting compost
Problems	Vine weevil, red spider mite
Availability	Commonly available as bedding plant in late spring; as seed from mid spring onwards
Uses indoors	Indoor or conservatory plant

Bulbs

With their erect, often tall stems, strap-shaped, glossy leaves and striking, sometimes scented flowers, bulbs make attractive features both indoors and in the conservatory. Many varieties flower in spring, others bloom in summer and autumn, and some provide much-needed winter colour. There are myriad options for displaying bulbs, and an impressive feature can be created by massing several plants in a container or conservatory bed, like the Darwin tulips shown here. Part of the attraction of growing bulbs lies in watching the dormant bulbs spring into life and push up the flower stems and leaves at an often spectacular rate.

Colchicum autumnale

These autumn-flowering bulbs have large, goblet-shaped flowers that are very similar to those of the Crocus. The long, lance-shaped leaves do not appear until flowering is finished. Colchicum flowers are mainly pink or mauve, with some white varieties. Colchicums look very effective planted in containers, and are ideal for the conservatory. After flowering has finished the plants can be moved to an inconspicuous position until the leaves have died down, lifted and divided. Varieties of interest include *C. a.* 'Album', with pure white flowers, *C. a.*'Roseum Plenum', with double rose-pink flowers and *C. a.* 'Waterlily', with double pink flowers. Wear gloves when propagating the Colchicum as the bulbs are poisonous.

COMMON NAME
Autumn Crocus

The Colchicum is best grown on a sunny windowsill

Plant type	Flowering bulb with upright habit
Season of interest	Autumn
Size	Flowers 15cm (6in) tall; leaves 51–64cm (8–10in)
Flower	Goblet-shaped, petals reflexing to star shape, to 15cm (6in) long, pink, purple or white, stalkless, single and double flowered varieties
Leaf	Lance-shaped, 20–25cm (8–10in) long, dark green
Temperature	−2–13°C (28–55°F)
Aspect/Light	Well-lit situation
Humidity	Moderate
Watering	Evenly moisten compost in autumn
Feeding	Feed with flowering plant liquid fertilizer just as flowers are dying to build up bulb for next year
Propagation	Every 3–5 years, divide clumps in mid-summer before flowering, remove bulbs and grow on for two years in pots before planting out
Potting	Bulb fibre or houseplant potting compost
Problems	Bulbs are poisonous
Availability	Commonly available from late summer to early autumn as dry bulbs
Uses indoors	Container plant for autumn colour in conservatory or greenhouse

Eucomis bicolor

A suitable plant for the conservatory, the Pineapple Lily has a thick spike of star-shaped flowers topped by a bushy tuft of leafy bracts which looks very much like the tuft on the top of a pineapple. The flowers themselves are bronze coloured with brown tip markings and are sweetly scented. This plant needs plenty of room as the flower spike grows from a rosette of leaves which can be up to 90cm (36in) in diameter; the flower spike itself is up to 30cm (12in) long. The flowers appear in late summer. After flowering the leaves die back and the plant should be allowed to dry out until growth starts again in spring.

COMMON NAME
Pineapple Lily

Group the Eucomis with plants of different heights and shapes

Plant type	Flowering bulb with erect habit
Season of interest	Late summer
Size	Height 60cm (24in); spread 90cm (36in)
Flower	Small star-shaped flowers in dense spike up to 30cm (12in) long, bronze coloured with brown tip marking, scented
Leaf	Lance-shaped, to 45cm (18in) long, dark green
Temperature	5–10°C (40–50°F)
Aspect/Light	Well-lit situation
Watering	Water regularly during growing season; allow to dry out as leaves wither in late summer
Feeding	Once every two to three weeks with flowering plant fertilizer during spring and early summer
Propagation	Divide bulbous clumps in autumn; sow seeds in seed and cutting compost at 16°C (61°F) in spring
Potting	Houseplant potting compost
Problems	None
Availability	Commonly available as dormant bulbs in early spring
Uses indoors	Container plant indoors or for conservatory or greenhouse
Other varieties	*E. comosa* – pale yellow flowers

Freesia hybrids

Sweet-smelling, colourful Freesias carry their tubular flowers on strong arching stems. Always popular as cut flowers, they will also provide a good display in the conservatory, where the bulbs can be grown in pots or wooden boxes with relative ease. The flowering period lasts from late winter to mid spring, and there are many different named cultivars in a wide range of colours from white and pale yellow, through orange, pink and red to mauve and blue. Freesias can be grown either from corms or from seed. When flowering has finished, continue to feed and water the plants well until the leaves start to die down. Then allow them to dry out and store in a well-aired place until the start of the next growing season.

COMMON NAME
Freesia

Plant type	Flowering bulb with arching habit
Season of interest	Late winter to mid-spring
Size	30–45cm (12–18in)
Flower	Tubular, 2.5–5cm (1–2in), white, yellow, orange, pink, red, mauve or blue
Leaf	Long, narrow, 22.5cm (9in), dark green
Temperature	Minimum 10–15°C (50–60°F)
Aspect/Light	Well-lit situation with sunlight
Humidity	Moderate
Watering	Keep compost evenly moist during growing period; allow to dry out once flowering is over and leaves begin to wither
Feeding	Once every two weeks with flowering plant fertilizer from appearance of flower buds until flowering is over
Propagation	Separate corm offsets in late summer; sow seeds in seed sowing compost at 15–21°C (60–70°F) in early spring
Potting	Soil-based potting compost
Problems	None
Availability	Corms widely available from late summer to autumn; seed from early to mid spring
Uses indoors	Container plant for conservatory or greenhouse

The Freesia is a good plant to grow in a wooden box filled with potting compost

Galtonia candicans

Also known as the Summer Hyacinth, and closely related to the true Hyacinth, this is a very attractive late summer-flowering bulb for the cool conservatory. The Galtonia has hanging, bell-shaped, scented white flowers on tall spikes, which are up to 90cm (36in) high. The upright flower stems grow from a rosette of strap-shaped, light-green leaves. The large, round bulbs are suitable for growing in a pot or tub. They should be planted in groups of three or five, for a good display, with the necks of the bulbs pushed just below the soil surface. After flowering has finished, the bulbs can be planted out separately, or lifted and stored dry for replanting in spring.

COMMON NAME
Summer Hyacinth

Plant type	Flowering bulb with upright habit
Season of interest	Late summer to early autumn
Size	60–90cm (24–36in)
Flower	Bell-shaped, 4cm (1½in) long, carried in groups of 12 or more along upright stems, scented, white shaded green
Leaf	Strap-shaped, 30–45cm (12–18in) long, upright, eventually spreading, light green to grey-green
Temperature	Minimum 5–10°C (40–50°F) in growing season
Aspect/Light	Full sun to light shade
Humidity	Moderate
Watering	Keep compost evenly moist while plant is in growth; keep dormant bulb dry
Feeding	Feed with liquid fertilizer as flowers fade
Propagation	Remove and replant bulblets every 5 years
Potting	Bulb fibre or houseplant potting compost
Problems	Slugs and snails can damage leaves and flowers
Availability	As dormant bulbs from late winter to early spring; as plants from mid to late summer
Uses indoors	Container plant for conservatory or greenhouse

Support the stems using green split canes and wire rings

Hippeastrum hybrids

A spectacular plant, producing boldly coloured, trumpet-shaped flowers with long, attractive stamens. The Hippeastrum is sold as a dormant bulb, either supplied loose with compost or gift-packaged in a pot. The bulb should not be completely buried but pushed about half-way into the compost. Once it has been watered and placed in full light, the plant will quickly spring into growth, often at a spectacular rate, with the flower stalk or stalks pushing ahead of the leaves. After flowering, the plant should continue to be watered, and feeding should commence in order to nourish the bulb. When the leaves begin to fade, watering and feeding can stop and the plant will die back to the bulb for the dormant period. In the winter or very early spring the plant can be started into growth again with water and increased warmth.

COMMON NAME
Amaryllis

When planting the bulb, ensure that it is not buried

Plant type	Bulb with erect habit
Season of interest	Late winter to early spring
Size	38–45cm (15–18in)
Flower	Trumpet-shaped, 10–15cm (4–6in), white, pink, orange or red, on one or sometimes two stalks, with two to four blooms per stem
Leaf	Strap-shaped, 38–45cm (15–18in), green, developing after flower stalks
Temperature	16–18°C (60–65°F)
Aspect/Light	Full sun
Humidity	Moderate
Watering	Evenly moisten compost in winter and spring; keep dormant bulb dry
Feeding	Once every two to three weeks with flowering plant fertilizer after flowering until mid summer
Propagation	Remove young bulbs from main bulb and plant singly in small pots; sow seeds at 21°C (70°F) in pans then pot singly from spring to mid summer
Potting	Houseplant compost
Problems	Relatively trouble free
Availability	Freely available as dormant bulbs from autumn to winter
Uses indoors	Any sunny window

Hyacinthus orientalis hybrids

This is an extremely popular plant with vividly coloured, tightly packed clusters of flowers that can fill a room with their distinctive scent. A variety of flower colours is available and the plant is sold in three different forms to suit individual needs. Prepared Hyacinths have been temperature-treated to encourage the bulbs to flower earlier, often in mid winter if they are planted indoors in late summer. Ordinary bulbs can be planted in a very cool place indoors to flower in late winter or early spring. Finally, the plant can be purchased actively growing from mid to late winter and very early spring. When planting bulbs, they should not be completely buried in the compost. They can also be grown in water but will rarely last for more than one season. After flowering, the bulbs can be planted outside to flower again.

COMMON NAME
Hyancinth

Heavy flower stems may need some support

Plant type	Flowering bulb with erect habit
Season of interest	Winter or spring
Size	15–20cm (6–8in)
Flower	Six-petalled, white, pink, yellow, red or blue, fragrant, in cylindrical arrangement around 15–20cm (6–8in) fleshy stalk
Leaf	Strap-like, thin, 10–20cm (4–8in) long, fleshy, green
Temperature	10–16°C (50–61°F)
Aspect/Light	Full sun when mature
Humidity	Moderate
Watering	Keep compost evenly moist in winter and spring; keep dormant bulb dry
Feeding	Not necessary
Propagation	Use new bulbs that are produced as offsets
Potting	Bulb fibre or houseplant potting compost
Problems	Not normally troubled by pests
Availability	Commonly available as dry bulbs in autumn and live plants in winter
Uses indoors	Limited life as feature plant for cool windowsill in kitchen or bedroom
Other varieties	*H. multiflorus* – multi-stemmed; white, pink or blue, fragrant flowers

Lilium hybrids

Lilies are perhaps the most spectacular of the summer-flowering bulbs, with large, scented flowers in a wide variety of colours. Many Lilium species grow well in containers and are ideal for the conservatory or as indoor plants as pots of forced bulbs can be purchased to flower at any time of year. Home-planted lilies need a good potting medium and adequate watering and feeding. Bulbs should be kept cold, dark and damp until they shoot, then moved into the light. It is best to plant out old bulbs in the garden and purchase new bulbs for pots. There are many varieties suitable for container growing.

COMMON NAME
Lily

Plant type	Flowering bulb with upright habit
Season of interest	Summer
Size	6–15m (24–60in)
Flower	Trumpet-, funnel- or turban-shaped, 10–25cm (4–10in) long, white, yellow, gold, orange, red
Leaf	Lance-shaped, 7.5–15cm (3–6in) long, glossy, mid to dark green
Temperature	Night-time temperature should remain under 10°C (50°F) during growing season
Aspect/Light	Well-lit situation out of direct sun
Humidity	Moderate
Watering	Keep compost evenly moist at all times during growing season; allow to dry out once flowering has finished and leaves start to yellow
Feeding	Houseplant liquid fertilizer as flowers are dying to build up bulbs for next season
Propagation	Remove and replant side bulblets
Potting	Houseplant potting compost
Problems	Slugs and vine weevils may damage bulbs; grow in pots for only one year
Availability	Commonly available autumn and early winter; late winter and early spring as dormant bulbs
Uses indoors	Conservatory or greenhouse plant or for cool room indoors

To propagate the Lily, remove the bubules and pot them up separately

Narcissus tazetta hybrids

A popular herald of spring, the Narcissus produces elegant, trumpet-shaped flowers on long stalks. The varieties range through all shades of yellow, white and cream, and many are scented. An attractive display can be created by massing several plants together in one pot. The Narcissus is sold either already growing or as a bulb to be planted in a pot, pan or bowl filled with bulb fibre or potting compost. The key to growing bulbs indoors is to ensure that the plants are kept cool and well lit. Too much heat will not only cause the growth to 'stretch' but also make the flowers dry up or fade very quickly. Too little light will also lead to stretched growth and possibly the collapse of the plant. Even plants that are grown in the correct conditions may need some support. After flowering, the Narcissus should be planted outside in the garden.

Plant type	Flowering bulb with erect habit
Season of interest	Winter or very early spring
Size	30–45cm (12–18in)
Flower	Six-petalled, trumpet-shaped, yellow, white, or cream, on 30–45cm (12–18in) stalk
Leaf	Strap-like, fleshy, 30–45cm (12–18in), green
Temperature	10–13°C (50–55°F)
Aspect/Light	Full sun
Humidity	Moderate
Watering	Evenly moisten compost during growing season
Feeding	Not necessary
Propagation	Separate bulb offsets from mid to late summer
Potting	Bulb fibre or houseplant potting compost
Problems	Bulb rot
Availability	Commonly available from mid winter to early spring
Uses indoors	Short-term feature plant to provide early colour in cool, well-lit room, such as bedroom

Use a simple framework to provide support

Nerine bowdenii

The bright pink flowers of this handsome South African bulb provide a welcome splash of colour in the conservatory. The flower heads have an elegant and highly distinctive shape, being composed of clusters of trumpet-shaped flowers and tall, straight stems. A good cultivar to grow is *N. b.* 'Pink Trumpet', a late-flowering variety that has silver-pink flowers with a more open shape. Nerines can be grown as pot plants in a sunny position indoors but they are best used as container plants in the conservatory. If possible, they should not be moved after flowering as any disturbance to their roots is likely to prevent them from producing any flowers the following season.

COMMON NAME
Nerine

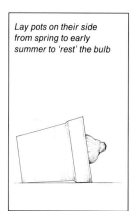

Lay pots on their side from spring to early summer to 'rest' the bulb

Plant type	Flowering bulb with erect habit
Season of interest	Late summer to autumn
Size	45–60cm (18–24in)
Flower	Narrow-petalled trumpets, 10–12.5cm (4–5in) wide, borne in clusters with or after foliage
Leaf	Strap-shaped, 45–53cm (18–21in) long, mid to dark-green
Temperature	0–3°C (32–37°)
Aspect/Light	Full sun
Humidity	Moderate
Watering	Keep compost evenly moist from spring to autumn; keep drier after flowering until new growth appears
Feeding	Once every two to three weeks with flowering plant liquid fertilizer once new leaves appear and continue until mid winter
Propagation	Plant dormant bulbs in mid to late summer; divide existing clumps in mid summer prior to flowering
Potting	Soil-based compost with 25 per cent extra grit or sharp sand
Problems	Root disturbance can prevent flowering the following year
Availability	Quite commonly available as dormant bulbs from late summer to early autumn or as pot plants in leaf in early spring
Uses indoors	Indoors in pots; in large containers in conservatory or greenhouse

Tulipa hybrids

Many tulips make excellent pot plants for the conservatory or indoors, where they can flower from as early as Christmas through to mid-late spring. A cool conservatory is ideal. Most tulips are suitable for container planting, from the early-flowering hybrids and species tulips to the taller Darwin and Lily-flowered varieties. They can be grown in bulb fibre and houseplant potting compost, or, if they are to be planted out after flowering, in seed and cutting compost. In this case they will need to be fed with flowering plant fertilizer from the time the flower buds appear to feed the bulbs for the next season.

COMMON NAME
Tulip

Pot bulbs in a bowl containing compost over a layer of bulb fibre

Plant type	Flowering bulb with erect habit
Season of interest	Winter to late spring
Size	12.5–75cm (5–30in)
Flower	6-pointed, oval or fringed petals, 4–8cm (1½–3in) wide and deep, white, cream, yellow, orange, pink, red, mauve, often variegated
Leaf	Lance-shaped, 15–23cm (6–9in) long, tapering, olive-green
Temperature	4–7°C (40–45°F)
Aspect/Light	Full sun to light shade
Humidity	Moderate
Watering	Evenly moisten compost throughout growing period, allowing to dry out a little before re-watering
Feeding	Once every two weeks after flower buds appear
Propagation	Plant dry bulbs from September to October
Potting	Bulb fibre and houseplant potting compost
Problems	None
Availability	Commonly available as dormant bulbs from late summer to early winter and in pots from mid winter to mid spring
Uses indoors	Container plant for indoors, conservatory or greenhouse

Vallota speciosa hybrids

An excellent plant for creating a colourful display on a sunny windowsill. The red, pink or white blooms are produced late in the summer, when the light intensity is high. This means that the Vallota normally produces well-balanced growth, and will only become top heavy or etiolated if the light is not strong enough. If the growth does start to 'stretch' or bend, the plant should be provided with a cane support to stop it collapsing. Vallota is an easy plant to grow, provided it is not over-watered, as this can cause the bulb to rot. After flowering, the plant produces bulbs as offsets and in the spring or early summer these can be removed and potted singly.
COMMON NAME
Scarborough Lily

Plant type	Flowering bulb with erect habit
Season of interest	Late summer
Size	45–60cm (18–24in)
Flower	Six-petalled, trumpet-shaped, 7.5–10cm (3–4in) across, white, pink or red, on 45–60cm (18–24in) stalks
Leaf	Strap-shaped, 30–45cm (12–18in), green
Temperature	13–20°C (55–68°F)
Aspect/Light	Full sun
Humidity	Moderate
Watering	Evenly moisten compost in spring and summer; keep on dry side during autumn and winter dormancy
Feeding	Once every two to three weeks with flowering plant fertilizer in spring and summer
Propagation	Remove bulbs produced as offsets in spring or early summer and pot singly in houseplant potting compost, first in 9cm (3½in) pots to become established, then in 13–18cm (5–7in) pots to mature and flower
Potting	Houseplant potting compost
Problems	Bulb rot; can become top heavy
Availability	Occasionally available from early to mid summer
Uses indoors	Windowsill plant or for display on furniture near window in lounge, dining room or kitchen

Support the flower stem with a cane if necessary

Veltheimia viridifolia hybrids

Although it is only rarely available the Veltheimia is well worth searching for. It produces a rosette of large, shiny green leaves and an unusual flower spike bearing many prettily coloured flowers. Flowering in the winter, the plant makes an attractive feature at a time of year when many other plants are dormant. The Veltheimia prefers to be grown in a situation that is both cool and well lit. This can make positioning in the home difficult as a lounge or dining room window would probably be too warm. One suitable location is a cool, sunny bedroom window, provided there is enough room for the plant. Like other bulbous plants, the Veltheimia produces bulbs as offsets, which can be removed and used for propagation.

Plant type	Flowering bulb with erect habit
Season of interest	Winter
Size	45–60cm (18–24in)
Flower	Tube-like, 2–2.5cm (¾–1in), pink and yellow or pink-mauve, clustered on 45–60cm (18–24in) stalk
Leaf	Strap-shaped, 30–45cm (12–18in), 7.5cm (3in) across
Temperature	10–16°C (50–61°F)
Aspect/Light	Full sun
Humidity	Moderate
Watering	Evenly moisten compost from summer to spring; keep on dry side during dormancy
Feeding	Once every four weeks with half strength flowering plant fertilizer as soon as the foliage is well formed until the plant begins to fade
Propagation	Separate bulb offsets in late summer or early autumn and pot singly in houseplant potting compost, first in 9cm (3½in) pots to become established, then in 13–18cm (5–7in) pots to mature and flower
Potting	Houseplant potting compost
Problems	Can become leggy if too warm
Availability	Rarely available in autumn and winter
Uses indoors	Windowsill or cool position close to window

Remove and pot small offsets in late summer or early autumn

Cacti and Succulents

Unlike other indoor plants, cacti and succulents are ideally suited to the dry, centrally-heated rooms of many homes, which resemble the conditions found in their natural habitat, the desert. These plants have a wide range of striking forms, and many bear attractive spines or hairs. When they flower, several varieties provide spectacular displays of colour, like the Trichodiadema shown here.

Agave americana 'Marginata'

An extremely tough and resilient plant with a pleasing, symmetrical habit of growth. Great care should be taken with the Agave as the barbed edges of the leaves and needle-sharp tips can be very dangerous. Ensure that it is placed well away from where people could brush against the leaves, and wear gardening gloves (and even goggles!) when tending to the plant. For potting and other activities it is advisable to wrap the Agave with newspaper for safety. The common name of Century Plant refers to the age at which it was once thought to flower. Although this is not true, the plant does not put forth its greenish yellow flowers for a long time. After flowering, the Agave will die, but not before it has produced several offsets, which can be removed and propagated.

COMMON NAME
Century Plant

Plant type	Succulent with erect rosette
Season of interest	All year round
Size	30–100cm (12–39in) (can grow larger)
Flower	Greenish-yellow on flower spike, rarely produced, in summer; plant dies after flowering
Leaf	15–45cm (6–18in) long, 5–7.5cm (2–3in) wide (will grow larger if space is available), fiercely serrated and pointed, fleshy, green and gold
Temperature	10–20°C (50–68°F)
Aspect/Light	Full light
Humidity	Tolerates warm, dry atmosphere
Watering	Moisten compost infrequently throughout year, keeping on dry side, particularly in autumn and winter
Feeding	Once every month with houseplant fertilizer in spring and summer
Propagation	Remove offsets when 10cm (4in) with greatest care (wear goggles and gloves)
Potting	Cactus and succulent compost
Problems	Very dangerous to children and others due to sharp leaves, pests generally tend to leave the plant alone
Availability	Occasionally available
Uses indoors	In full light but never at eye level and well away from people
Other varieties	A. 'Medio-picta' – yellow stripe down centre

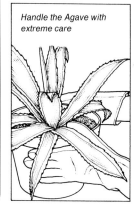

Handle the Agave with extreme care

Aloe variegata

A highly distinctive succulent with a rosette of very thick, triangular leaves coloured dark green with whitish bands and edges. In spring the plant produces a long flower spike bearing a number of tubular flowers. The Aloe can tolerate a wide range of conditions and a certain amount of neglect. It is at its most attractive when young and compact. After a while the stem tends to become rather untidy and the plant can become top-heavy, losing its original elegant, symmetrical shape as it leans to one side. Although a clay pot will help to provide stability, the appearance of the plant may eventually become so lopsided as to warrant being replaced with a younger specimen. New plants can be propagated fairly easily from offsets that grow in the soil.

COMMON NAME
Partridge-breasted Aloe

Plant type	Flowering succulent with erect habit
Season of interest	Spring to early summer
Size	15–80cm (6–32in)
Flower	Tubular, 2.5cm (1in), pink, on 10–20cm (4–8in) stem, produced from early spring to summer
Leaf	Pointed, 7.5–12.5cm (3–5in) long, 2.5–4cm (1–1½in) wide, thick, fleshy, dark green with whitish bands and edges, borne in rosette on stem
Temperature	10–28°C (50–82°F)
Aspect/Light	Well-lit situation with some sunlight
Humidity	Low
Watering	Evenly moisten compost in spring and summer, allowing to dry a little before re-watering; water just enough to prevent dehydration in autumn and winter
Feeding	Once every three to four weeks with flowering plant fertilizer in spring and summer
Propagation	Remove offsets and plant in cactus and succulent compost at 18–20°C (65–68°F) in late spring to early summer
Potting	Cactus and succulent compost
Problems	Mealy bug, root mealy bug, rot from too much water
Availability	Commonly available throughout year
Uses indoors	Windowsill or conservatory
Other varieties	A. aristata – more compact rosette; orange flowers

Remove damaged or withered leaves with a sharp knife

Aporocactus flagelliformis

The extraordinary Aporocactus can produce trailing stems up to two metres (six feet six inches) long in ideal conditions. It makes an excellent subject for a hanging pot or basket in a very sunny situation. Great care needs to be taken with positioning, as the fine, prickly spines can cause injuries and are very difficult to remove from the skin. When hanging the plant, ensure that it is anchored well in the pot or basket as any unbalanced growth can cause it to fall out. The Aporocactus is at its best in spring when it produces attractive reddish pink, tubular flowers. Although the individual flowers only last about a week the plant can remain in flower for up to two months.

COMMON NAME
Rat's Tail Cactus

Propagate the plant from sections of stem

Plant type	Flowering cactus with trailing habit
Season of interest	Spring
Size	30–90cm (12–36in)
Flower	Tubular, 5cm (2in), reddish pink, produced in spring
Leaf	Long, trailing, prickly, ribbed, cylindrical stems, 1.25cm (½in) wide, up to 2m (78in) long, although more usually 30–90cm (12–36in) long indoors
Temperature	10–28°C (50–82°F)
Aspect/Light	Well-lit situation with exposure to direct sunlight
Humidity	Low
Watering	Evenly moisten compost in spring and summer, allowing to dry out somewhat before re-watering, water just enough to prevent dehydration in autumn and winter
Feeding	Once every three to four weeks with flowering plant fertilizer in spring and summer
Propagation	Plant 10–15cm (4–6in) tip or stem cuttings in cactus and succulent compost at 20–22°C (68–72°F) in spring or summer
Potting	Cactus and succulent compost
Problems	Mealy bug
Availability	Occasionally available throughout year
Uses indoors	Good hanging basket or hanging pot plant for display in south facing window

Ceropegia woodii

A curious plant with trailing stems that can grow extraordinarily long, silvery grey leaves with purple undersides, and unusual, tube-like flowers. The Ceropegia's thin habit makes it an ideal subject for a hanging pot or basket in a confined space. The plant will tolerate high light intensities and a certain level of neglect as far as watering is concerned. Indeed, if too much water is provided the roots will rapidly fail and rot, and the plant will probably die. As the roots fail the plant can quite easily fall apart, resulting in loss of anchorage that can cause the stems to drop from the pot. Stems that become bare should be cut back to encourage new leaves to grow. Although it is best as a trailing plant, the Ceropegia can be anchored to a low support if preferred.

COMMON NAMES
Rosary Vine, Hearts Entangled, String of Hearts

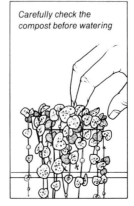

Carefully check the compost before watering

Plant type	Trailing succulent with thin habit
Season of interest	All year round
Size	60–90cm (2–3ft) trailing
Flower	Unusual, tube-like, 2.5cm (1in), pink with bulbous purple end, produced in summer
Leaf	Heart-shaped, 2–3cm (¾–1¼in), fleshy, succulent, silvery green with pink underside
Temperature	18–21°C (65–70°F)
Aspect/Light	Full light
Humidity	Low
Watering	Water carefully, keeping on dry side, throughout year
Feeding	Houseplant fertilizer once every four weeks at half strength in spring and summer
Propagation	Plant 5–7.5cm (2–3in) stem cuttings or tubers from trailing stems in mid spring to early summer at 18–21°C (65–70°F) in cactus and succulent compost
Potting	Cactus and succulent compost
Problems	Root rot causing plant to fall apart and fail
Availability	Infrequently available
Uses indoors	Hanging basket or hanging pot plant that can be displayed in or very near to window

Echeveria setosa

The Echeveria is an appealing succulent with a compact and tidy habit of growth. The rosette of leaves is attractive throughout the year, but the plant becomes even prettier in spring, when it flowers. The small, cup-shaped flowers, which are borne on erect spikes, can last for several weeks. When propagating the Echeveria, it is difficult to strike a balance between taking good propagation material and minimizing damage caused to the parent plant. Removing the lowest leaves causes the least damage, although this may reduce the chances of success with propagation. Conversely, a well-formed leaf from the middle of the rosette may provide better chances of success, but the plant could easily be damaged or disfigured. Select a leaf that is not too old and is in a position that will cause minimum damage.

COMMON NAME
Firecracker Plant

Plant type	Flowering succulent with compact rosette habit
Season of interest	All year round, especially spring
Size	10–15cm (4–6in)
Flower	Cup-shaped, red and yellow, on 10–15cm (4–6in) spike, produced in spring
Leaf	Compact, 2.5–5cm (1–2in), green, covered with white, downy hairs
Temperature	13–30°C (55–86°F)
Aspect/Light	Full sun
Humidity	Low
Watering	Evenly moisten compost in spring and summer, allowing to almost dry out before re-watering; keep almost dry in winter, watering just enough to prevent dehydration
Feeding	Once every two to three weeks with half strength flowering plant fertilizer in spring and summer
Propagation	Cut off and plant a rosette or offset or insert a leaf in cactus and succulent compost at 20–22°C (68–72°F)
Potting	Cactus and succulent compost
Problems	Mealy bug
Availability	Occasionally available in spring
Uses indoors	Very good windowsill plant
Other varieties	E. agavoides – larger leaves
E. derenbergii – orange and yellow flowers
E. elegans – flour-like covering on foliage

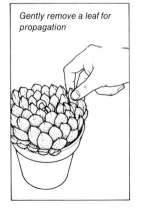

Gently remove a leaf for propagation

Echinopsis multiplex

The extraordinarily large, fragrant flowers of the Echinopsis are quite outstanding. Although the individual flowers last for only a day, the plant remains in flower for some time. To get the best from the plant, it is important not to expose it to any artificial light at night, as it needs darkness to begin flowering. In Europe the Echinopsis is very popular, especially as it is quite hardy and tolerates relatively low temperatures. It is important to keep the compost on the dry side. One of its common names, Windowsill Cactus, suggests the plant's favoured position. As with many other cacti the spines can cause quite painful injuries, so always wear protective gloves when tending to the plant.

COMMON NAMES
Easter Lily Cactus, Windowsill Cactus

Plant type	Flowering cactus with low globular habit
Season of interest	Summer
Size	10–15cm (4–6in)
Flower	10cm (4in) wide, pink, fragrant, produced in summer
Leaf	Globular, ribbed, green stem with spines radiating from woolly areoles
Temperature	10–30°C (50–86°F)
Aspect/Light	Full sun
Humidity	Low
Watering	Evenly moisten compost in spring and summer, allowing to get quite dry before re-watering; keep almost dry in autumn and winter, watering only enough to prevent dehydration
Feeding	Once every two to three weeks with half strength flowering plant fertilizer in spring and summer
Propagation	Remove and plant offsets in spring or summer, sow seeds in cactus and succulent compost at 24–28°C (75–82°F) in spring; wear gloves when handling the plant.
Potting	Cactus and succulent compost
Problems	Mealy bug
Availability	Occasionally available in the spring
Uses indoors	Good windowsill plant
Other varieties	E. eyriesii – white flowers

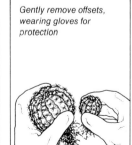

Gently remove offsets, wearing gloves for protection

Epiphyllum × 'Ackermannii'

Few plants can produce anything to match the large and extraordinarily beautiful flowers of the Epiphyllum. The flowers appear along the edges of the curious, flat or angular stems, which are initially erect, but lay outwards as they grow. It may become necessary to support the stems with a stake. Take care when performing this task or otherwise tending to the plant as the stems bear spines. Unlike most other cacti, this cactus is an epiphytic or tree-living plant. Not only does it prefer compost with a higher humus content, but it also dislikes direct sunlight, requiring a position with light shade.

COMMON NAME
Orchid Cactus

Provide support for wayward stems

Plant type	Flowering cactus with erect habit
Season of interest	Spring, occasionally summer
Size	30–45cm (4–6in)
Flower	10–15cm (4–6in), red, with radiating petals with protruding stamens, produced in spring/summer
Leaf	Erect, angular, flattish, green stems, 30–45cm (12–18in) long, 2.5–5cm (1–2in) wide
Temperature	10–24°C (50–75°F)
Aspect/Light	Moderate light with some light shade
Humidity	Moderate to high
Watering	Evenly moisten compost in spring and summer; keep on dry side in autumn and winter, watering only enough to prevent dehydration
Feeding	Once every two to three weeks with flowering plant fertilizer from early spring until flowers are well formed
Propagation	10–15cm (4–6in) cuttings or side shoots in cactus and succulent compost at 20–22°C (68–72°F) in mid spring to early summer, sow seeds at 24–27°C (75–80°F)
Potting	Cactus and succulent compost or houseplant potting compost
Problems	Mealy bug
Availability	Occasionally available in spring
Uses indoors	Good in lounge, dining room, kitchen or lightly shaded conservatory
Other varieties	*E. × 'Cooperi'* – fragrant, white flowers

Euphorbia milii splendens

As its common name suggests, the Crown of Thorns should be treated with great care. Apart from the fierce thorns, which can cause a nasty injury, the milky white sap is poisonous and all contact with it should be avoided. When taking tip cuttings, strong gardening gloves should be used to prevent injury and to protect against the sap, which will freely ooze from the cut stem. To help stop the flow of sap, ground charcoal may be sprinkled on to the wound before the cutting is dibbed into the compost. This may help to improve the success of propagation, as plant material that loses too much sap will not produce roots easily. Unlike many other succulents, the Euphorbia can become dehydrated if it is allowed to dry out.

COMMON NAME
Crown of Thorns

Handle the plant with gardening gloves

Plant type	Flowering succulent with upright habit
Season of interest	Spring and summer
Size	30–90cm (12–36in)
Flower	Insignificant, with paired red bracts, 0.5–1cm ($\frac{1}{4}$–$\frac{1}{2}$in), produced spring/summer
Leaf	Oval, sometimes spade-shaped, 2.5–5cm (1–2in), mid-green
Temperature	13–28°C (55–82°F)
Aspect/Light	Full sun
Humidity	Moderate
Watering	Evenly moisten compost in spring and summer, allowing to dry somewhat before re-watering; keep on the dry side in autumn and winter, but avoid drying out
Feeding	Once every two to three weeks with flowering plant fertilizer in spring and summer
Propagation	Plant 7.5–10cm (3–4in) tip cuttings in cactus and succulent compost at 21°C (70°F) in mid spring to early summer, take extreme care and wear protective gloves
Potting	Cactus and succulent compost
Problems	Can rot off if kept too wet
Availability	Quite commonly available in the spring and early summer
Uses indoors	Windowsill well away from where it could be a hazard; probably better for higher window in lounge or bedroom

Faucaria tigrina

With its unusual, jaw-like leaves, this plant is particularly popular with children. The 'jaws' are in fact quite soft and will not cause injuries if brushed against. The attractive, daisy-like yellow flowers are produced in the autumn.

The Faucaria can be over-watered quite easily and needs to be carefully looked after. However, it is a versatile succulent, which can be grown on its own in a pot or displayed in a mixed planting with other succulents in a bowl. When propagating the Faucaria by division, take great care not to cause any damage to the parent plant as this could kill it.

COMMON NAME
Tiger's Jaws

Plant type	Flowering succulent with low-growing habit
Season of interest	Autumn
Size	10–12.5cm (4–5in)
Flower	5cm (2in), daisy-like, yellow, produced in autumn
Leaf	Triangular, jaw-like with tooth-like protuberances along edge, succulent, greenish grey, 4–5cm (1½–2in)
Temperature	10–28°C (50–82°F)
Aspect/Light	Direct sun
Humidity	Low
Watering	Evenly moisten compost in spring and summer, allowing to dry a little before re-watering; keep on dry side in autumn and winter, but avoid drying out
Feeding	Once every three to four weeks with half strength flowering plant fertilizer in spring and summer
Propagation	Divide plants and plant in cactus and succulent compost at 21°C (70°F) in late spring to early summer
Potting	Cactus and succulent compost
Problems	Susceptible to over-watering
Availability	Not commonly available, but may be seen in summer
Uses indoors	Good windowsill plant for most sunny rooms, ideal for mixed succulent planting or mini-garden

Carefully separate clumps for propagation

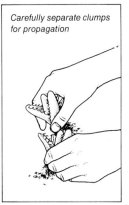

Gymnocalycium andreae

The diminutive Gymnocalycium is a small plant that makes a worthwhile contribution to a collection of cacti and succulents grown either on a sunny windowsill or in a conservatory. It is attractive throughout the year, but at its best when it comes into bloom, producing yellow flowers that are so large they almost dwarf the plant. The chin-shaped nodules, or tubercles, on the plant have earned it the common name of Chin Cactus. As with propagating other cacti, it is wise to allow the cut edges of the offsets to dry out a little for a day or so before inserting them into the compost. Take care when choosing the varieties of the plant, as some produce quite fierce spines for their size.

COMMON NAME
Chin Cactus

Plant type	Flowering cactus with low-growing, globular habit
Season of interest	Summer
Size	5cm (2in)
Flower	Radiating petals forming yellow flowers, 2.5cm (1in) wide
Leaf	Globular, greyish green stem with small spines
Temperature	7–30°C (45–86°F)
Aspect/Light	Direct sun
Humidity	Low
Watering	Evenly moisten compost in spring and summer, allowing to dry out a little before re-watering; keep on the dry side in autumn and winter, watering just enough to prevent dehydration
Feeding	Once every two to three weeks with half strength flowering plant fertilizer in spring and summer
Propagation	Plant offsets in cactus and succulent compost at 21–22°C (70–72°F) in late spring to early summer
Potting	Cactus and succulent compost
Problems	Mealy bug
Availability	Occasionally available in spring and summer
Uses indoors	Warm and sunny windowsill or in conservatory
Other varieties	G. baldianum – pink or red flowers G. denudatum – white flowers

Leave offsets for a couple of days to allow the cut surfaces to dry and heal

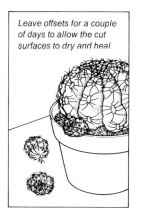

Gymnocalycium mihanovichii hybrids

This extraordinary cactus is not one plant but two, and is also man-made rather than naturally occuring. The plant is created by preventing the Gymnocalycium from producing the normal green chlorophyll in favour of an artificial-looking hue of rosy pink, or sometimes orange or yellow. Without the green chlorophyll the plant is unable to produce food and must be grafted on to another plant from which it can take nutrients. The plants normally used for this are Hylocereus and Trichocereus. In time the Gymnocalycium might flower, although this is unusual. It is more likely to produce offsets of the same colour, which can be removed and grafted on to other plants. Match the two wounded areas on stock and graft together, and anchor them with matchsticks until the graft has taken.

COMMON NAME
Ruby Ball

Grafting may be attempted by marrying the two wounded areas of stock and graft

Plant type	Novelty cactus of columnar and globular habit
Season of interest	All year round, especially summer
Size	7.5–12.5cm (3–5in)
Flower	White or pink rayed flowers 2.5cm (1in), produced in summer
Leaf	Globular, pinkish red on green, angular stem
Temperature	10–28°C (50–82°F)
Aspect/Light	Well-lit situation with some light shade
Humidity	Low
Watering	Evenly moisten compost in spring and summer, allowing to dry out a little before re-watering; keep on the dry side in autumn and winter, watering just enough to prevent dehydration
Feeding	Once every three to four weeks with half strength flowering plant fertilizer in spring and summer
Propagation	Remove 2.5cm (1in) offsets and graft onto Hylocereus or Trichocereus, matching wounded areas and supporting with toothpicks or matchsticks at 21–22°C (70–72°F) in late spring or early summer
Potting	Cactus and succulent compost
Problems	Mealy bug
Availability	Occasionally available in spring and summer, sometimes at other times
Uses indoors	Novelty plant for display on lightly shaded windowsill

Kalanchoe blossfeldiana hybrids

This attractive, shrubby plant is one of the most popular succulents, and is widely available. Commercially grown specimens produce their flowers late in the year, at a time when few other plants are in bloom. A further benefit is that the flowering period can last up to three months. The plant prefers a sunny windowsill and can be displayed either on its own or used as part of a group arrangement. A number of flower colours are available, including red, pink and orange. As it gets older, the plant can become rather leggy and straggly and may not flower as readily. For this reason, it is usually thrown away once the first flowering has finished. New plants can be propagated quite easily from tip cuttings removed in spring.

Tip cuttings may be removed for propagation

Plant type	Flowering succulent with shrubby habit
Season of interest	Autumn, winter and spring
Size	15–30cm (6–12in)
Flower	Red, pink, orange or yellow, in clusters, on erect, 10–20cm (4–8in), spikes, produced autumn/winter/spring
Leaf	Roughly heart-shaped, slightly serrated, green, fleshy, 2.5–7.5cm (1–3in)
Temperature	10–20°C (50–82°F)
Aspect/Light	Full sun
Humidity	Low
Watering	Water moderately in spring and summer, allowing compost to dry out a little before re-watering; keep drier in autumn and winter
Feeding	Once every two to three weeks with flowering plant fertilizer when in bud and flower
Propagation	Take 7.5cm (3in) tip cuttings with sharp knife in mid to late spring, leave to dry for two to three days to form callus, then dib in cactus and succulent compost at 21–22°C (70–72°F)
Potting	Cactus and succulent compost
Problems	Mealy bug
Availability	Commonly available in spring, autumn and winter
Uses indoors	Provides useful splash of colour for short term display in a bowl planting or on its own; prefers windowsill

Kalanchoe daigremontiana

An unusual and attractive plant with a curious method of self-propagation. Tiny plantlets, complete with roots, are produced along the edges of the leaves, and when fully formed they drop on to the compost where they easily root and grow. If they are not wanted, the plantlets can of course be weeded out. In time, the plant will become rather leggy and straggly, and will need to be staked. When this happens it might be better to grow a fresh plant from one of the plantlets. In the autumn or winter this Kalanchoe produces small, tube-like flowers at the top.

COMMON NAME
Devil's Backbone

Plant type	Foliage succulent with upright habit
Season of interest	All year round
Size	30–60cm (12–24in)
Flower	2.5cm (1in), tube-like, pink, flowers in autumn and winter
Leaf	Arrow-head-shaped, 7.5–12.5cm (3–5in), green and brown, with tiny plantlets along edge
Temperature	10–28°C (50–82°F)
Aspect/Light	Well lit situation, but out of direct sunlight
Humidity	Low
Watering	Evenly moisten compost in spring and summer, allowing to dry a little before re-watering; keep on dry side in autumn and winter
Feeding	Once every four weeks with flowering plant fertilizer in spring and summer
Propagation	Dislodge plantlets from the leaf and place them on surface of cactus and succulent compost at 20–22°C (68–72°F)
Potting	Cactus and succulent compost
Problems	Mealy bug
Availability	Occasionally available throughout year
Uses indoors	Novelty plant for lounge, dining room, kitchen or bedroom

Plantlets are readily produced along the edges of the leaves

Lithops bella

The common name of Living Stones is very descriptive of these most unusual succulents, which look just like small pebbles or stones. Lithops varieties are most effective when mixed together against a background of small stones, chippings or pebbles. To cultivate these plants successfully, it is essential to be very frugal with watering, even during the growing season. In winter the plant must not be watered at all. Watering should commence in spring when the new leaves are produced. Take care not to splash water on to the foliage, as this can cause marking or scorching.

COMMON NAME
Living Stones

Plant type	Flowering succulent with very low-growing habit
Season of interest	Late summer, early autumn
Size	1–4cm (½–1½in)
Flower	Daisy-like, rayed, white, 2.5cm (1in), produced late summer/early autumn
Leaf	Greyish green, fleshy, in pairs
Temperature	10–28°C (50–82°F)
Aspect/Light	Full sun
Humidity	Low
Watering	Evenly moisten compost from spring to early autumn, allowing to dry out a little before re-watering; do not water again until the following spring
Feeding	Not usually necessary
Propagation	Gently tease apart plants and pot separately, or in small clumps, using cactus and succulent compost at 20–22°C (68–72°F) in late spring or early summer; sow seeds as above in mid to late spring
Potting	Cactus and succulent compost
Problems	Can easily be over-watered
Availability	Not commonly available
Uses indoors	Windowsill display in small collections in small bowl or planter
Other varieties	L. helmutii – bright yellow flowers; grey-green leaves
L. marmorata – white flowers; grey-green leaves

Always water the Lithops from below

Lobivia backebergii

If cared for correctly, the Lobivia will reward the owner with a spectacular display of colourful flowers, quite out of proportion to the diminutive plant that bears them. Although the individual flowers do not last very long, they are produced in succession and the display may last for several weeks. The appeal of the plant is further enhanced by the fact that the flowers open in the morning and close in the evening. Particular care should be taken with watering, as too much water can quite easily cause root rot followed by the loss of the plant. This is especially important during the winter when the plant is dormant.

COMMON NAME
Cob Cactus

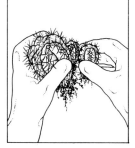

Gently tease offsets apart, wearing gloves for protection

Plant type	Flowering cactus with globular habit
Season of interest	Late spring and summer
Size	7.5–10cm (3–4in)
Flower	Rayed petals forming red flowers, 2.5–5cm (1–2in), produced late spring/summer
Leaf	Globular, ribbed, green stem becoming more cylindrical with age
Temperature	10–28°C (50–82°F)
Aspect/Light	Well-lit situation in full sun
Humidity	Low
Watering	Evenly moisten compost in spring and summer, allowing to dry a little before re-watering; provide only sufficient to prevent dehydration in autumn and winter
Feeding	Once every two to three weeks with half strength flowering plant fertilizer in spring and summer
Propagation	Carefully tease apart offsets and pot in cactus and succulent compost at 20–22°C (68–72°F) in spring and summer
Potting	Cactus and succulent compost
Problems	Mealy bug, root mealy bug, root rot from over-watering
Availability	Occasionally available spring and early summer
Uses indoors	Windowsill or conservatory display on its own or as part of a collection
Other varieties	*L. hertrichiana* – slightly larger; red flowers

Opuntia microdasys albispina

The Opuntia is a popular cactus, with an unusual, unpredictable habit of growth. The leaf pads are produced in an irregular pattern so that each plant looks different. The tissue on the pads is dotted with areoles from which hooked bristles called glochids emerge. The glochids look attractive, but can be a nuisance as even the most casual contact will dislodge them from the plant. Once in the skin they are very difficult to remove and produce a pain or irritation not dissimilar to that caused by fibres of fibreglass. With all Opuntia avoid leaving water droplets on the plant, as marking or scorching can easily occur in sunlight. Opuntia are good plants to use in cactus gardens.

COMMON NAMES
Prickly Pear, Bunny Ears

Glochids can be removed from the skin with adhesive tape

Plant type	Ornamental cactus with upright habit
Season of interest	All year round
Size	10–30cm (4–12in)
Flower	4cm (1½in) wide, yellow, rarely produced, in summer
Leaf	Oval leaf pads, 5–7.5cm (2–3in), green with reddish brown glochids
Temperature	10–28°C (50–82°F)
Aspect/Light	Full sun
Humidity	Low
Watering	Evenly moisten compost in spring and summer, allowing to dry a little before re-watering; water only enough to prevent dehydration in autumn and winter
Feeding	Once every two to three weeks with half strength flowering plant fertilizer in spring and summer
Propagation	Remove pad in spring or summer; allow wound to dry for a few days to produce a callus, then pot in cactus and succulent compost at 20–22°C (68–72°F); sow seeds as above in spring
Potting	Cactus and succulent compost
Problems	Mealy bug, root mealy bug
Availability	Occasionally available throughout year
Uses indoors	Windowsill or conservatory plant for use in cactus garden or similar display
Other varieties	*O. m. rufida* – reddish brown glochids *O. robusta* – larger; pronounced spines

Pachypodium saundersii

The Pachypodium is rather grotesque in appearance, with a swollen stem armed with fiercesome spines. Although the plant will flower, it does so only occasionally, when conditions are right. In addition to the white-flowered variety, there are also yellow, orange and red forms. After flowering, the plant produces fruit with seeds that have a parachute device to aid their dispersal by the wind. The seeds can be removed once the fruits are ripe, and germinated in the spring. The leaves produced at the top of the stem are deciduous, being shed just before the rest period, when the plant should be kept on the dry side. The Pachypodium is susceptible to leaf spot and any leaves that become infected should be removed immediately.

Plant type	Ornamental succulent with erect habit
Season of interest	All year round
Size	15–30cm (6–12in)
Flower	White, occasionally produced, in summer
Leaf	Elongated oval, 5–10cm (2–4in), green, on thick, cylindrical stem with fierce spines
Temperature	13–28°C (55–82°F)
Aspect/Light	Full sun
Humidity	Low
Watering	Evenly moisten compost in spring and summer, allowing to dry somewhat before re-watering; water only enough to prevent dehydration in autumn and winter
Feeding	Once every two to three weeks with half strength flowering plant fertilizer in spring and summer
Propagation	Sow seeds in cactus and succulent compost at 20–22°C (68–72°F) in spring
Potting	Cactus and succulent compost
Problems	Mealy bug, leaf spot
Availability	Occasionally available
Uses indoors	Windowsill or conservatory plant, well away from people, especially children

Remove leaves that are infected with leaf spot

Parodia mutabilis

The Parodia is a very attractive cactus, producing pretty, boldly coloured flowers in summer. The individual flowers may last several days and are produced on and off throughout the summer. However, the plant requires expert care, as it easily suffers from root problems. It is best to keep this plant on the dry side, for if the compost becomes a little too moist, especially in cooler weather, the Parodia will often shed its roots and may never recover. Plants that have suffered root damage or loss need particularly careful attention. Provided it can be cared for correctly this cactus makes an ideal subject for a windowsill or a conservatory.

Plant type	Flowering cactus with globular habit
Season of interest	Summer
Size	7.5cm (3in)
Flower	Rayed, 2.5cm (1in), yellow or orange, produced in summer
Leaf	Globular, green stem with brown and white spines
Temperature	10–28°C (50–82°F)
Aspect/Light	Well-lit position in direct sunlight
Humidity	Low
Watering	Evenly moisten compost in spring and summer, allowing to dry a little before re-watering; water only enough to avoid dehydration in autumn and winter
Feeding	Once every three to four weeks with half strength flowering plant fertilizer in spring and summer
Propagation	Remove offsets in early summer, allow them to dry for a couple of days, then pot them in cactus and succulent compost at 20–22°C (68–72°F); sow seeds as above
Potting	Cactus and succulent compost
Problems	Root rot, mealy bug, root mealy bug
Availability	Occasionally available spring and summer
Uses indoors	Windowsill or conservatory plant for display singly or in arrangement
Other varieties	P. sanguiniflora – cylindrical habit; red flowers

Always check the compost before watering

Rebutia senilis 'Elegans'

For its size the Rebutia is a prolifically flowering plant, becoming virtually smothered in fiery-red blossoms for several days. The small plants produce clumps of offsets, as well as seedling plants, which occasionally grow to 15–20cm (6–8in) wide. The effect, when in flower, is quite spectacular. Offsets develop the colour of the parent plant and can complement the display as the population grows, whereas seedlings often produce a range of colours due to their mixed parentage, including white, yellow, orange and red. As well as being suitable for display on its own, the Rebutia can be used effectively in bowl arrangements.

Gently tease offsets apart, wearing gloves for protection

Plant type	Flowering cactus with globular habit
Season of interest	Late spring, early summer
Size	5cm (2in)
Flower	2.5–4cm (1–1½in), fiery-red flowers, produced in late spring/early summer
Leaf	Small, globular green stem with soft white spines
Temperature	10–28°C (50–82°F)
Aspect/Light	Full sun
Humidity	Low
Watering	Evenly moisten compost in spring and summer, allowing to dry a little before re-watering; keep on the dry side in autumn and winter, watering only enough to prevent dehydration
Feeding	Once every two to three weeks with flowering plant fertilizer in spring and summer
Propagation	Remove offsets in late spring to early summer and plant in cactus and succulent compost at 20–22°C (68–72°F); sow seeds in spring
Potting	Cactus and succulent compost
Problems	Mealy bug, root mealy bug
Availability	Quite commonly available in spring and summer
Uses indoors	Windowsill and conservatory plant, which can be displayed on its own or in an arrangement
Other varieties	*R. fiebrigii* – orange flowers

Rhipsalidopsis rosea

When its flowers open fully, the Rhipsalidopsis provides a spectacular display of colour, which is particularly enhanced by the open spreading habit. When young it can be effectively grown as a pot plant, but as it grows it is better suited to a hanging pot or basket, where the cascading foliage and flowers may be viewed to greater benefit. As buds and flowers are produced, great care should be exercised to avoid any fluctuations of temperature, moisture and light, as any of these may result in the sudden loss of the flower buds. Where plants are grown in a position with light from one side, they should be regularly turned to keep the growth in balance and to encourage even production of flowers.

COMMON NAME
Easter Cactus

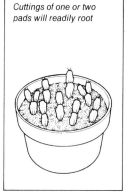

Cuttings of one or two pads will readily root

Plant type	Flowering cactus with upright, bushy, semi-trailing habit
Season of interest	Spring
Size	15–30cm (6–12in)
Flower	Star shaped, 2.5cm (1in), rosy-pink
Leaf	Flat or angled leaf-like pads 2cm (¾in), green, with fine bristles, produced in spring
Temperature	10–28°C (50–82°F)
Aspect/Light	Reasonably well-lit situation, but with some light shade
Humidity	Moderate to high
Watering	Just moisten compost in summer, autumn and winter, allowing to dry a little before re-watering; provide more water in spring during flowering period; after flowering, keep on the dry side for a few weeks
Feeding	Once every two to three weeks with half strength flowering plant fertilizer from production of flower buds to end of flowering
Propagation	Remove one or two pads and pot in cactus and succulent compost at 20–22°C (68–72°F) in spring or summer
Potting	Cactus and succulent compost or houseplant potting compost
Problems	Mealy bug
Availability	Commonly available in spring
Uses indoors	Feature plant for lounge, dining room or kitchen; suitable for hanging basket

Schlumbergera truncata hybrids

Unlike most other cacti and other succulents, which originate in the drier regions of the world, such as deserts and semi-arid regions, the Schlumbergera comes from the rainforest, where it grows on tree trunks. The trees are a rich source of humus, and this cactus prefers a high humus content when grown indoors. It is also used to slightly less light, with some shade, and a higher level of humidity than other cacti. Apart from being effective as a pot plant displayed on a table, the Schlumbergera makes a superb hanging basket plant, where the flowers can be appreciated fully.

COMMON NAME
Christmas Cactus

Plant type	Flowering cactus with upright, spreading, semi-trailing habit
Season of interest	Winter
Size	10–20cm (4–8in)
Flower	2.5–4cm (1–1½in) wide, 4–5cm (1½–2in) long, red, pink or white, with pronounced stamens and petals, produced in winter
Leaf	Flattened pads, 4–5cm (1½–2in), green, with spiky protrusions
Temperature	10–28°C (50–82°F)
Aspect/Light	Well-lit situation with some shade
Humidity	Moderate to high
Watering	Evenly moisten compost until end of flowering period, then keep on drier side for a few weeks, allowing compost to dry a little before re-watering
Feeding	Once every two to three weeks with half strength flowering plant fertilizer throughout year except for a few weeks after flowering
Propagation	Remove two pads and pot in cactus and succulent compost at 20–22°C (68–72°F) in spring and summer
Potting	Cactus and succulent compost, preferably with a high humus content
Problems	Mealy bug
Availability	Commonly available late autumn and early winter
Uses indoors	Feature plant for lounge, dining room or kitchen

The Schlumbergera is ideal for a hanging basket

Sedum rubrotinctum

An unusual plant with foliage that changes colour from green to a reddish pink. The flowers are not spectacular, but the plant is quite hardy and can be displayed outside during the summer to expose it to as much sunlight as possible. In autumn it should be brought back indoors again before any cool and damp conditions cause problems. Care should be taken with watering at all times, as excessive moisture can cause stem and root rot, resulting in the loss of the plant. The Sedum is best when it is kept low-growing and compact, as it can look untidy if the stems are allowed to become leggy.

COMMON NAME
Christmas Cheer

Plant type	Succulent with upright, bushy habit
Season of interest	All year round
Size	10–15cm (4–6in)
Flower	Yellow, rarely produced indoors, in spring
Leaf	Sausage shaped, 1–2cm (⅜–¾in), glossy, fleshy, green with red tinges
Temperature	10–28°C (50–82°F)
Aspect/Light	Full sun
Humidity	Low
Watering	Evenly moisten compost in spring and summer, allowing to dry a little before re-watering; keep on drier side in autumn and winter
Feeding	Once a month with half strength flowering plant fertilizer in spring and summer
Propagation	Remove 5cm (2in) tip cuttings in mid to late spring and leave to dry for a couple of days, then insert in cactus and succulent compost at 20–22°C (68–72°F)
Potting	Cactus and succulent compost
Problems	Stem and root rot
Availability	Occasionally available all year round
Uses indoors	Bowl or hanging basket plant in window

Propagate the Sedum by inserting tip cuttings into compost

Senecio rowleyanus

As its name suggests, this plant produces unusual, bead-like leaves on trailing stems. It is a good subject for a small hanging basket or pot, and is best displayed in or near to a window, where the higher light intensities will help to keep it well balanced and healthy. For a more massed effect, plant several specimens together in the same container. As with many other cacti and succulents, great care should be taken with watering, as the plant will quickly suffer if the compost is kept too moist. Furthermore, because it is a trailing species the weight of the foliage puts more of a strain on the roots, so any damage to the roots will rapidly affect the plant. In the early winter the Senecio produces small, whitish, fragrant flowers.

COMMON NAME
String of Beads

To propagate the plant, insert pieces into compost

Plant type	Succulent with trailing habit
Season of interest	All year round
Size	45–60cm (18–24in) trails
Flower	Uninteresting, white, fragrant, produced late spring/early autumn
Leaf	Globular, 1cm (½in), green, on string-like trailing stems
Temperature	10–28°C (50–82°F)
Aspect/Light	Full sun
Humidity	Low
Watering	Evenly moisten compost in spring and summer, allowing to dry a little before re-watering; keep on dry side in autumn and winter
Feeding	Once a month with half strength flowering plant fertilizer in spring and summer
Propagation	Remove 7.5–10cm (3–4in) pieces in spring or early summer and pot in cactus and succulent compost at 20–22°C (68–72°F)
Potting	Cactus and succulent compost
Problems	Aphid
Availability	Occasionally available all year round
Uses indoors	Hanging basket plant in or near window

Stapelia variegata

The Stapelia is an unusual plant with fleshy, angular stems that spread across the pot. The flowers, produced from summer to autumn, are also unusual, being quite fleshy, arranged in a star-like pattern, and borne at a strange angle at the side of the plant. In proportion to the plant they are also quite large. However, the most unusual characteristic of the plant is the smell of the flowers, which is quite revolting and resembles the smell of carrion, hence the common name of Carrion Flower. This smell has the purpose of attracting flies, which would normally feast on rotting meat, to pollinate the flowers. The odour can be so strong that it fills a room, in which case the flower is perhaps best removed.

COMMON NAMES
Carrion Flower, Star Flower, Toad Plant

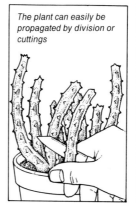

The plant can easily be propagated by division or cuttings

Plant type	Flowering succulent with low-growing, erect, spreading habit
Season of interest	Summer, autumn
Size	7.5–15cm (3–6in)
Flower	Star-like, five-lobed, 6.5cm (2½in), yellow with reddish brown flecks and lines, with revolting smell of carrion, produced summer/autumn
Leaf	Angular, branching stems, 7.5–15cm (3–6in), fleshy, grey-green
Temperature	10–28°C (50–82°F)
Aspect/Light	Full sun
Humidity	Low
Watering	Barely moisten compost in spring and summer, allowing to almost dry out before re-watering; keep on the dry side in autumn and winter
Feeding	Once a month with half strength flowering plant fertilizer in spring and summer
Propagation	Sow seeds in cactus and succulent compost at 20–22°C (68–72°F) in mid spring; divide or cut 10cm (4in) stem and plant as above from late spring to mid summer
Potting	Cactus and succulent compost
Problems	Mealy bug, root mealy bug, root rot
Availability	Occasionally available spring and summer
Uses indoors	Windowsill or conservatory plant
Other varieties	*S. hirsuta* – purplish brown flower

Bromeliads

Strange and exotic, bromeliads are among the most rewarding of all plants. Typically they produce a rosette of glossy leaves, from which arises a variety of beautifully shaped and coloured flower spikes. Most species are ideal for use as individual specimens, providing a focal point in a room or conservatory. If space allows, though, several plants grouped together will produce an even more spectacular display. In their natural state, in the tropics, bromeliads grow on trees, collecting rainwater in the cup formed by the foliage. Subjects grown indoors should also be watered through this cup, as shown in the Neoreglia pictured here.

Aechmea fasciata

One of the most popular bromeliads, the Aechmea produces a long, brightly coloured flower head from a rosette of arching, saw-edged leaves. The leaves form the central cup or 'urn' from which the plant gets its common name, and which it uses in its natural environment to catch rainwater. If the plant is to thrive indoors, this reservoir should be kept topped up with fresh water. As it is an epiphytic or tree-living plant, it produces a very small root system, and can easily be kept in a 13cm (5in) pot. The flower spike is produced when the plant is three or four years old, and remains attractive for about six months. After flowering, the plant will produce two to three offsets at the base, which grow to maturity as the mother plant dies. When they are large enough the offsets can be potted up singly.

COMMON NAME
Urn Plant

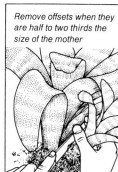

Remove offsets when they are half to two thirds the size of the mother

Plant type	Flowering bromeliad with erect, radiating habit
Season of interest	All year round
Size	45–60cm (18–24in)
Flower	Small, blue and red, produced amongst many spiny bracts at end of 45cm (18in) pink spike, usually produced spring or summer, but sometimes at other times
Leaf	Broad, arching, strap-shaped, with a serrated edge, 30–60cm (12–24in), dark green with silver-grey coating
Temperature	16–21°C (60–70°F)
Aspect/Light	Moderate to full light
Humidity	Moderate to high humidity
Watering	Keep 'urn' formed by rosette of leaves filled with water throughout year
Feeding	Once a month with half strength houseplant fertilizer in spring and summer
Propagation	Remove offsets when half to two thirds the size of the mother plant in spring to early summer
Potting	Houseplant potting compost and sphagnum moss peat in equal parts
Problems	Aphid on flower spike, root mealy bug
Availability	Quite commonly available, usually from late spring to mid summer
Uses indoors	Good for lounge or dining room
Other varieties	*A. chantinii* – reddish-orange flower spike

Ananas comosus variegatus

An attractive plant that is closely related to the wild pineapple, although its fruit does not ripen sufficiently indoors to become edible. The Ananas has very sharp leaf tips and edges, so must be positioned well out of the way. The bright pink flower head bears tiny blue flowers. To encourage flowering, place under the plant two or three ripe apples and cover the whole with a clear polythene bag. After a few days, the ethylene gas given off by the apples should stimulate the plant to flower and the bag can be removed. After flowering, the Ananas will produce offsets, which can be removed and potted.

COMMON NAME
Variegated Pineapple

To promote flowering, place apples under the plant and cover it with a bag

Plant type	Flowering bromeliad with erect habit
Season of interest	All year round
Size	30–60cm (12–24in)
Flower	Tiny, blue, from pink bracts on rosette of leaves produced on 30–60cm (12–24in) spike, followed by small, pink, inedible fruit 7.5cm (3in) produced at almost any time of year
Leaf	45–60cm (18–24in), with sharply toothed edge, cream striped with green edges
Temperature	18–24°C (64–75°F)
Aspect/Light	Full sun
Humidity	Moderate
Watering	Evenly moisten compost in spring and summer, allowing to dry a little before re-watering; keep on drier side in autumn and winter
Feeding	Once every two to three weeks with flowering plant fertilizer in spring and summer
Propagation	Remove rosette from top of fruit or offsets from base of plant and pot in seed and cutting compost at 24°C (75°F) from mid spring to mid summer
Potting	Houseplant potting compost
Problems	Mealy bug, leaves may scorch in places with too much sun
Availability	Occasionally available throughout year
Uses indoors	In or near window in lounge or dining room, but away from people

Billbergia nutans

A very hardy plant, the Billbergia can tolerate lower temperatures than many other bromeliads, down to 10°C (50°F). It does not have a specific flowering season, and can bloom at almost any time of year, producing attractive, pendulous flowers from its pink-bracted flower stems. Offsets are formed prolifically and if not removed the display can look untidy. Leaf tips that wither due to dehydration can be trimmed off, taking care to leave a small edge of dead tissue. However, it is obviously better to avoid the need for this by maintaining the level of humidity.

COMMON NAME
Queen's Tears

Plant type	Flowering bromeliad with upright habit
Season of interest	Varies according to plant and situation
Size	30–45cm (12–18in)
Flower	Small, pink and blue, hanging from 5–7.5cm (2–3in) long, pink bracts, borne on 30cm (12in) spikes, produced at any time of year
Leaf	Strap-like, thin, 30–45cm (12–18in) long
Temperature	10–20°C (50–68°F)
Aspect/Light	Well-lit position with some direct sunlight
Humidity	Moderate to high
Watering	Evenly moisten compost throughout year, allowing to dry a little before re-watering
Feeding	Once every two to three weeks with houseplant fertilizer in spring and summer
Propagation	Remove 10–15cm (4–6in) offsets in spring and pot in houseplant potting or bromeliad compost at 18–20°C (64–68°F)
Potting	Houseplant potting or bromeliad compost
Problems	Mealy bug, dehydration of leaf ends in dry atmosphere
Availability	Occasionally available from spring to summer
Uses indoors	In or near window in bedroom, dining room or kitchen

Trim untidy leaf ends with a sharp pair of scissors

Cryptanthus bivittatus

The low-growing Cryptanthus produces insignificant flowers but has quite attractively coloured and patterned foliage. The wavy edged leaves are green with cream stripes, which turn pink or red in bright light. Other Cryptanthus plants produce quite different foliage, such as C. zonatus, which has brownish green and white stripes running across the leaves. An effective display can be created by massing several species together in a trough or planter. The Cryptanthus produces offsets in the shape of a small rosette in the centre of the plant. These can easily be dislodged and potted on.

COMMON NAME
Earth Star

Plant type	Bromeliad with low-growing habit
Season of interest	All year round
Size	5–7.5cm (2–3in) tall, 10–12cm (4–5in) across
Flower	Uninteresting, small, white, produced infrequently throughout year
Leaf	Semi-rigid, leathery, pointed, 7.5–10cm (3–4in), green striped cream, pink or red, in rosette
Temperature	16–22°C (61–72°F)
Aspect/Light	Reasonably well-lit situation with some light shade from direct sun
Humidity	High
Watering	Evenly moisten compost throughout year, allowing to become almost dry before re-watering
Feeding	Once a month with half strength houseplant fertilizer in spring and summer
Propagation	Remove offsets in spring or early summer and pot in houseplant potting or bromeliad compost at 20–22°C (68–72°F)
Potting	Houseplant potting or bromeliad compost
Problems	Mealy bug, root mealy bug, root rot from over-watering
Availability	Occasionally available throughout year
Uses indoors	Good for bowl gardens and terrariums
Other varieties	C. acaulis – grey-green foliage C. zonatus – brown-green and white

To propagate the plant, remove the rosettes from the centre and pot them

Fascicularia bicolor

This native of Chile is one of the finest bromeliads. Although it comes from a warm climate, its herbaceous, perennial habit, and close, spiny, leathery rosettes of leaves help it to tolerate a wide range of conditions. It has pale blue flowers surrounded by ivory-coloured bracts with serrated edges. Given a peaty soil with sand added to improve drainage, it can be successfully cultivated in many locations. It can even be grown without a pot, simply by putting a layer of moss with a mixture of peat and sand over some rocks. The Fascicularia is an ideal plant for the cooler conservatory, provided the temperature is kept over 3°C (37°F).

To propagate the plant, remove the side shoots and pot them up singly

Plant type	Flowering bromeliad with horizontal, radiating habit
Season of interest	All year round
Size	50–60cm (18–24in)
Flower	Up to 3.5cm (1¼in) long, surrounded by ivory-coloured bracts, up to 4cm (1½) long, serrated
Leaf	Lance-shaped, 50cm (18in) or more long, green
Temperature	3–28°C (37–82°F)
Aspect/Light	Light shade
Humidity	Moderate
Watering	Evenly moisten compost in spring and summer; keep on drier side in autumn and winter; never allow compost to become waterlogged
Feeding	Liquid houseplant fertilizer in late spring
Propagation	Remove offsets in spring or early summer and pot in houseplant potting or bromeliad compost at 27°C (80°F); slow to root
Potting	Houseplant potting or bromeliad compost
Problems	Whitefly, mealy bug
Availability	Quite commonly available in spring and summer
Uses indoors	Indoor or conservatory plant

Guzmania lingulata

With its bright red or orange bracts and bright green, glossy leaves, the Guzmania makes a bold feature plant. Several specimens planted together provide a striking display. It is one of the more delicate bromeliads and particular care must be taken to avoid cold and damp conditions. These can lead to rot setting in and killing the flower spike, which is produced in winter when conditions are least favourable, or even the whole plant. As with most bromeliads, water should be poured into the central cup formed by the leaves and replaced at least once a month with tepid water before it becomes stagnant. The plant can be propagated from offsets removed from the base and potted singly.

COMMON NAMES
Orange Star, Scarlet Star

Guzmania and other bromeliads can be grown on a branch with moss

Plant type	Flowering bromeliad with upright, radiating habit
Season of interest	Late winter to early spring
Size	30–45cm (12–18in)
Flower	Small, yellow, growing from pointed, 5cm (2in) reddish bracts on 30cm (12in) spike, produced in winter/spring
Leaf	30–45cm (12–18in), pointed, strap-shaped, bright green, glossy, in rosette
Temperature	19–24°C (66–75°F)
Aspect/Light	Reasonably well-lit situation with some shade from direct sun
Humidity	High
Watering	Keep central cup full at all times except when plant is in flower, when level should be allowed to drop a little
Feeding	Once every two to three weeks with half strength houseplant fertilizer poured into central cup in spring and summer
Propagation	Remove 10–12.5cm (4–5in) offsets in spring and pot in houseplant potting or bromeliad compost at 22–24°C (72–75°F)
Potting	Houseplant potting or bromeliad compost
Problems	Rotting of spike if cold and damp
Availability	Occasionally available from winter to early spring
Uses indoors	Feature plant for lounge, near window
Other varieties	*G. l. cardinalis* – larger; red bracts *G. l. minor* – slightly more compact

Neoregelia carolinae 'Tricolor'

The common name of Blushing Bromeliad aptly describes this plant, as just before flowering, the centre of the rosette turns a bright red. The boldly striped leaves form an unusual, compressed habit, which does not grow very tall but requires quite a lot of horizontal space as it radiates outwards. In order to thrive, the Neoregelia needs a fairly high level of humidity, so is best grown in a mixed planting. Like other bromeliads, the plant dies after flowering, but not before it has produced several offsets, which can be separated when they are large enough, and potted up singly.

COMMON NAMES
Cartwheel Plant, Blushing Bromeliad

Plant type	Bromeliad with horizontal, radiating habit
Season of interest	All year round
Size	15–20cm (6–8in) tall, 45–60cm (18–24in) across
Flower	Insignificant, bluish, in centre of cup, produced at almost any time of year
Leaf	Shiny, pointed, strap-shaped, 20–30cm (8–12in), green and yellow striped with rose-pink central cup, which turns red prior to flowering
Temperature	16–22°C (61–72°F)
Aspect/Light	Well-lit situation with some shade from full sunlight
Humidity	Moderate to high
Watering	Replace water in central cup every month with fresh, tepid water; keep cup full at all times, except in winter, when level should be allowed to drop
Feeding	Once every two to three weeks with half strength houseplant fertilizer poured on to compost in spring and summer
Propagation	Remove 10–15cm (4–6in) offsets in spring or early summer and pot in houseplant potting or bromeliad compost at 20–22°C (68–72°F)
Potting	Houseplant potting or bromeliad compost
Problems	Leaf scorch with excessive direct sun
Availability	Frequently available throughout year
Uses indoors	Feature plant for lounge or dining room

When large enough, the offsets can be removed and potted individually

Nidularium innocentii lineatum

Like Neoregelia, this bromeliad 'blushes' bright red at the centre of the rosette before flowering. The Nidularium must be positioned with great care as, although it likes a well-lit situation, exposure to direct sunlight will quickly bleach or scorch the leaves. The best position is on furniture that is near to, but not in front of, a sunny window. If the plant should suffer some minor damage to the leaves, this can be trimmed off with sharp scissors, taking care to leave a small edge of dead tissue. The Nidularium can either be displayed on its own or grouped with other bold-leaved plants. It requires a high level of humidity so stand the pot on a tray of moist pebbles and mist the foliage regularly.

COMMON NAME
Blushing Cup

Plant type	Bromeliad with horizontal habit
Season of interest	All year round
Size	25–30cm (10–12in) high, 45–60cm (18–24in) across
Flower	Insignificant, white, in centre of rosette
Leaf	Broad, strap-shaped with toothed edge, 20–30cm (8–12in) long, shiny, green and white striped along length, with red base to central vase
Temperature	16–22°C (61–72°F)
Aspect/Light	Reasonably well-lit situation with some shade from direct sunlight
Humidity	High
Watering	Keep compost evenly moist throughout year, allowing to dry a little before re-watering
Feeding	Once every two to three weeks with half strength houseplant fertilizer in spring and summer
Propagation	Remove 10–15cm (4–6in) offsets in spring or early summer and pot in houseplant potting or bromeliad compost at 20–22°C (68–72°F)
Potting	Houseplant potting or bromeliad compost
Problems	Root mealy bug, scorching of leaves
Availability	Occasionally available throughout year
Uses indoors	Feature plant for lounge or dining room, fairly close to window
Other varieties	N. innocentii – green leaves / N. i. nana – more compact

Regularly mist the leaves with tepid water

Tillandsia cyanea

The Tillandsia is one of the smallest bromeliads and also one of the most attractive. The unusual, flat flower spike is made up of a series of overlapping bracts, coloured a beautiful shade of pink. For several weeks it produces a succession of blue-violet flowers. The spike itself remains attractive for over two months. As it is an epiphytic or tree-living plant, the Tillandsia has a very weak root system. Water and food are therefore best applied directly to the foliage, with a hand mister or a fine-rosed watering can. In warm conditions the plant may need to be sprayed nearly every day.

COMMON NAME
Pink Quill

Remove faded flowers before they rot and mark the bracts

Plant type	Flowering bromeliad with upright, arching habit
Season of interest	Varies according to plant and situation
Size	20–30cm (8–12in)
Flower	Three-petalled, blue-violet, produced from flattened, oval, 7.5–12cm (3–5in), pink-bracted spike
Leaf	Pointed, thin, 20–30cm (8–12in) long, greyish green, radiating from centre
Temperature	16–22°C (61–72°F)
Aspect/Light	Reasonably well-lit situation with some shade
Humidity	High
Watering	Spray foliage with mister, allowing to dry a little before re-watering
Feeding	Once a month with half strength houseplant fertilizer in spring and summer
Propagation	Remove 7.5–10cm (3–4in) offsets in spring or early summer and pot in seed and cutting compost at 18–22°C (68–72°F)
Potting	Seed and cutting or bromeliad compost
Problems	Dehydration and leaf scorch if foliage is not moistened regularly and atmosphere is too dry
Availability	Frequently available throughout year
Uses indoors	Small feature plant or as part of mixed arrangement in bowl or planter in lounge or dining room

Vriesia splendens

A striking plant with a bright red, spear-shaped flower spike, borne above attractively banded foliage. The spike lasts for several months, growing up to 60cm (24in) and eventually producing a succession of short-lived, yellow flowers. Like other bromeliads, the Vriesia may flower at any time of year, depending on the individual plant and the conditions in which it is grown. After flowering, the plant dies but not before it has formed offsets at the base, which can be removed when they are large enough and potted on. Take care when positioning the Vriesia as, although it likes some direct sunlight, too much can scorch the leaves. It is best placed on a low table where the foliage and flower head can be seen to best effect.

COMMON NAME
Flaming Sword

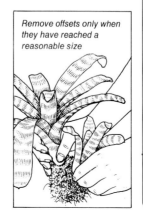

Remove offsets only when they have reached a reasonable size

Plant type	Flowering bromeliad with upright habit
Season of interest	Varies according to plant and situation
Size	30–60cm (12–24in)
Flower	2.5–5cm (1–2in), yellow, borne on flattish, spear-shaped, 20–30cm (8–12in), red-bracted spike, produced at almost any time of year
Leaf	Broadly strap-shaped 20–40cm (8–16in), green with purplish horizontal bands, forming a central cup
Temperature	16–22°C (61–72°F)
Aspect/Light	Well-lit situation with some sunlight
Humidity	High
Watering	Keep central cup filled with water, changing every month or so
Feeding	Once a month with half strength houseplant fertilizer in spring and summer
Propagation	Remove 10–15cm (4–6in) offsets in spring or early summer and pot in houseplant potting or bromeliad compost at 20°C (68°F)
Potting	Houseplant potting or bromeliad compost
Problems	Mealy bug, root mealy bug, aphid on flowers, leaf scorch
Availability	Commonly available throughout year
Uses indoors	Feature plant or as part of mixed grouping in lounge or dining room
Other varieties	*V. psittacina* – red and yellow flowers *V. saundersii* – yellow flowers

Index

Acknowledgments

The publishers would like to thank the following for providing plants, containers and facilities for photography:

Keith Butters Ltd; Stuart Lowe Ltd; Royal Botanic Gardens, Kew; The Chelsea Gardener; Clifton Nurseries; The Garden Centre, Alexander Palace.

The publishers would also like to thank the following for supplying photographs for this book:

Page 1 Zefa; 3 Biofotos; 5 (left) Brian Davis, (centre, top right and bottom right) Harry Smith, (centre right) Garden Picture Library; 6 Garden Picture Library; 8 Garden Picture Library; 13 Biofotos; 14 Garden Picture Library; 15 Garden Picture Library; 16 Harry Smith; 17 (left) Brian Davis; 18 (left) Flower Council of Holland; 23 (left) Harry Smith; 24 (left) Flower Council of Holland, (right) Peter Stiles; 25 (left) Brian Davis; 26 (left) Flower Council of Holland; 27 (right) Brian Davis; 28 Harry Smith; 29 (left) Brian Davis; 33 (left) Brian Davis; 37 (left) Peter Stiles; 40 (left) Brian Davis; 43 (left) Brian Davis; 44 (left) Garden Picture Library; 46 (left) Garden Picture Library; 48 (left) Harry Smith; 50 Harry Smith; 51 (left) Flower Council of Holland; 52 (right) Flower Council of Holland; 53 (right) Pat Brindley; 55 Harry Smith; 59 Harry Smith; 62 Harry Smith; 63 (left) Zefa; 64 (left) Brian Davis, (right) Flower Council of Holland; 65 (left) Harry Smith, (right) Flower Council of Holland; 66 (left) Flower Council of Holland; 67 (right) Flower Council of Holland; 68 (left) Harry Smith; 69 (right) Harry Smith; 72 Flower Council of Holland; 73 (right) Brian Davis; 74 (left) Brian Davis, (right) A-Z Botanical Collection; 75 (right) Brian Davis; 76 (left) Brian Davis, (right) Harry Smith; 77 (left) Harry Smith, (right) Brian Davis; 78 (left) Brian Davis; 79 (right) Brian Davis; 80 (left) Brian Davis; 81 (left) Brian Davis; 82 Garden Picture Library; 83 (right) Flower Council of Holland; 84 (left) Flower Council of Holland; 84 (right) Harry Smith; 85 (left) Brian Davis, (right) A-Z Botanical Collection; 86 (left) Harry Smith, (right) Flower Council of Holland; 87 (left) Harry Smith; 88 (left) Brian Davis; 89 (right) Garden Picture Library; 90 (right) A-Z Botanical Collection; 92 (left) Flower Council of Holland; 93 (right) Brian Davis; 94 (right) Brian Davis; 95 Brian Davis; 96 (left) Brian Davis; 97 (left) Harry Smith, (right) A-Z Botanical Collection; 99 (right) A-Z Botanical Collection; 100 (right) Brian Davis; 101 (left) Harry Smith, (right) Flower Council of Holland; 102 (left) Flower Council of Holland, (right) Brian Davis; 103 (left) Brian Davis, (right) Harry Smith; 104 (left) Brian Davis, (right) Harry Smith; 106 (left) Harry Smith, (right) Garden Picture Library; 107 (left) A-Z Botanical Collection; 108 (right) Flower Council of Holland; 109 (right) Garden Picture Library; 110 Harry Smith; 111 Brian Davis; 112 (left) Brian Davis, (right) Harry Smith; 113 Brian Davis; 114 Brian Davis; 115 Brian Davis; 116 (left) A-Z Botanical Collection, (right) Brian Davis; 117 (left) Flower Council of Holland; 118 (left) Brian Davis, (right) Harry Smith; 119 (left) A-Z Botanical Collection, (right) Brian Davis; 120 (left) Flower Council of Holland, (right) Harry Smith; 121 Harry Smith; 123 Flower Council of Holland; 124 (right) Harry Smith; 125 (left) Harry Smith; 126 Harry Smith; 128 (right) Harry Smith; 129 (left) Harry Smith; 131 (left) Harry Smith; 132 (left) Harry Smith; 133 (left) Flower Council of Holland, (right) Harry Smith; 134 Harry Smith; 135 (right) Flower Council of Holland; 136 (left) Harry Smith, (right) Flower Council of Holland; 137 (left) Harry Smith; 138 (right) Harry Smith.

All other photographs by Paul Forrester.